"This collection of essays presents a range of voices and critical perspectives on America's system of mass incarceration. Its notable strengths include the thoughtful pieces by incarcerated men and women and the historical perspective gained by including older essays with recent scholarship. This book makes a clear, honest, and smart case for radical reappraisal of the practice of imprisonment. It deserves a wide audience among those who care about violence and justice."

—Rebecca Ginsburg,
Director of the Education Justice Project,
University of Illinois at Urbana-Champaign

And the Criminals with Him

And the Criminals with Him

Essays in Honor of Will D. Campbell
and All the Reconciled

EDITED BY
Will D. Campbell
Richard C. Goode

CASCADE *Books* · Eugene, Oregon

AND THE CRIMINALS WITH HIM
Essays in Honor of Will D. Campbell and All the Reconciled

Cascade Books
An Imprint of Wipf and Stock Publishers
199 W. 8th Ave., Suite 3
Eugene, OR 97401

www.wipfandstock.com

ISBN 13: 978-1-61097-946-7

Cataloging-in-Publication data:

And the criminals with him : essays in honor of Will D. Campbell and all the reconciled / edited by Will D. Campbell and Richard Goode.

vi + 298 p. ; 23 cm. —Includes bibliographical references and index(es).

ISBN 13: 978-1-61097-946-7

1. Christianity and justice. 2. Prisoners. 3. Reconciliation. 4. Capital punishment—Religious aspects—Christianity. I. Title.

HV7419 A55 2012

Manufactured in the U.S.A.

Contents

Part 1: Introduction | 1

1 From Institution to Community—*Richard C. Goode* | 3

2 The Good News from God in Jesus is Freedom to the Prisoners
—*Will D. Campbell and James Y. Holloway* | 16

3 Law and Love in Lowndes—*Will D. Campbell* | 22

Part 2: Naming the Powers | 29

4 What Has Happened Since 1973?—*Preston Shipp* | 33

5 The Societal Impact of the Prison Industrial Complex, or Incarceration for Fun and Profit . . . Mostly Profit—*Alex Friedmann* | 43

6 Why It Pays to Imprison: Unmasking the Prison-Industrial Complex—*Andrew Krinks* | 54

7 Why I am a Prison Abolitionist—*Lee Griffith* | 70

Part 3: A Demonic Principality | 87

8 Security and Rehabilitation and God in a Godless World
—*A. Puchalski* | 93

9 The Incarcerated Village—*Shelly A. Breeden* | 103

10 What Prison Has Taught Me—*Crystal Sturgill* | 112

11 Transformations: How Prison Changed Me—*Donna McCoy* | 119

Part 4: By and with Death | 129

12 My Friend Steve—*Stacy Rector* | 135

13 The Diary of an Execution: Is Lethal Injection Really Painless?
—*William Stevens* | 144

14 Tearing down the Temple to Rebuild the Kingdom
—*Jeannie Alexander* | 173

Part 5: The Scandal of Community in this Institution | 181

15 Questioning Society's Criminal Justice Narratives
—*Randy Spivey* | 185

16 The Confession and Correction of a Former Correctional Chaplain
—*Marlin Elbon Kilpatrick* | 193

17 Freedom out of Bondage: The Baptism of Walter Pride
—*Jeannie Alexander, illustrations—Nathan Miller* | 199

18 On Fear and Following: Reading the Beatitudes in Prison
—*Richard Beck* | 203

Part 6: Reconciliation is Our Story | 209

19 Punitive Justice vs. Restorative Justice: A Meditation on the Spirit of
Punishment and the Spirit of Healing—*Harmon Wray* | 213

20 Misjudging: A Reconciliation Story
—*Cyntoia Brown and Preston Shipp* | 225

21 Reframing Academy and Community: The Prison and the Power of
Art—*Laura Lake Smith* | 235

22 The Transformation of X, Y, and We—*Felicia Ybanez* | 243

23 To See and Be Seen—*Janet Wolf* | 252

Contributors | 273
Acknowledgments | 277
Bibliography | 279
Scripture Index | 289
Subject Index | 291

PART 1

Introduction

1

From Institution to Community

RICHARD GOODE

WISDOM LITERATURE TEACHES "THERE is nothing new under the sun," (Eccl 1:9). In Nashville we dignify our tendencies for artistic and intellectual recycling by announcing that we're "doing a cover" of another's work; imitation being, of course, the highest form of flattery. In that Music City spirit, readers might think of this collection as a "cover" of the Winter-Spring 1972 issue of *Katallagete*. A couple essays are from that original '72 edition, while many new additions make for an updated rendition.

In its 25-year run, *Katallagete*, the journal of the Committee of Southern Churchmen [COSC], published an occasional "themed" issue.[1] Selected topics, for example, ranged from "Vocation" (Fall-Winter 1972), and relations with "the World" (Spring 1974), to "Non-violence" (Winter 1974).[2] Early in '72, the COSC published a collection of 13 essays on prisons, penned principally by individuals with first-hand experience of incarceration.[3] Some authors were convicted felons, while others had been locked up for acts of civil disobedience, e.g., Freedom Riders who endured time in Mississippi's notorious Parchman Prison a decade earlier. The goal

1. For more information on the Committee of Southern Churchmen see Campbell and Goode, *Crashing the Idols*, 40–47.

2. In December 1967, Thomas Merton told Sisters of Loretto, on retreat at Gethsemani, "There is one very good non-violent group you should keep praying for, called the Committee of Southern Churchmen . . . One of their leaders is a friend of mine, Will Campbell, a marvelous fellow who visits here often." See Thomas Merton, *The Springs of Contemplation*, 30–31.

3. Kris Kristofferson designed the artwork for the issue.

of this 1972 issue, however, was more than consciousness raising, i.e., that some 200,000 sisters and brothers were incarcerated. Aiming for more than guilt-pricked consciences, *Katallagete*'s publisher, Will D. Campbell, and editor, James Y. Holloway, peppered the issue with a series of invitations to action.

> In your immediate community there are prisons and prisoners. Get some folk—neighbors, students, church groups, teachers, men and woman at the bar—to find out who has no one to visit them and go to them once each week. Tell them your story and they will tell you theirs. Things will happen from there. (15)

> "For when I was hungry, you gave me food; when thirsty, you gave me drink; when I was a stranger you took me into your home, when naked you clothed me; when I was ill you came to my help, when in prison you visited me." Then the righteous will reply, "Lord, when was it that we saw you hungry and fed you, or thirsty and gave you drink, a stranger and took you home, or naked and clothed you? When did we see you ill or in prison, and come to visit you?" And the king will answer, "I tell you this: anything you did for one of my brothers here, however humble, you did for me." (20)

> Yes money. People in prison and recently out are in desperate need of money, just a little bit of money. We found that we could not just publish an account of what it is like to be in prison and think that we had done our bounden duty toward the captives. We have given of our own resources where we have found great need and where it has been asked—five dollars here, twenty there, ten elsewhere. If you will send a small offering for that purpose it will be put to good use. We are setting up a discretionary fund for captives. It will be for their personal use, for the "little things." There will be no administrative cost taken out, no skimming off the top. Every dollar sent will be given to someone in prison, or recently out . . . It's a little thing. Unless you are the one in prison. (36)

> It is not enough to read and bleed about people in prison. As we worked on this issue of KATALLAGETE it became immediately apparent to us that it was not enough just to write about them either. WE CALL UPON YOU AS A READER TO JOIN US IN A SIMPLE ACTION. Some of the writers on these pages are now out of prison and need jobs. There are many others who

have not written here but are recently out of prison and who also need jobs. Send us word of a job available and we will try to match it. That is a small thing for us who seek to release the captives. But it is a big thing for the captive. Find a possible job. Then let us know. We'll take it from there. (46)

If America's prison system demanded active engagement in '72, consider what the prison-industrial complex has become in the last 40 years. Today's correctional system is a massive, multifaceted principality wielding crushing power over millions of lives. Part 2 of this collection, "Naming the Powers," will detail some of these developments over the last four decades. Despite the system's size and appetite today, the church still finds it easy to ignore what the prison is, and what it does. We know those "red letter" words of Jesus are in Matthew 25 and Luke 4, yet we've become rather adept at spiritualizing such directives away. Not only with our words but more so in our lives, we confess that the gods of gaol have conquered the Prince of liberation.

Will D. Campbell

Occasionally people ask, "Who's Will Campbell?" When that happens I'm speechless. Initially, I'm incredulous that folks could somehow not know of Will. Then panic sets in as I realize that my conversation partners expect me to describe the indescribable Will. Discrete biographical facts are insufficient, of course, so I sometimes start with, "Well, do you know the Rev. Will B. Dunn character from Doug Marlette's comic strip 'Kudzu'?" This gambit often fails when they say, "No. Should I?" How exactly does one describe a man whose nonconformity is as well worn as his ubiquitous cherry walking stick? How to introduce a man whose charm is, in part, his defiance of categories and whose trademark is his resistance of labels? Groping for words, I often then say something like "Will is an iconoclast," which is about as accessible to most folks as shaped note music is to a Roman Catholic. Reality is, Will has made a career of flouting society's most revered and sacrosanct institutions—whether they be the "steeples," the government, or the Academy.[4]

"Iconoclasm" often carries connotations of destruction, and insofar as Campbell has sought to contest the principalities and powers, he is an iconoclast. Nevertheless, his deconstruction is consistently for the purpose of building (or rebuilding); a means to a creative, constructive,

4. Campbell, *Writings on Reconciliation and Resistance*, 89–232.

hopeful end. He has sought to identify and remove that which impedes and obstructs the opening of more desirable possibilities. His iconoclasm, in other words, creates space for the Beloved Community to emerge, where individuals are respected, nurtured, sustained, and loved for being the image of God that they are. To incarnate such an alternative community requires an indefatigable opposition against—a subversive resistance of—the manipulative arrogance, condescending bigotry, the usurious chauvinism, and self-righteous activism that functions as political science and conventional wisdom of our world. To be what God created and Christ redeemed us to be, requires a contravention—a breaching—of the principalities and their powers that seduce us into oppressing and dehumanizing our sisters and brothers. This kind of iconoclasm reveals Campbell at his prophetic and pastoral best.

When it comes to the hope that has sustained him, Will has never composed a systematic theology. Nevertheless, his life and writing have consistently operated from four core interconnected points: reconciliation, human unity, the difference between institutions and communities, and the idolatry of heroism.[5]

Reconciliation

As proclaimed in 2 Cor 5, Christ accomplished reconciliation—once and for all. Our task as disciples, therefore, is neither to contrive new efficient ways, nor more effective means for promoting reconciliation. Our political agendas, educational curricula, or social gimmicks are idols that cannot promote greater progress toward reconciliation because reconciliation is an accomplished fact. There's nothing more to *do*. Christ has done it. For those who believe this good news, our task is to *be* (e.g., to live out, or to incarnate) Christ's reconciliation.[6]

---

5. Readers will find more detail on the first two themes (reconciliation and human unity) in *Writings on Reconciliation and Resistance* and *Crashing the Idols*. Because the second two themes (i.e., institutions vs. community, and the idolatry of heroism) received less attention in those volumes, more discussion is offered here.

6. Campbell, *Writings on Reconciliation and Resistance*, 1–86; Campbell and Goode, *Crashing the Idols*, 1–67.

Human Unity

Campbell's encouragement to "be reconciled" *could* read like an overly saccharine Hallmark card, complete with Thomas Kinkade art work. "Reconciliation," in other words, might be misconstrued as a bland encouragement to be kind, civil, and nice; to exude affability, gentility, and mannerliness. Those who have read Campbell know that he has seldom provided such placid, feel-good "Kumbaya moments."

Grace, according to Campbell, is the great, scandalous equalizer. We all need it, and we all have received it. At the end of the day, therefore, we're all the same. Those of us who use colorful expletives, enjoy Jack's Tennessee sour mash with Fidel's elicit cigars, steal another's widescreen TV, defraud our employees, conspire to organize and inflame racist bigots, or assassinate a national hero, we are all the same. "We're all bastards, but God loves us anyway." Quickly dispatching with any "caste system of grace," Campbell reminds us that our reconciliation puts all of us on exactly the same footing.

Common sense might caution against taking this egalitarian ethic too far, right? Will's not so sure. For him distinctions such as "us" and "them" simply do not exist. In community there's only "we." To illustrate how far he would carry this Radical community ethic, Will once told an interviewer that he could imagine former Israeli Prime Minister, Golda Mier, chasing Adolph Hitler around Heaven for a thousand years. When Mier eventually catches the old Führer, she will pin a Star of David on him and the two will laugh together.[7] At the end of the day, even the most notorious offender in modern history is reconciled—just like everyone else?

The Difference between Institutions and Communities

"Principalities can best be understood in modern language as institutions," Will asserts. "All are blasphemy for they usurp the authority of the one true God."[8] His assertion that institutions are inherently evil and irredeemable[9] often evokes consternation and confusion. Institutions may have their problems and limitations, people admit, but the idea that these entities, which structure and preoccupy our lives, are inherently evil? Well, *that's* just a step too far. "How will we ever get things done?" "Doesn't Will

---

7. "God's Will."

8. Campbell, *And Also With You: Duncan Gray and the American Dilemma*, 248.

9. Ibid., *Writings on Reconciliation and Resistance*, 151.

want to make a difference in the world?" "Isn't Will just setting himself up to live the life of a hermit, never cooperating with others?"

In some ways, such questions expose how domesticated or colonized our thinking has become. We presume that institutions—be they political parties, denominations, social service agencies, universities, corporations, or nation-states—serve *us* by organizing our energies and achieving our objectives. Instead, we serve *them*. Institutions impose membership crite¬ ria, coerce compliance, and determine an individual's livelihood. Fail to advance the institutional mission, fail to enhance the institution's position, exhaust one's utility, or embarrass the institution, and one is a "liability"— best dismissed before damaging "the brand." The institution's first and greatest commandment is, "Thou shalt perform."

Stressing performance, institutions have predictable organizational structures and systems, with strategic plans for growth, prestige, and power. Toward those ends, institutions seek effective, charismatic, admin- istrators who—presuming to know better than others how to get things done—recruit, inspire, harness, and orchestrate the institution's talent for the institution's good and overall security. These administrators execute the institution's authority, and do the things necessary (e.g., eradicate risks, browbeat the uncooperative, dismiss the excess or unproductive), to protect and advance the institution.

To measure success and progress, institutions are preoccupied with rankings. Whether the yardstick is net worth, market share, social prestige, or might and power, the goal is upward mobility, control, and domination. The institution might sell diplomas, salvation, or widgets, but the ethic is essentially the same. Public or private, for-profit or non-profit, sacred or secular; whether the institution is the United States of America, the Republic of Iraq, the New York Yankees, Lipscomb University, the Crips, the Bloods, or the mafia, the ethic is the same. Win.

For decades, Will Campbell has been unmasking the inherent evil of institutions by practicing the scandalous alternative of community. One insight into Will's thinking on community comes from *And Also With You*. The book may be a biography of Duncan Gray, but Will's depiction conveys as much about him as it does about Bishop Gray. Campbell de- scribes how an employee of the Sewanee Inn discovered that Will was in the Monteagle, TN, area researching Bishop Gray. Initially, she offered standard, letter-of-recommendation adjectives for Gray, e.g., "personable" and "approachable." But the line that caught Campbell by surprise was her insight, "He's not up to anything." That, for Campbell, is the description of people living the community ethic of reconciliation. By their very nature, institutions and their administrators—the principalities and their powers—are always "up to something." Gray, by contrast, interacted with sisters and brothers humbly, not as someone scheming to manipulate humans as resources for some institutional advancement, or personal exploit. He treated people as neighbors bearing God's image, not pawns to be artfully managed for strategic outcomes. Instead of a bureaucrat masterfully controlling events and people, Gray was "content to be a clay pot, an earthen vessel, the treasure within radiating the Light of the World, affecting change, making things better wherever he went."

> For the moment the thought of his not being up to anything lingered. It seemed somehow incongruous with the way so many have viewed Duncan Gray over the years: liberal, radical, social activist, crusader, disturber of the status quo; a priest of doing. Then, looking back and reflecting on what I had learned of him, I realized the woman at the inn was right. He really wasn't up to something. Why should he be? For him there is nothing left to do. Simply something to be. Not trying to do anything at all. Just trying to live, and lead others to live, knowing what has already been done, knowing that celebration of liturgy brings the past to present. Free in obedience. Be what you already are: reconciled to God and all creation.[10]

Admittedly, communities can go awry, seduced into becoming like the institutions around them. Even well-intentioned communities can lose their calling and succumb to institutional ethics. Somewhat akin to Clarence Jordan's Koinonia Farm in Sumter County, Georgia, the Providence Community of Holmes County, Mississippi—founded by the Fellowship of Southern Churchmen—sought to create an island of justice in an ocean of oppression. Providence, for example, would practice racial and economic *shalom*, extending a hand of healing and uplift to the mid-state. In the early '50s Will relished the presence of this Mississippi community. Then "something went wrong." The Providence Community had weathered threats from without, but seemed to collapse from within. From all appearance, one wouldn't suspect failure.

> These were all men who devoutly yearned for the success of what they started. What was it? They were all men of note. Reinhold Niebuhr was one of the most distinguished theologians of his time. Sherwood Eddy was a social critic and Christian

10. Campbell, *And Also With You*, 241–46.

layman, known around the world for his zeal for human bet-
terment. William Amberson was a brilliant teacher, medical
scholar, and humanitarian. Sam Franklin was a Presbyterian
missionary to Japan, before and after his years with the cooperative farm. What then is one to make of this behavior, which at
times seemed a blend of schoolyard scuffle and political party
bosses contending for control? Was it nothing more, nor less,
than what the theologians among them know as original sin,
that indefinable flaw in the human condition that magnifies
pride, ego, thinking more highly of ourselves than we ought to
think until it controls all else? Was it that, from the beginning to
this day, under the system there was no other way to do it? That
no matter how highborn the notion, a plantation [institution]
has a built-in modus operandi?[11]

Folks may be up to something good, Campbell warns, but benevolent goals notwithstanding, once an institutional *modus operandi*
is invoked the outcome is unavoidable. The founders of Providence, for
example, labored to build a community that bore the fruit of the Spirit—
nothing sinister or evil there. But when they hit a tough patch and chose
to protect the viability of their enterprise at the expense of the people it
was to serve, it was "game over." "The Christian virtues of equality, love,
and forbearance seemed to wane when the institution was threatened,"
Campbell explains. Institutional thinking came before community ethic.
"It was not a new story in the history of humankind. Institutional survival, even institutional well-being, becomes sacred. We search in vain
for exceptions."[12]

So, how is a community different from an institution? First and
foremost, a community always values the worth of an individual—each
and every individual—over and above the well-being or reputation of an
abstract, impersonal construct such as an "institution." Communities are,
therefore, faithful to individuals, sacrificing for each individual—even at
great cost to the collective. In communities, individuals are not assessed
by their ability to perform, or conform, to a mission statement. Communities take risks on individuals, while institutions risk individuals.

Communities turn institutional models of authority on their heads.
As Gerhard Lohfink explains, a trademark of distinctly Christian communities is the "authority of the Crucified."[13] Instead of a controlling

11. Campbell, *Providence*, 229–30.
12. Ibid., 224.
13. Lohfink, *Jesus and Community*, 120.

administrator, Christ emptied himself of privilege and power, becoming vulnerable. The genius of the Passion—the trademark of our ethic—is that the one who actually was omnipotent, became impotent. Or as Jean Vanier reveals, communities move beyond visions of grandeur.

> A community is only being created when its members accept that they are not going to achieve great things, that they are not going to be heroes, but simply live each day with new hope, like children, in wonderment as the sun rises and in thanksgiving as it sets. Community is only being created when they have recognized that the greatness of humanity lies in the acceptance of our insignificance, our human condition and our earth, and to thank God for having put in a finite body the seeds of eternity which are visible in small and daily gestures of love and forgiveness. The beauty of people is in this fidelity to the wonder of each day.[14]

Where institutions trust management systems, endowments, laws, contracts, secured pledges, weapons and other forms of coercion and leverage, Christian communities trust love. Consequently, communities need not insist on their own ways and outcomes. Because Christian communities love, they can "bear all things, believe all things, hope all things, endure anything from everyone." Trusting in sacrificial, self-emptying love, Christian communities know they will not fail. Communities, therefore, live by hope rather than business plans. They can forgive rather than punish, include those discarded by society, eradicate lines of distinction, and listen rather than announce. Communities reassure an individual that she need not prove her worth, or earn her keep from the institution. She is always welcome. This community can always be her home. Communities are remarkably "inefficient," "irresponsible," and often "inconvenient." Communities, moreover, look foolish because they keep serving those who abuse and take advantage of the community's grace.[15] This practice is more than a strategy or tactic. It is, according to Vanier, even "more than a way of life. It is a hope, an incarnation of love;" made manifest in the community's "sharing, obedience, and poverty."[16]

A critical difference between communities and institutions, therefore, is that institutions may love constructs and concepts (e.g., "our

14. Vanier, *Community and Growth*, 109.

15. As Merton taught, "mercy is not credible to a lot of people, because it's not very profound. That is why we have to bear witness to the word of God" (*The Springs of Contemplation*, 34).

16. Vanier, *Community and Growth*, 151.

country," "our party," "our church"), but communities love actual human beings—the abrasive, the obnoxious, the infuriating, and the offensive. Communities love bastards.

The Idolatry of Heroism

"Be ye significant!" This, to paraphrase Ernest Becker, is the "central calling" that makes us "hopelessly absorbed with ourselves." If we're not the center of attention, we just don't matter.[17]

Will Campbell has made a career of resisting the cultural forms and practices that make some lives count more than others—that elevate selected folks to iconic hero status. Lives matter, Will insists, not because of our list of accomplishments, our incomparable vita, or some unique "contribution" made. Remember, at the end of the day we're all the same. We don't have to go out and make a difference; God has already made the difference.[18]

Nevertheless, we mortals still have this insatiable, idolatrous desire to be in charge, because, we reason, if we had the power we could finally get things done correctly. We can set things right, and fix our neighbor's failures and limitations.[19] Even if we don't expect to be *the* savior, we still play a pretty good, self-righteous martyr—a visionary who is just too smart for her peers. Our hope is that someday others will finally awaken and appreciate our brilliance. Then they'll realize that they should have listened to us all along, because we were—as we always knew—right. At that point we'll have both our revenge and the recognition we're due. Will,

17. Becker notes that culture defines the contributions that elevate one to heroic status. In the US, for example, the contribution might be the wielding of political influence in D.C., or manipulating economic trends on Wall Street. Whatever the contribution might be, Becker concludes, this power actually functions as a "religion" insofar as this contribution defines life's meaning for, and life's value in, that society. (See *Denial of Death*, 1–11.)

18. Thomas Merton, for a time something of Will's spiritual director, once counseled that if we must be heroic, we should cultivate a "heroic humility." Instead of clamoring to be the cultural icon—instead of insisting that one knows better than God what one is gifted to be—have the humility to accept God's initiative and work. That which makes us exceptional, therefore, is not our accomplishments, but our self-abnegation. (See Merton, *New Seeds of Contemplation*, 100.)

19. Lee Griffith captures this idolatrous logic by explaining, "If I wield power, there is no reason to fear what I will do with it. I will use it only for the good. But the question that is seldom asked is what *it* does to me. In order to have been effective at acquiring the power, I will have already been thoroughly imbued with pragmatic calculations about how to win people over and how to win over people" (*God is Subversive*, 114).

however, has been adept at avoiding such hero complexes. He's never been inclined to launch a campaign, lead a crusade, or champion a cause. He's chaffed at titles like "activist," or recoiled from epithets like "Movement leader." Simply stated, he is just uninterested in being in charge, and he's not even too keen on mastering all the schematics for group stability and networking.[20] (Given Will's leadership model, it's no small miracle that the *Katallagete* team produced as many volumes as they did. We won't discuss how successful they were at publishing respective issues on time.) For those who can forego the temptation to be the self-ordained omniscient and omnipotent hero, Will can be one of the more non-judgmental, affirming, loyal individuals ever encountered. He is the witty, eccentric, and sagacious brother you long to have in community.[21] For those, however, zealous to control and run the community as some kind of a political, ecclesiastical, or educational institution, he will make life hell.

Prisons Cannot Reconcile

Given these four elements of Will's theology (reconciliation, human unity, the difference between institutions and community, and the idolatry of heroism), it's easy to anticipate his response to prisons. Here is an institution announcing to more than 2 million, "You don't matter. Because of what you've done, your life doesn't count." Prisons segregate and silence offenders. Their institutional mission is to make an example of offenders by exerting sufficient power to break and recreate them into the kind of resource that society can use.

To discern Will's idea of criminal justice, consider his "Good News to the Prisoners" and "Law and Love in Lowndes." The former takes the politically blasphemous position of announcing that Christ called for the abolition of incarceration—also championed here by Lee Griffith. We might dismiss Will's thesis by arguing that it's easy to think such utopian notions while writing in one's log cabin in Mt. Juliet, Tennessee, but who would really follow through with such ludicrous claims? Will did. In 1965, he took the unpopular position (risky too, for a new periodical) of arguing in "Law and Love in Lowndes" that Jon Daniels'

20. An example of Campbell's indictment of the idolatry of heroism and power, is his resistance to the National Council of Churches in the late '50s and early '60s. See Campbell and Goode, *Crashing the Idols*, 26–39.

21. Charles Campbell has rightly placed Will Campbell in that storied tradition of "holy fools" in Christian history.

murderer, Tom Coleman, should go free.[22] Good, progressive institutional ethics—at least outside the South—argued that Tom Coleman had broken the law and violated Daniels' rights. For his offense Coleman should pay for his crime. Order, public safety, justice, whatever one calls it, all demanded Coleman's punishment.

Albeit for radically different reasons, a Lowndes County jury and Will Campbell agreed. Coleman should go free. Will argues that according to the we're-all-bastards community ethic, the adversarial nature of the justice system is nonsensical (perhaps even tacky). Given our reconciliation there can be no "us vs. them," "righteous vs. sinner." Besides, exactly who is the sinless one to throw the first stone at Coleman? If we're all just bastards, it's just "us" now. Tom Coleman is a valued, needy member of the community—no better, no worse, no different than Jon Daniels.

So, how will we live reconciled? Do nothing. Listen to Shelly and Crystal, Donna, Cyntoia, Alex, Bill and Felicia and what they have to say here. Be in community with the incarcerated and those released. Consider your reading of what they have to say here as a first act of community.

Plea

This collection differs from "prison writings" in the traditional sense.[23] All the authors have first-hand experience with the prison industrial complex, but not all of us have a felony conviction on our record. More importantly, the focus is less on our respective stories in this collection, and more on you the reader. Because our essays are appeals to you, our "hook" (or refrain), in keeping with the '72 edition, is "here's what *you* need to know."

If not a formal thesis, this collection has a plea. When you hear the word "prison," try not to think of tattooed convicts caged behind razor-wired fences, guarded by surveillance towers and other paramilitary apparatus. (In other words, turn off MSNBC's weekend programming.)

22. Daniels was the young Episcopal Theological School seminarian who had traveled to southern Alabama to work in the Selma campaign. After spending about a week in the Haynesville jail, Daniels and other civil rights workers were released on August 20. That afternoon Thomas Coleman shot and killed Jon Daniels, wounding others. A month later an all-white Lowndes County jury acquitted Coleman. For one of the great, unsung pieces of the Civil Rights Movement, see Jonathan Myrick Daniels, "But My Heart is Black," *The Texas Observer* (October 29, 1965).

23. For the genre of prison literature, readers have numerous and compelling options. Wally Lamb and the Women of York Correctional Institution's *Couldn't Keep It to Myself: Testimonies from Our Imprisoned Sisters*, is a wonderful example.

When you hear "prison," please see sisters and brothers; neighbors to whom Christ has reconciled you. And as you start to see, then listen to their wisdom that can pull back the cloak on this veiled institution. Hear their wisdom that can move us from institutions of incarceration to the incarnation of community.

At the end of the day we are up to nothing more than encouraging folks to find messy, inefficient, unsecure communities with *all* our fellow bastards. Perhaps in so doing we might reclaim the scandal of our story, replicating the humble trust of St. Dismas who took quite a risk in requesting community with a fellow criminal being executed on Good Friday. Not a bad place to start.

So we begin this first-hand look at prisons with two of the most outrageous essays imaginable. What do you, the reader, need to know about the prison-industrial complex? According to Will, it ought not exist, period.

2

The Good News from God in Jesus is Freedom to the Prisoners

WILL D. CAMPBELL and JAMES Y. HOLLOWAY

Katallagete (**Winter-Spring 1972**)

WHY [IN LUKE 4:16-30] did Jesus use that Isaiah passage [Isa 61] to announce that the news from God was good?

Talk to prisoners. Be a prisoner. Here is the clear account of what Jesus says about prisoners and prisons. It is not we Christians on the outside—safe with our money, respectability and connections—who tell the prisoners the Scriptures. It is the prisoners who tell us. This is what *Katallagete* is all about.

Jesus read a passage of Gospel from Isaiah, and announced that God was coming through on his promises, reconciling all men to each other, and to Himself. The hatred, warfare and death between and among us is over: God is with us the way He is with us in Jesus. The promises, "fulfilled in your hearing" in Jesus, come not in law, but in life. The promises are not about moral principles, but people: not generalizations, but specifics; not pieties about God, and man, but deeds between them. Immanuel! God is with us! God with us, not "for-example-prisoners," but with prisoners, specifically, literally. A concrete deed as a first notice about the meaning of reconciliation. Freedom to prisoners!

The announcement then, and now, throws us into fear, trembling and terror because it shatters our worship of self; that is, our money,

16

career, social security, law-abidingness, morality, education, politics and culture. It is the announcement from God which frightens us to install new locks on our doors, burglar bars on our windows, sign up in the neighborhood security system, submit to more taxes for more police protection, abrogate lofty, school-book political principles about individual rights and due process, and believe that everything that is against our middle-income morality is political conspiracy or organized crime. In Jesus God proclaims freedom for those in prison. The prisoners are to be turned loose. Literally. This is the good news from God. In Jesus God is not reform. Not rehabilitation. Nor parole. In Jesus God is freedom. Liberation. Freedom to the criminals inside the walls of stone and so to criminals on the outside who use prison as a shield against what is done against one another, against God, and against the criminals that are hidden from sight inside the walls of stone.

Jesus' news is specific, immediate, indifferent to moral codes. It is an event as close to us as brothers, children, neighbors, bedrooms and bars and the poor and black who stand as judgment on our citizenship and our confessions about Jesus as Lord. Criminals are proclaimed free by God's deed in Jesus, and that, literally: "Today in your very hearing this text has come true." It is difficult to be more specific than that. We do not believe that Jesus was speaking of enlightened chaplains who, using the latest techniques of pastoral counseling, lead the prisoners into an adjustment—into a life of great books, celibacy, good behavior points. Nor was He talking of the chaplains who, through the art of preaching, win a soul here and there to a decision which says, "I am free wherever I am, for 'if God be for us who can be against us?'" What Jesus is talking about is unlocking the doors, dismissing the Warden and his staff, recycling the steel bars into plowshares, and turning the prisoners loose. But let us be clear at all points. This means James Earl Ray as well as Angela Davis; William Calley as well as Phil and Dan Berrigan.

Well. Of course Jesus' neighbors in the congregation at Nazareth were dismayed and angry: "Today in your very hearing this text has come true." The one thing society cannot do is free the prisoners. Society can only make prisoners, and rehabilitate, adjust and then parole them . . . to itself. Society cannot free the prisoners. Thus does Jesus' word from God undermine the claims of absolutism lurking in all political orders—whether religious (Israel) or secular (Rome). All any political order can do is to rest its legitimacy and make its distinctions between criminals and free men on the basis of power deals and arrangements. It is never good news to say to those who stake their lives on the political order and its distinctions that God frees the prisoners. Now, and here, not there and later, God announces freedom to prisoners. Literally, not symbolically. That is how God in Jesus overcomes society. No guns. No plastic bombs or napalm or anti-personnel missiles. No conspiracy that will have to be tried in a court of law. In Jesus God is freedom to the prisoners. Society is overcome. Not destroyed. Overcome.

In his time Jesus had to go. God was made a prisoner and executed. To good religious people, as a religious fanatic; to good citizens, and a political "king." But in any case, he had to go. Society's law in both religious and political dimensions makes Jesus a prisoner and executes him in the company of other criminals. And as a wise man reminds us, there, at Jesus' crucifixion at the place called The Skull, there "was the first Christian fellowship, the first certain, indissoluble and indestructible Christian community . . . directly and unambiguously affected by Jesus' promise and his assurance . . . to live by this promise is to be a Christian community." Thus, in their time John the Baptist was a criminal, a prisoner, and executed so; thus, Paul, Peter and others in the earliest communities who confessed Jesus as Lord; thus the prophets through whom God had spoken his words of reconciliation "to our fathers of old." Prison and the threat of prison were the necessary part of the life of Jeremiah, Amos, Isaiah, Micaiah, Joseph, Samson. . . . The news that God proclaims freedom to the prisoners is the word that overcomes society and politics. It is the word and deed of freedom which overcomes the words and deeds of inhumanity. Society and politics can only answer by Crucifixion, as God answers Crucifixion by freedom, liberation, resurrection.

Prison is all that society and law know to do when there are violations of its codes, values, moralities, prejudices. Society and society's law cannot acquit, liberate, reconcile, free, resurrect. Rehabilitation? What would the prisoners be "rehabilitated" from? And to? From the very codes, values, arrangements, moralities and prejudices which put them in prison? To a society that sees men—all men or any man—as sovereign over these codes, values, arrangements, moralities and prejudices? Never. Society can only "rehabilitate" the man from himself and his violations of the codes which placed him in prison, and to the society which lives by these codes. That is all society can ever know to do to those it judges "criminals." Jesus' word about this arrangement is not that it is "bad" and must therefore be destroyed, but that it is inhuman, unfree, of the order of necessity, death . . . but, that God overcomes it.

So the proclamation about freedom to the prisoners: the news from God in Jesus is another word, a Word about, and to, men. Prisoners are proclaimed free, delivered from the walls of stone: a paradigm, a first-sign, but a literal one, to all men, inside and out of prison, a notification about the specifics of the Gospel—specifics, according to Paul, that occur "while still in life . . . a new order has already begun." It is the good news from God that is an outrage: a concrete action. A deed. Freedom. Resurrection.

So the Bible looks at prisons without illusion. Their accounts of men in prison, and why they are in prison, are straightforward without rhetoric, whether men are imprisoned by Philistines or Israelites, Babylonians, Judeans or Romans. No explanation is to be found, nor is one needed, about violations of due process or about a system of justice gone mad under the pressure of external enemies or internal tyrannies. Both Testaments understand all prisoners to be political prisoners. Murderers, rapists, sodomists, insurrectionists, assassins, thieves of millions in a stock fraud or a loaf of bread to keep the family alive—the only thing society can do with those it judges criminals is to make prisoners. Therefore, to the Scriptures, it is always, in Dr. Menninger's phrase, "the crime of punishment"—a situation more characterized by inhumanity's necessity than by a delicate and evil conspiracy. . . . All this takes us back to Jesus, and to Calvary. . . . We hear no call for prison reform. We do not find instructions to the disciples to become involved in prison reform. Visit the prisoners, yes. But visit them as the prisoners Jesus talked about: no questions asked about their "crimes," about their "motives," else we tell as lie about the quality of the good news from God. Here is another basis for "visit the prisoners," inasmuch as those separated from the Lord at the final judgment would have visited the prisoners had they know that Jesus the Lord was in jail. Yet, they didn't, and we don't because we deny the Lord is a criminal. "Visit the prisoners" has never been taken seriously by the churches. Yet, we constantly discover men and women who have been in various types of prisons for decades without one single visitor having signed their record card. We have suggested on other occasions that each institutional church adopt three prisoners purely and simply for purposes of visitation—so that at least once each week every man and woman and child behind bars could have one human being with whom he could have community, to whom the prisoner could tell his story. And the visitor his. We have advocated that because we are convinced that this elementary act of charity alone would provide all the prison reform that society could tolerate. And we're not talking about visiting Phil and Dan [Berrigan]—in truth, they "visit" us when we talk to them in prison, not we, them—but about visiting the poor and the unknown and forgotten. For brutality and injustice is meted out far less often to those the world is watching than to those who are ignored by the world.

But it is not of reform that our scriptures speak. Rather, it is that prisoners remind us again that Jesus is not a social reformer. So neither were (and are) those who call him Lord! Lord! God's good news in Jesus to the prisoners calls us to the reality that Jesus means freedom, not reform. That is what Jesus' life is, and does. Those who call him Lord! Lord! are ambassadors of, witnesses to, freedom to the prisoners, not messengers of reform of prisons. (The fate of Quaker "reforms" in an earlier century might serve as a plumb-line for the realism of the Gospel at this point.)

Perhaps it is not good news to Jewish or Roman or to any society to proclaim freedom to those whom society has made prisoners. Perhaps it is to blur if not reject the distinctions between innocent and guilty on which societies necessarily exist. Those who call him Lord! Lord! should never forget what happened when Jesus first spoke about freedom to the prisoners. He was speaking to his own people, his friends and neighbors and relatives: ". . . they were infuriated. They leapt up, threw him out of the town, and took him to the brow of the hill on which it was built, meaning to hurl him over the edge"—the town, his town, Nazareth, like all towns built on moralities, prejudices, codes, fears, power arrangements, prestige and a worship of security. And finally Jesus' people, religion and secular people, did the only thing they knew to do with him: make him a criminal, imprison him, and execute him along with others they had judged criminals and prisoners.

And that is why the news from God in Jesus is good. All society knows to do about criminals and prisoners is to do what they did to Jesus and to those executed with him. But God in Jesus did and does free the prisoners. Resurrection. Jesus is prisoner in our place. He is executed in our place. So we might be free. So we might be resurrected. "Free?" Yes, free to be with God and with neighbors and enemies the way Jesus was with God and with neighbors and enemies. But free also in and from prisons of stone and concrete.

The texts, but more critically the lives of Jesus and the prisoners, admit no demythologizing, no re-mythologizing, no hermeneutic contortions, no theologizing about symbolic or other hidden meanings. Jesus proclaims freedom to the prisoner. That is the good news in its first-fruits. Men's crimes against God and therefore against society are taken up, they are assumed by the imprisoned and executed Jesus. Jesus in our place. But we in His. Free. Resurrected. So why not "free the prisoners?" God has. All of us, inside and outside prison. "Worldly standards have ceased to count in our estimate of any man" (II Corinthians 5: 16). So what could the freed "prisoners" do to us that we are not already doing to ourselves? Murder us? Pervert us? Steal from us? Use us? Lie to us? Is not the freedom that Jesus means the very option to humanity that the murderer, conspirator, dope-pusher and user, sodomist, and thief cannot find in the prisons and the paroles of society?

It is not to oppose "reform" of prison life, but to overcome prison, to preach and live the good news of freedom to the prisoners as a first-fruit of freedom to us all.

We cannot blot our Christmas and Easter. Jesus became a criminal and prisoner of society and was executed for us. All! Everyone! When we call him Lord! Lord! we are therefore calling upon a Lord who was and is a prisoner. . . . We cannot take refuge in our law-abidingness, our good citizenship and economics, for our Lord was himself executed as a criminal and thus brings freedom, resurrection, to them.

If, as we believe, the first certain Christian community was those three criminals and prisoners at their execution on Calvary, then we who call him Lord! Lord! must bear witness to His promise to the criminals and prisoners: "I tell you this: today you shall be with me in Paradise."

The good news from God in Jesus is freedom to the prisoners.

3

Law and Love in Lowndes

WILL D. CAMPBELL

Katallagete (December 1965)

IF ONE THING IS clear in the New Testament it is the central theme of the triumph of grace over law. While St. Paul stopped short of a rigid antinomian position, a complete disregard for law, he did make it clear that to abide in grace is more radical than to abide by law. And such law as he did emphasize was not law in the sense of entreaties of the State to make us behave, but an ethic, the fruit of the spirit, resulting from being "in Christ." Far more radical than law was the acceptance of this freedom.

Unless and until the Christian civil rights movement goes to the white segregationist—or the Negro segregationist—with that radical word we will continue to be little more than a pitiful addendum to the humanistically oriented organizations which got along quite well without us during our long period of silence and inactivity.

The real issue now is the failure of law in the racial crisis. (If anyone sees a few recent "convictions" as a denial of this let him understand that "failure of law" does not have to do with conviction or acquittal, but with the fact that the acts were committed.) So to go on crying, "More law!" or "Better law!" or even "Federal law!" is to beg the question. It is akin to using aspirin for a headache long after it is discovered that the headache is caused by a brain tumor. There is no question that aspirin is a remarkable drug and continues to have its place even in the presence of a brain tumor. But to rush around to find better aspirin—aspirin with buffering, aspirin that will dissolve minutes faster, aspirin with a combination of ingredients—simply because that is all the pharmacist could provide, is to place too much confidence in the pharmacist and too little in his allies of medical science. The patient is dying. We are suspicious of surgery for brain tumors because Dr. John R. Brinkley and other quacks used it to graft goat reproductive organs onto human beings with the claim that it would restore one to youthful vitality.

The Christian doctrine of grace is suspect in the area of civil rights because "the South has had that preached to it for two hundred years and it hasn't done any good." The only trouble with that claim is that it simply is not true. The folk religion of the South has been a religion of law, not of grace, and it continues to be such. As Harry Caudill observed in his recent book, *Night Comes to the Cumberland*, concerning the Appalachian South, we also have never been the Bible Belt in the sense of a depth of understanding of the Bible. He points out that many rural folk of that area—and the same is true of the lower South—did not even have Bibles, and if they had them seldom could read them.

The religion that developed in the South was a strange combination of Indian lore, old wives tales, bits of Stoic doctrine passed on by the educated aristocracy, and superstitions based on biblical quotations remembered from the time the Methodist or Baptist itinerant preacher spent the night on his way to Natchez.

The religious problem of the South is not biblical literalism but biblical illiteracy.

When religion in the formal sense did move South, it was generally in the form of a rigid legalism, and for much the same reason that legalism is what we are promoting today in civil rights. That reason is to solve a problem, to get people to behave in a certain way. It was assumed that it would work. The drunkenness, knife fighting, and general unruliness of the frontier South was not conducive to the success of mine, mill, and field. What better way to control that than to proclaim that the Devil will get you if you don't watch out. Thou shalt not fight, thou shalt not get drunk or cause others to get drunk through the making and selling of the stuff, and above all, thou shalt not come to work late on Monday or run away if you are a slave. That is not biblical literalism and it is certainly not New Testament literalism, unless one wants to twist Paul's letter to Philemon into a letter to Onesimus.

And it failed. The South has the finest laws but without a corresponding relationship to its crime rate. (It is true that the F.B.I. recently rated Mississippi as having the second lowest crime rate in the nation—next to Alaska—but if one considers seventeen men accused of murdering three civil rights workers, and none of them have been either indicted or convicted, one can see that the crime rate would be accordingly lowered.)

Legalism is failing again. Whether we can see it or not, it is failing. It fails because the first lesson man learned was how to deal with the requirements of the law. From Eve to Thomas Coleman it has been the same. The way to handle law is to interpret it. Thus, "Thou shalt not steal," means children should not take apples from other children's lunch baskets, but it does not have anything to do with price fixing, cheap labor, or the stock market. "Thou shalt not commit adultery," means unless your wife doesn't understand you. "Thou shalt not kill," means one man does not take a gun and shoot a fellow he admits he hates, but it does not apply to a nation killing thousands of men, women, and children whom it claims to love.

Yet, if we seem now to advocate the repeal of recently enacted civil rights laws or oppose the passage of others we are being less than clear. And certainly we are not suggesting that love and law are contrary to each other. The point is that those of us who should be interested in relating the two seem not to be relating them at all, but to be promoting the one and ignoring the other. The further point is that the one we insist on promoting continues to let us down.

If law is for the purpose of preventing crime, then every wail of a siren calls out its failure. Every civil rights demonstration attests to the courts' inability to provide racial justice. Every police chief who asks for a larger appropriation because of the rising crime rate is admitting his own failure. Every time a law has to be enforced it is a failure.

The simple fact is that for the Christian, law is an inadequate minimal. Do not even the publicans do the same? If this is all we have to offer the world, then Jesus Christ was of all men most mad.

Still we hear, "But the Thomas Colemans must be restrained." Exactly! Then where is the fruit? When will he be restrained? The truth is that he now sees a truce being signed between his two traditional enemies, Negro leaders and the Federal government. No doubt, this has been necessary in moving in the direction of simple justice, especially when he has declined offers to be a party to the truce. Be that as it may, the rejections continue, the killings go on, the hostilities mount and intensify, perhaps to be set loose wholesale again on another day when the Feds and Marchers have all gone home, or turned to stopping the war with Venus, and what we see as the gains of this day turn out to be the rack rent of that day.

If the argument now is on the basis of what will work, then let us put it there.

Few criminologists today see punishment, and especially capital punishment, as an effective deterrent to crime. I have had the frustrating experience during the past six months of working with a group on a frantic, around-the-clock, basis in an effort to abolish capital punishment. The argument that got the most votes in the legislature was the above finding of leading criminologists. Since that time, some of those same individuals have marched in the streets over the acquittal of Thomas Coleman. When they hear, "You are after revenge," they reply, "No, not revenge. Preventative." Now this is sheer madness.

What then do we say? Certainly, we cannot say we are not interested in stopping the killings all around us. And a Christian who is not involved to his maximum in correcting the injustices of the Southern region had best examine his commitment to Christ. Certainly, we cannot say we are not interested in the success of the civil rights movement. Too long we debated the number of angels on a needle point while our brothers were in chains. Certainly, we cannot advocate retreating from the world into the security of established religion. God knows that didn't work! But the question is, what is one's maximum involvement? Is it law or is there a still deeper issue and involvement?

What distinctive word, what message of hope does the Christian have for the racial crisis? It may be that he has no word of hope in the sense that hope is understood generally. But he certainly has a distinctive word. That word is The Word. The Word become flesh.

And that Word leads us to the death of Jonathan Daniels and our response to it. What can one say when a brother whom we have set apart and sent forth is dead? We can say, "Our brother is dead. Let's go bury him." Then we can say a benediction. And perhaps nothing more is appropriate.

But we who set Jon Daniels apart and sent him forth have said far more than that. We got immediate appointments with the highest official of the Department of Justice. We pressured through releases and statements and marches and court stays for Federal intervention. We have said such things as: "We must have Federal initiative and involvement in the investigation and prosecution of murders . . ." And now we are considering civil proceedings of our own against the murderer of our brother. We have indicated that the President is a scoundrel for not "doing something." And worst of all we have said that unless the conditions which we have set forth are met, Jonathan will have died in vain.

Yes, that is the worst of all because nothing, absolutely nothing, any of us do or do not do now will cause his death to have been in vain. That is out of our hands. He can never have died in vain because he loved his killer. By his own last written words he loved his killer. (If one is looking for a martyr in it all, to die at the hands of one you love for a cause in which you believe strongly enough to let the beloved kill you is coming mighty close.) If he had loved only the Negroes with whom he lived and ate and worshipped it might have been different. Then one might set up conditions and issue ultimatums in order to get mileage out of his death, in order to have his death "mean something." But since he loved his murderer his death is its own meaning. And what that means is that Thomas Coleman is forgiven. If Jonathan forgives him, as he did when he came to love him, then it is not for me to cry for his blood. Any act on my part which is even akin to "avenging" his death is sacrilege. Vengeance negates martyrdom. It never confirms it. The sacramental act was Jonathan's, not mine.

When he loved his killer he set him free, for that is what love is. We might at least have learned that much from two thousand years of punishing Jews for killing Christ.

But apart from that, for the Christian to invoke the law of the State in this case is as absurd as it would have been for the early Christians to have gone to Court following the death of Polycarp in 155, or for the Gospel Missionary Union to have lobbied for a war with Ecuador when Nathaniel Saint was killed at the hands of a savage Jinaro Indian mob in 1958. Jonathan was as certainly an evangelist as Polycarp. He was as certainly a missionary as Nathaniel. And any time a Christian is set apart and sent forth to proclaim the bold and offensive Word, death is apt to be the outcome. While I cannot find it within me to rejoice in this death, we at least must know that what happened was the worst that they could do, that all Satan can produce is death and that that enemy has been conquered by The Word. . . . And might the truth of the matter be that we don't quite, not after all this time, learning, and protestations of faith, trust the central theme of the Gospel, the triumph of grace over law.

The notion that a man can go to a store where a group of unarmed human beings are assembled, fire a shotgun blast at one of them, tearing his lungs, heart, and bowels from his body, turn on another and send lead pellets ripping through his flesh and bones, and that God will set him free is almost more than we can stand. But unless that is precisely the case then there is no Gospel, there is no good news. Unless that is the truth we are back under law, and Christ's death and resurrection are of no account.

When Thomas killed Jonathan he committed a crime against the state of Alabama. Alabama, for reasons of its own, chose not to punish him for that crime against itself. And do we not all know what those reasons were?

When Thomas killed Jonathan he committed a crime against God. The strange, the near maddening thing about this case is that both these offended parties have rendered the same verdict—not for the same reasons, not in the same way, but the verdict is the same—acquittal.

The Christian response here is not to damn the "acquittal by law," but to proclaim the "acquittal by resurrection." One frees him to go and kill again. The other liberates him to obedience in Christ. Acquittal by law was the act of Caesar. Render unto him what is his. The State, by its very nature and definition, can do anything it wills to do—Hitler proved that much. Acquittal by resurrection was the act of God. And he has entrusted us with that message.

Thomas also committed a crime against Jonathan. And Jonathan rendered a similar verdict when he loved him.

But he also committed an offense against us, against those of us who set Jonathan apart and sent him forth. Thus far we have come out worst of all.

Perhaps it is because we are afraid of the Colemans of this world. Perhaps it is because he rebuffed us in the Delta and elsewhere. But worse than either of these it may be that we just plain do not love him.

The blood that is on our hands is more than that of Daniels and [James] Reeb, [Michael] Schwerner and [Herbert] Lee, [James] Chaney and [Andrew] Goodman, [Medgar] Evers and [Jimmy Lee] Jackson. The blood that is on our hands is the immortal souls of the Colemans and the [Lawrence] Raineys. They did it in the name of Jesus Christ.

That makes them blasphemers. If we, the righteous ones, the children of light, can offer them only law for their deliverance, we are approaching the point of joining them in that offense.

If he persists in his blasphemy, and we in ours, we may yet be integrated with him—but in hell. What then have we overcome?

PART 2

Naming the Powers

"WORDS WILL NEVER HURT me"? Words, of course, command the power of freedom and captivity, inclusion and exclusion, life and death. Label someone an "illegal immigrant," for example, and you can expel her from your society. Tag another "enemy," and you can extinguish his life. Brand yet a third "criminal," and you can deny human rights, caging her in perpetuity. All such terms, David Dark notes, are "death sentences that generate a sort of verbal totalitarianism, cutting off real-live people."[1]

Over the years Will Campbell has been especially prophetic in exposing the vocabulary that we as a society will utter and tolerate. Will recounts how his friend, Thad Garner, was on a radio call-in show, and how so many callers seemed offended by Johnny Cash's use of a "bad word" on a recent TV show. Garner asked one of the callers to tell him what Cash had said.

> [The caller] hesitated, stammered, and then said, "Wellll. I can't repeat it. It was a bad word and I don't say bad words."
>
> "I understand, ma'am," Thad said quickly. "I'm glad you don't say bad words. Now, I tell you what. I know some bad words, so I'll call them out one by one, and you just tell me yes or no if that's what he said. Okay. Here goes" He was barking like a drill sergeant. "Did he say 'death'?"

1. Dark, *The Sacredness of Questioning Everything*, 122.

"Wellll. No," the woman said in the same grating voice.

"Very good," Thad said. "Did he say 'nuclear war'?"

"Wellll. No. That's not what he said." Her voice was showing irritation.

"Good. Okay. Did he say 'electric chair'?"

Thad waited for the woman to answer. Instead there was the noise of the heavy slamming of the telephone.

"I'm sorry you left us, ma'am. Hope you're still listening. That's three of the nastiest, filthiest, ugliest, most vile words I know. If Johnny Cash didn't say any of those, and if you can't tell me what he did say, well, I guess I can't help you."[2]

Why are some expletives vulgar and unutterable, while "verbal totalitarianism that cuts off real-live people" draws hardly a notice? What does that (in)tolerance reveal about us?

George Orwell is right in encouraging us to break all grammatical rules "sooner than say anything outright barbarous."[3]

Who, for example, would dare call the grammatically flawless directions for operating the gas chambers in a concentration camp, "good writing"? Communicating well and rightly neither devalues, nor diminishes a neighbor.

In that spirit, Dark explains, good words "uplift the way bad language degrades." They "dismember death," and rightly "RE-member" our communities. They perform that miracle by deconstructing oppressive systems and unmasking abusive practices. That's the prophetic act. Prophets shatter what's normative, and contest the doublespeak that violence obtains peace, or retribution achieves justice. Prophets utilize vocabulary we know, but in such "enlivening" ways that we catch a totally different vision—"rethinking, reappraising, and redeeming" what we thought we knew to be right and true. If we join in their "emancipating conversations," the world and our practices will never look quite "normal" again.[4]

The essays in this section perform this prophetic act. They exhibit good writing insofar as they pull back the veil and expose a heinous, death-dealing system and its profane logic—a way of thinking that has been building exponentially for the last forty years. The authors here invite you, the reader, into that emancipating, redemptive exploration. Perhaps they will inspire us—in the name of reconciliation—to foreswear

2. Campbell, *Forty Acres and a Goat*, 187–88.

3. Orwell, "Politics and the English Language," http://www.mtholyoke.edu/acad/intrel/orwell46.htm

4. Dark, *The Sacredness of Questioning Everything*, 121–40.

some expletives of verbal totalitarianism like "felon," "prisoner," and "retribution."

Richard C. Goode

4

What Has Happened Since 1973?

PRESTON SHIPP

NEARLY FOUR DECADES HAVE passed since Will Campbell and the Committee of Southern Churchmen published their ". . . *and the criminals with him . . .*" volume of *Katallagete*, and Paulist Press reprinted the issue in 1973. In that year, Richard Nixon occupied the White House, and the Vietnam War drew to a close with the signing of the Paris Peace Accords. "Killing Me Softly With His Song," by Roberta Flack and "Crocodile Rock," by Elton John were on the radio. At the Academy Awards ceremony on March 27, "The Godfather" won the Oscar for Best Picture. Secretariat won the Triple Crown, and Billie Jean King defeated Chris Evert at Wimbledon. There was no Internet, no DVDs, and no cellular telephones. If a person wanted to play a video game, she went to an arcade, as the Atari, much less the Playstation or Xbox, had yet to be released. The average cost of a new house was $32,500. 1973 also marked the beginning of the oil crisis, when Arab members of the Organization of Petroleum Exporting Countries restricted the flow of oil to countries supporting Israel. And in an opinion rendered on January 22, 1973, the United States Supreme Court held that a woman has a constitutional right to obtain an abortion.[1]

More importantly for the purposes of this work, however, was the Supreme Court's decision one year earlier in *Furman v. Georgia*, in which the Court held that the death penalty, as applied, violated the Eighth and Fourteenth Amendments to the United States Constitution because it was discretionary, haphazard, and discriminatory in so far as it was inflicted

---

1. *Roe v. Wade*, 410 U.S. 113, 93 S. Ct. 705, 35 L. Ed. 2d 147 (1973).

in only a small number of the total possible cases and primarily against certain minority groups.[2] Thus, at the time the *Katallagete* issue and subsequent book was first published, the death penalty was unconstitutional. Given the relentless pursuit of retribution which is the American criminal justice system, however, little time passed before numerous states devised a scheme to resume the killing of their own citizens. To that development we shall soon return.

Perhaps the most notable change in the criminal justice landscape since 1973, however, is the sheer growth in size of the American prison population. In 1973, approximately 200,000 people were incarcerated in the United States. In 2009, however, approximately 2.3 million people were incarcerated in federal and state prisons and jails.[3] Thus, since the first publication of this work, the population of incarcerated persons in the United States has increased tenfold. While the United States has less than 6 percent of earth's population, it currently warehouses almost 25 percent of its prisoners.[4] Additionally, another 5 million people were on probation or on parole as of 2008. Therefore, 3.2 percent of all U.S. adult residents, or one in every thirty-one adults, are under the supervision of the American corrections system.[5]

Warehousing this many American citizens is not cheap. According to December 2009 information from the United States Bureau of Justice Statistics (BJS), $68,747,203,000 was spent on corrections in 2006.[6] The average annual operating cost per state inmate in 2001 was $22,650, or $62.05 per day; among facilities operated by the Federal Bureau of Prisons, it was $22,632 per inmate, or $62.01 per day.[7] The colossal amount of money being poured into the prison system raises the question, where is all that money going? But considering the price tag for feeding and providing medical care to 2.4 million people, the salaries paid to all of the wardens and corrections officers, the electric and water bills generated by all of the prisons across the country, simply paying for that many pillows or light bulbs or that much fencing, it becomes clear why incarcerating such a large segment of the American population amounts to a vast money pit.

2. *Furman v. Georgia*, 408 U.S. 238, 92 S. Ct. 2726, 33 L. Ed. 2d 346 (1972).

3. http://bjs.ojp.usdoj.gov/index.cfm?ty=pbdetail&iid=2200

4. http://www.nytimes.com/2008/04/23/us/23prison.html.

5. http://bjs.ojp.usdoj.gov/index.cfm?ty=tp&tid=11. For an excellent analysis of the devastating collateral social consequences of such mass incarceration, particularly for low-income, minority communities, see James Samuel Logan's *Good Punishment?*

6. http://bjs.ojp.usdoj.gov/content/glance/tables/exptyptab.cfm.

7. http://bjs.ojp.usdoj.gov/index.cfm?ty=tp&tid=16.

Other financial concerns related to the prison system are also worthy of consideration. With the advent of private, for-profit prison corporations came the opportunity to turn the prison population into an investment opportunity. Private corporations capable of operating prisons more efficiently, i.e., cheaply, than the federal or state governments receive lucrative contracts to manage the institutions and prisoners. The government pays the corporation a per diem or monthly rate for each prisoner confined in the facility. One of the most prominent private prison companies is Nashville-based Corrections Corporation of America (CCA). CCA, founded in 1983, builds, manages, owns, and operates correctional facilities and detention centers on behalf of all three federal corrections agencies and nearly half of the states.[8] CCA is the fourth-largest corrections system in the nation, behind only the federal government, California, and Texas. CCA alone warehouses approximately 75,000 offenders and detainees in more than 60 facilities, 44 of which are company-owned. According to its website, "CCA employs nearly 17,000 professionals nationwide in security, academic and vocational education, health services, inmate programs, facility maintenance, human resources, management and administration. The company has been named among 'America's Best Big Companies' by *Forbes* magazine . . . The company also provides valuable economic benefits to its local community partners by paying property, sales and other taxes, and by providing a stable employment base that focuses on building careers with unlimited growth and development opportunities." Thus, James Samuel Logan notes that "[t]oday, private prison management represents one of the fastest growing sectors of the U.S. economy."[9] In short, crime is business, and with 2.4 million Americans incarcerated and recidivism rates hovering around 70 percent, business is booming.

Even more troubling from an ethical perspective is that in 1994, CCA joined the New York Stock Exchange. Therefore, since the government pays the corporation a flat rate for each prisoner, an investor in CCA stock has a financial interest in the company warehousing as many people as possible as cheaply as possible. Under this paradigm, an empty prison bed represents lost profits, and a repeat offender constitutes repeat business. We have exchanged Jesus' proclamation of release of the prisoners in Luke 4, for an opportunity to line our pockets.

8. Information about Corrections Corporation of America came from the company's website, www.correctionscorp.com.

9. Logan, *Good Punishment?*, 51.

Furthermore, the U.S. prison population, which is roughly the size of the city of Houston, is a source of cheap labor for numerous large companies. IBM, Dell, Eddie Bauer, Microsoft, Victoria's Secret, Texas Instruments, and AT&T have all been linked to prison labor. For the tycoons at the helms of these corporations, the immense prison population is a goldmine. The companies pay prison workers a fraction of what they would have to pay outside workers, and no longer worry over strikes, paying unemployment insurance, vacations, or comp time. Courts have repeatedly held that the Fair Labor Standards Act does not apply to prisoners, who are therefore without leverage to secure just working conditions. Also, the pittance that the incarcerated workers earn, places artificial downward pressure on the wages of free-world workers. "Indeed, it would be no exaggeration to say that prison culture has effectively introduced a significant slave-like class into the American social fabric, one of whose significant functions is that of feeding profits to big business."[10] For corporations that exploit prisoners as a source of cheap labor, every tough-on-crime piece of legislation that mandates longer prison sentences represents dollars in their pockets. Accordingly, since the first publication of this book, America has heralded the birth of the prison-industrial complex. The vast prison-industrial complex consists of all of the businesses and organizations involved in the construction and operation of correctional facilities, including private corrections companies, corporations that contract prison labor, construction companies, companies that supply necessary materials, and lobbyists promoting the interests of such organizations. In short, the American prison system has become a leviathan, a principality and power if ever there was one.

The dramatic expansion of the American prison population over the past forty years is a complex issue that is not the product of any one event or actor. Numerous parties—from police unions to legislators to investors in private, for-profit prison corporations—bear responsibility for the social dilemma of mass incarceration. However, to gain a basic understanding of the root of this human crisis, we need look no further than the war on drugs, which was declared by President Nixon in 1971 and has been subsequently waged by every President since. The unprecedented number of people being locked away from their families and communities has been fueled by the drug war, which shows no signs of being won any time soon.

The war on drugs came on the heels of the tumultuous 1960s, when the recreational use of narcotics increased significantly. Two years after

10. Ibid., 56.

President Nixon's declaration of a drug war, in which he claimed that drug abuse was "public enemy number one," the Drug Enforcement Administration (DEA) was established. The DEA consolidated agents from several other agencies, and allowed the federal government to assume a much greater role in fighting all aspects of the drug problem.

When Ronald Reagan entered the White House in 1980, the war on drugs gained momentum as a top priority, utilizing a law-enforcement-oriented approach. First, between 1980 and 1984, money allocated to the FBI for anti-drug initiatives increased from $8 million to $95 million.[11] Second, in 1984, Nancy Reagan's "Just Say No" campaign began, which largely targeted white, middle-class children. Third, President Reagan signed the Anti-Drug Abuse Act in 1986, an enormous omnibus drug bill, which appropriated $1.7 billion to fight the drug crisis and $97 million to build new prisons. Additionally, the bill created mandatory minimum penalties for drug offenses. These mandatory minimums were criticized over the years for promoting significant racial disparities in sentencing. Most notably, those convicted of crimes involving crack cocaine, which was commonly associated with inner-cities and the African-American population, were punished on a 100-to-1 ratio compared to those whose crimes involve cocaine in powder form. Thus, possession of five grams of crack cocaine would trigger a mandatory five-year prison sentence, while it would require trafficking 500 grams of powder cocaine to receive the same sentence.[12]

Following the Anti-Drug Abuse Act of 1986, with its heavy emphasis on punishing crack cocaine users, federal and state courts were dominated by crack cases. The result was minorities, specifically young African-American men, being shipped to prison in record numbers. Between 1980 and 1999, the incarceration rate of African-Americans in federal prisons more than tripled, and this despite clear evidence that the majority of crack cocaine users are white.[13] "In 1996, ninety percent of the prison admissions for drug offenses were either African-American or Latino/a."[14] In 2002, 47 percent of prison inmates serving time for drug offenses were black, although blacks constituted only 15 percent of illicit drug users.[15]

11. Provine, *Unequal Under Law*, 103.

12. This disparity remains to this day, although the Fair Sentencing Act of 2009, as amended, would reduce the current 100:1 sentencing disparity to 20:1.

13. Provine, *Unequal Under Law*, 127.

14. Logan, *Good Punishment?*, 68.

15. Benavie, *Drugs: America's Holy War*, 4

It is also well documented that blacks are more likely to be sentenced to prison than whites convicted of the same offense, and once in prison, they serve longer sentences than their white counterparts.[16]

The war on drugs had a disproportionate effect on women as well. At the beginning of President Reagan's first term, 10 percent of incarcerated females were serving sentences for drug-related offenses. Twenty years later, the number had climbed to one in three.[17] Throughout the remainder of Reagan's presidency and the subsequent administrations of Presidents Bush, Clinton, and George W. Bush, increasing numbers of people were serving increasingly long prison sentences, often for possessing a relatively small amount of drugs. Regardless of who sat in the Oval Office or which party controlled Congress, there was little concern for the price, in either human or financial terms, of mass incarceration. Accordingly, the American prison population has continued to swell.

The result of this massive drug war, which costs approximately 50 billion dollars per year, is that today, drug offenders make up almost 60 percent of the federal prison population.[18] Nearly three-fourths of these inmates have no history of violence.[19] Over 100,000 people are currently incarcerated in American prisons for simply possessing, not selling, illegal drugs.[20] Marijuana arrests constitute 45 percent of the 1.5 million drug arrests that occur annually in the U.S., and around 80 percent of these arrests are for possession alone.[21]

The war on drugs was wrong-headed almost from its genesis. Only during the remainder of President Nixon's administration did the majority of funding go toward prevention and treatment, rather than law enforcement initiatives. "By 1986, 80 percent of the federal drug-fighting budget went for interdiction and law enforcement, rather than treatment."[22] Between 1987 and 1998, the federal budget for fighting the war on drugs increased from $6 billion to $20 billion, and two-thirds of this money went to law enforcement and prisons.[23] Thus, the American approach to the

16. Ibid., 67–68
17. Logan, *Good Punishment?*, 73.
18. Provine, *Unequal Under Law*, 17.
19. Ibid.
20. Benavie, *Drugs: America's Holy War*, 4
21. Provine, *Unequal Under Law*, 18, 100; and Benavie, *Drugs: America's Holy War*, 33.
22. Ibid., 96.
23. Ibid., 119

drug problem has been increasingly skewed in favor of punishment in the form of incarceration, even of nonviolent offenders. Nixon's establishment of the Drug Enforcement Administration in 1973 set the punishment-oriented tone for the drug war that remains today. As Laura Magnani and the late Harmon Wray noted in their important book, *Beyond Prisons*, "It is imperative that drug and alcohol addiction be treated as a health problem and not as a political or moral issue calling for punishment. As long as resources are squandered on punishment, the United States will never be able to meet the demands for treatment."[24] Wray's prophetic words come too late for many incarcerated persons and their families.

Perhaps the most damnable fact about the American war on drugs is that, as a practical matter, it constitutes an assault against the nation's poor, mostly urban minorities. The tendency of people in physical or emotional pain, as so many modern Americans are, to self-medicate is not germane to either rich or poor. The rich, however, have access to physicians who, with a quickly scribbled signature, can legitimate a drug addiction. The poor, on the other hand, settle for what can be purchased on a street corner. Therefore, Angela Y. Davis argues that "those unfortunate enough to become addicted to crack can be arrested and thrown in jail, while their middle-class counterparts, who have access to licit drugs such as Valium or Prozac, are free to indulge their drug habits."[25] It is against the drugs of the poor, most notably crack cocaine, that the drug war is violently waged.

Possession of crack cocaine is punished more severely in the federal system than most violent offenses, with an average sentence of approximately ten years.[26] Over 90 percent of people convicted of crack cocaine offenses are minorities.[27] Although African-American males make up less than seven percent of the U.S. population, they compose approximately 37.5 percent of the incarcerated population, and when combined with African-American females, the two groups constitute half of the nation's inmates.[28]

Jeffrey Reiman notes the racially skewed practice of law enforcement more aggressively policing the sale of illegal drugs in low-income neighborhoods, where much more social interaction, including drug

24. Magnani and Wray, *Beyond Prisons*, 66
25. Davis, "Race, Gender, and Prison History," 36.
26. Provine, *Unequal Under Law*, 3, 17; Benavie, *Drugs: America's Holy War*, p. 15.
27. Ibid., 17, 120.
28. Logan, *Good Punishment?*, 67–68.

transactions, occurs in the open than it does in the suburbs.[29] Reiman also points out that rather than discourage criminal activity, the war on drugs has the practical effect of encouraging crime.[30] First, when a product for which there is a demand is made illegal, the value of the item skyrockets due to the risk involved in producing, transporting, and selling it. The inflated price of the drug enriches all who risk prison time in order to make it available. Thus, during the prohibition era of the 1920s and 1930s, when alcohol was illegal, gangsters such as Al Capone became rich and powerful by manufacturing and bootlegging alcohol due to the increased value of the product. With such outrageous profits to be made from the sale of illicit substances, there will be a steady supply of people who are willing to break the law by providing them. "Numerous studies show that arrested drug dealers in inner-city neighborhoods are quickly replaced" by the next person who is willing to risk time in prison for the chance to make money as a drug dealer.[31] Simply locking up drug offenders is an exercise in futility. By criminalizing the sale and use of drugs, the government has provided a financial incentive to be involved in the drug trade. The immutable laws of supply and demand renders the war on drugs unwinnable.

Additionally, the exorbitant cost of illegal drugs renders it impossible for a user to fund her habit with an honest salary. Normal people, particularly low-income people, cannot afford a drug habit of several hundred dollars per day. Thus, people resort to other, more harmful crimes, such as theft, burglary, or robbery—all acts predicated on the need to fund the use of illegal drugs. The Bureau of Justice Statistics determined that a third of robbers and burglars had committed their crimes to obtain money for drugs.[32] Were drugs not illegal, their cost would plummet, and people would not be seduced to pursue other criminal activity to obtain money to buy more drugs.

Finally, because the sale of illegal drugs is so lucrative, drug traffickers engage in violent turf wars over the money to be made. Competing gangs, which are organized around the illegal drug trade, resort to homicide in an attempt to obtain a larger piece of the drug market. It is not the drugs themselves that cause such violence, but the increased value of the drugs that results from their illegality. "Legal drugs don't spawn violent drug

---

29 Reiman, *The Rich Get Richer and the Poor Get Prison*, 117–18.

30. Ibid., 37–44.

31. Ibid., 43.

32. Benavie, *Drugs: America's Holy War*, 18, 41.

cartels. . . ."[33] If marijuana and cocaine could be safely and legitimately purchased for reasonable prices, profit-motivated violence between rival gangs would cease. Meanwhile, the money being devoted to the futile drug war could be funneled into more prudent programs focused on treatment and education.

> When drug addicts cannot obtain their fix legally, they will obtain it illegally. Because those who sell it illegally have a captive market, they will charge high prices to make their own risks worthwhile. To pay the high prices, addicts must, will, and do resort to crime. Thus, every day in which we keep the acquisition of drugs a crime, we are using the law to protect the high profits of drug black marketeers, *and* we are creating a situation in which large numbers of individuals are virtually physically compelled to commit theft. In sum, we have an antidrug policy that is failing at its own goals and succeeding only in adding to crime.[34]

Thus, since the first publication of this work in 1973, the issues that gave Campbell such concern have been magnified almost beyond measure. "The war against drugs [has served] as the pretext for police and military campaigns and an obscene proliferation of prisons and jails."[35] With the ten-fold increase in the size of the American prison population and the privatization of correctional institutions came an investment opportunity for Wall Street players and a source of cheap labor for megacorporations eager to cut production costs in order to maximize profits. The ongoing war on drugs has proven ineffective in reducing the drug trade, despite virtually limitless spending. The drug war is, in fact, foolish and unwinnable because its very existence creates the incentive to engage in criminal activity, either by selling drugs to make a profit, committing theft, burglary, or robbery in order to finance one's addiction, or by resorting to lethal violence in order to protect or enlarge one's slice of the illegal drug trade. The war on drugs is a failed policy that unfairly targets poor minorities, who are being incarcerated at a rate that would have been hard for Campbell to imagine thirty-seven years ago.

As noted earlier, the principality and power that is the American criminal justice system, comprised as it is of voters, lobbyists, legislators, police officers, prosecutors, judges, prison wardens and guards, is not

33. Reiman, *The Rich Get Richer and the Poor Get Prison*, 36.
34. Ibid., 195 and 43.
35. Davis, *The Angela Y. Davis Reader*, 230.

content merely to warehouse its criminals. After the Supreme Court declared the death penalty unconstitutional in the 1972 decision of *Furman v. Georgia,* because it was applied in a discriminatory manner, only four years passed before the Court was presented with a more structured, systematized, methodical, organized method of dolling out death sentences in the case of *Gregg v. Georgia.*[36]

The State of Georgia presented the court with a new statutory scheme for imposing the death penalty that included a bifurcated trial composed of a guilt phase and a sentencing phase; the opportunity to present additional argument and additional evidence in mitigation or aggravation of punishment; the requirement that the trier of fact find at least one aggravating circumstance to exist beyond a reasonable doubt before the death sentence may be imposed; automatic appeal of a death sentence to the state supreme court; and proportionality review to ensure that the death sentence was not excessive or disproportionate to the penalty imposed in similar cases. The United States Supreme Court found that capital punishment, as imposed under Georgia's new scheme, did not run afoul of the constitutional protection against cruel and unusual punishment because the new procedures eliminated the potential for the death penalty to be applied in an arbitrary or discriminatory manner. The Court also noted that, since its decision in *Furman,* no less than thirty-five states had enacted new statutes in an attempt to address the Court's concerns and place the death penalty back on the books in a form that would withstand constitutional scrutiny. Americans thirsty for the blood of the criminals among them won the day.

The enduring war on drugs, the resulting dramatic increase in the U.S. prison population, the advent of the prison-industrial complex, and the reinstatement of capital punishment all demonstrate that in the past four decades, America has become more vengeful. Instead of working for justice, as the criminal justice system claims to do, we have settled for mere retribution. Content to punish the bad acts, whether they be possession of marijuana or murder, we fail to address the underlying context in which the actions were committed, which include poverty, prior victimization, lack of education and access to employment that pays a living wage, and mental illness. If ever there was a time to be mindful that Lord Jesus died a convicted criminal in the company of two other condemned persons, and to contemplate that He is incarnated in each and every one of our 2.4 million prisoners, the time is now. For as we do unto these, we do unto Him.

36. 428 U.S. 153, 96 S. Ct. 2909, 49 L. Ed. 2d 859 (1976).

5

The Societal Impact of the Prison Industrial Complex, or Incarceration for Fun and Profit . . . Mostly Profit

ALEX FRIEDMANN

A T THE BEGINNING OF the 1980s there were no privately-operated adult correctional facilities in the United States. As of 2009, more than 129,300 state and federal prisoners are housed in for-profit lock-ups.[1] Prison privatization has become an acceptable practice, and the private prison industry is a multi-billion dollar business. How did this drastic expansion of incarceration-for-profit occur, and more importantly how has it rearranged the criminal justice landscape?

The prison and jail population in the United States has increased exponentially over the past several decades, from 648,000 in 1983 to more than 2.3 million as of 2009. That doesn't include another 5 million on parole and probation, plus millions more who were formerly incarcerated and are no longer under correctional supervision. Spending on prisons has outstripped expenditures on higher education in at least six states, including Michigan, Connecticut, and California, as lawmakers engage in one-upmanship to prove who's tougher on crime.

Why has our nation's prison population grown to epic proportions, until the U.S.—with only 5 percent of the world's population—now has 25 percent of the world's prisoners? The succinct answer is because imprisonment has become enormously profitable as a result of politically-influenced

1. "Prisoners in 2009," U.S. Dept. of Justice, Bureau of Justice Statistics (NCJ 231675, Dec. 2010), Table 19.

decisions as to who should be locked up and for how long. In the 1980s and 90s a series of tough-on-crime laws were enacted, spurred by the so-called War on Drugs and the corporate media's steady and often sensationalistic coverage of violent offenses. Those laws included mandatory minimum sentences, truth-in-sentencing statutes, and three-strikes laws, which required lengthy prison terms or life sentences for certain offenders.

Consequently, more and more people were arrested, prosecuted, convicted, and sent to prison, where they served longer periods of time under harsher sentencing statutes. Concurrently, prison release policies became more restrictive. For example, parole in the federal prison system was abolished in 1987. With more people entering the prison system to serve longer sentences, and fewer leaving, the U.S. prison population grew exponentially—increasing over 350 percent from 1983 to the present.

This prison population boom created a market for companies that found they could profit by providing correctional services, and a multi-billion dollar industry was born to capitalize on crime and punishment. This industry, commonly referred to as the "prison industrial complex," is composed of a confluence of businesses and special interest groups that collectively profit from incarceration. The most overt members include private prison companies such as Corrections Corporation of America (CCA), GEO Group (formerly Wackenhut Corrections), MTC, Cornell (acquired by GEO in 2010), and a bevy of smaller firms that operate detention facilities.

Beyond companies that own or operate prisons there are a number of other businesses that benefit from the prison boom—ranging from corporations that provide prison and jail food services (e.g., Aramark, Canteen Services); prison medical care (Prison Health Services, Correctional Medical Services); private probation supervision services (Sentinel Offender Services); and prisoner transportation services (TransCor, PTS of America); to the banks and investment firms that provide bond financing for new prisons; the construction companies that build them; suppliers of razor wire, surveillance cameras, and other security equipment, etc. In short, the expansion of the U.S. prison population created an enormously profitable market opportunity. CCA alone grossed $1.67 billion in revenue in 2009; its closest competitor, GEO Group, grossed $1.27 billion.[2]

---

2. CCA's 2010 annual report (http://phx.corporate-ir.net/External.File?item=UGF yZW50SUQ9NDE5MTEwfENoaWxkSUQ9NDMyMjg1fFR5cGU9MQ==&t=1); and GEO Group, *Annual Report 2010* (www.geogroup.com/AR_2010/HTML2/default.htm).

The private companies that comprise the prison industrial complex have thus reaped substantial benefits by surfing the wave of overincarceration that has swept our nation's criminal justice system. They are the ones that most obviously benefit from putting more people in prison for longer periods of time. But what are the collateral consequences of for-profit incarceration as social policy?

Frustrating Prison Reform Efforts

Criminal justice policies in the U.S. are based in large part on capacity—that is, the capacity of state and federal prison systems, plus sentencing and parole policies that govern the number of inmates entering prison and being released. The need for prison beds created by our nation's burgeoning prisoner population has outstripped existing capacity, leading states and the federal government to go on a prison-building binge and, when that solution failed to accommodate growing numbers of prisoners, to overcrowd correctional facilities by double or triple-bunking cells and installing beds in prison gyms, classrooms, and even chapels.

However, overcrowding—which leads to increased violence, decreased access to medical care for prisoners, and a host of other problems—can only go so far. At some point it becomes impossible or impractical to cram more prisoners into already-packed cells, and too expensive to build more prisons. Enter CCA, GEO Group, and other companies that finance and build their own correctional facilities, which provide public prison systems with extra bed space capacity. Notably, if private prison firms did not provide such additional beds, then state and federal governments would be forced to address the harsh sentencing laws and prison release policies that have resulted in over-incarceration and prison overcrowding.

Thus the private prison industry—the moving force behind the prison industrial complex—has served to stymie criminal justice reform efforts over the past several decades, particularly in regard to sentencing and prison release policies. Rather than being forced to deal with the repercussions of such policies, government officials have used private prisons as a safety valve. As an analogy, if our prison system was a bucket being filled to overflowing by a steady stream of prisoners, the extra bed space provided by the private prison industry allows prisoners to be siphoned off into another bucket. So long as this extra capacity is provided by private prisons, government officials can postpone dealing with the politically-unpopular issues of sentencing reform or increasing the number of people being released from prison.

Although private prisons house only 8 percent of state and federal prisoners, that is an important 8 percent. In 2009, private prisons were utilized by the federal government and 32 states, of which some have become dependent on privatization to maintain their prison population levels. As of the end of 2009, ten states have 20 percent or more of their prisoners in privately-operated facilities, including New Mexico (43.3 percent), Montana (39.8 percent), Vermont (30.1 percent), and Hawaii (28 percent).[3] The Federal Bureau of Prisons houses 16.4 percent of its population in for-profit facilities—which does not include detainees held by Immigration and Customs Enforcement (ICE) in private detention centers.[4] By leveraging a relatively small number of beds nationwide, the private prison industry has managed to forestall much-needed criminal justice reform that would address the problems of over-incarceration and overcrowding in the U.S. prison system.

Creating Worse Criminals and Increasing Recidivism

Another deleterious aspect of the private prison industry is that, contrary to the claims of for-profit prison companies, prisoners held in privately-operated facilities are subjected to higher levels of violence. Also, when prisoners are released from such prisons they are less likely to be rehabilitated and more likely to recidivate.

Realizing why private prisons have higher levels of violence requires an understanding of the business model of the private prison industry and how the industry generates profit. At a basic level, public and private prisons have many similarities: both require cell blocks, fences, security staff, medical units, etc. In terms of operating costs, approximately 70–75 percent of a prison's expenses are related to staffing. Specifically, how many staff members are employed, how much they are paid, what benefits they receive, and the amount of training provided.

Since such a high percentage of operating expenses are related to staffing, that is where private prison firms cut costs to generate profit. On average they employ fewer staff members than comparable public prisons; they pay less than in the public sector; they offer fewer (or less

3. "Prisoners in 2009," U.S. Dept. of Justice, Bureau of Justice Statistics (NCJ 231675, Dec. 2010), Table 20.

4. Ibid.

costly) benefits; and they provide less training. These tactics undeniably reduce expenses for private prison operators and boost their bottom line, but at what cost?

There is substantial evidence to support the business model of the private prison industry as described above. For example, according to the 2000 Corrections Yearbook, the average starting salary for private prison officers was $17,628 while the average starting salary in public prisons was $23,002.[5] More recently, when CCA announced plans not to renew its contract to operate the Hernando County Jail in Florida effective August 2010, the sheriff said he would resume control over the jail. He also said he would increase the salaries of qualified CCA employees retained at the facility by more than $7,000 annually, to bring them in line with the salaries of the county's corrections deputies—indicating the pay differential between the public and private sector.[6]

In terms of training for corrections employees, CCA vice president Ron Thompson stated in June 2010 that the company provided "a minimum of 200 hours of initial training, along with at least 40 hours of annual training."[7] However, this is significantly less than the training that employees in some state prison systems receive. California, for example, requires "a sixteen-week, formal, comprehensive training program" consisting of 640 hours. In Alabama, state prison guards must "successfully complete 480 hours of correctional officer training at an approved Academy." The New Jersey Department of Corrections requires a "14-week, in-residence NJ Police Training Commission course."[8] Less training allows private prison companies to cut costs, but at the expense of employing officers who are less prepared for work in a prison setting.

In regard to job benefits, private prison employees do not enjoy government retirement plans, civil service protection, or generous health insurance available in the public sector.

5. *The Corrections Yearbook 2000*, Private Correctional Facilities (p. 98) and Adult Corrections (p. 150).

6. *Hernando Today*, August 27, 2010.

7. Ron Thompson, "Private prison firm provides quality care at an affordable price," Honolulu *Star Advertiser*, June 29, 2010.

8. California Dept. of Corrections and Rehabilitation (www.cdcr.ca.gov/Career_Opportunities/POR/COTraining.html); Alabama Peace Officers Standards and Training Commission, Rule 650-X-4-.01 (www.apostc.state.al.us/Portals/0/Rulebook%20Update%20—%202-09.doc); State of New Jersey Dept. of Corrections (www.state.nj.us/corrections/pages/careers.html).

As a result of paying lower wages, supplying less training, and providing fewer benefits, private prisons have much higher staff turnover rates than their public counterparts. According to the last self-reported data from the private prison industry, published in the 2000 Corrections Yearbook, the average turnover rate at privately-operated facilities was 53 percent. The average rate in public prisons was 16 percent.[9] More recently, a Texas Senate Committee on Criminal Justice report released in December 2008 found that the "correctional officer turnover rate at the seven private prisons [in Texas] was 90 percent (60 percent for the five privately-operated state jails), which in either case is higher than the 24 percent turnover rate for [state] correctional officers during FY 2008."[10]

High staff turnover rates, in turn, mean less experienced employees who lack institutional knowledge about the facilities where they work, which results in greater instability in private prisons. Higher turnover also leads to understaffing, as employees who resign or are terminated leave vacant positions that are not immediately filled. The 2000 Corrections Yearbook found that public prisons had an average prisoner-to-staff ratio of 5.6 to 1 compared with a ratio of 8 to 1 in private prisons—which reflects significantly less staffing at privately-operated facilities.[11]

Understaffing, instability, and fewer experienced employees result in higher levels of violence. Several studies have shown that privately-operated prisons experience more violence, including a 2004 report in the *Federal Probation Journal* that found private prisons had over twice as many inmate-on-inmate assaults than in public prisons, and a 2001 Bureau of Justice Assistance report that found private prisons had 65 percent more inmate-on-inmate assaults and 48 percent more inmate-on-staff assaults than public prisons with comparable security levels.[12]

There is also anecdotal evidence that security problems and violence are more likely to occur at private prisons as a result of the industry's business model, which results in high staff turnover and thus inexperienced

9. *The Corrections Yearbook 2000*, Private Correctional Facilities (p.100) and Adult Corrections (p.152).

10. Interim Report to the 81st Legislature, Texas Senate Committee on Criminal Justice (December 2008), 9.

11. *The Corrections Yearbook 2000*, Private Correctional Facilities (p.88) and Adult Corrections (p.157).

12. "Private and public sector prisons – A comparison of select characteristics," *Federal Probation*, Vol. 68, No. 1 (June 1, 2004); "Emerging issues on privatized prisons," U.S. Dept. of Justice, Office of Justice Programs (NCJ 181249, Feb. 2001), Table 20.

staff and greater institutional instability. As just one example, during a four-month period from May to September 2004, CCA experienced four major riots at prisons in Colorado, Oklahoma, Mississippi, and Kentucky, plus a hostage-taking at a jail in Florida.[13]

A report by the Department of Corrections following the uprising in Colorado found that just 33 CCA guards were watching over 1,122 prisoners at the time of the riot—a ratio 1/7th that at state prisons. Some CCA employees had literally been "on the job for two days or less." The CCA facility had a 45 percent staff turnover rate, and CCA guards were paid an average salary of $1,818 per month compared with $2,774 for public prison officers. As indicated above, these deficiencies result from the business model of the private prison industry.[14]

Certainly, public prisons experience riots, violence, and other problems, too, but the frequency and severity of such incidents in private prisons imply that those facilities are more prone to unrest and instability as a direct result of how the private prison industry cuts costs in order to generate profit.

A related issue concerns the rehabilitation of prisoners in privately-operated facilities. Consider that for-profit prison firms have a vested interest in maintaining—and increasing—the number of people behind bars. The sole purpose of companies like CCA and GEO Group is to make money, not to ensure public safety, aid in the rehabilitation of offenders, or reduce recidivism and thus decrease the amount of crime and victimization in our communities.

During CCA's annual meeting on May 14, 2010, CCA vice president Dennis Bradby confirmed that the company had not conducted any studies to determine whether the rehabilitative programs offered at its for-profit prisons were effective in terms of reducing recidivism. Independent research, however, has found that private prison inmates have a higher rate of reoffending.

A 2003 study by the Florida Department of Corrections, Florida State University, and Correctional Privatization Commission found that while there were no significant differences in recidivism rates among

13. "Uprising at CCA prisons reveal weaknesses in out-of-state imprisonment policies," *Prison Legal News* (Jan. 2005) 26; "CCA Florida jail operations: An experiment in mismanagement," *Prison Legal News*, (July 2006) 1.

14 After Action Report, Inmate Riot: Crowley County Correctional Facility. See:http://www.inthepublicinterest.org/sites/default/files/Colorado%20Dept%20of%20Corrections_After%20Action%20Report.pdf; and *Pueblo Chieftain*, July 25, 2004 and Sept. 21, 2004; *Rocky Mountain News*, Oct. 13, 2004.

prisoners in private and public facilities, in "only one of thirty-six comparisons was there evidence that private prisons were more effective than public prisons in terms of reducing recidivism."[15] More tellingly, a research study published in *Crime and Delinquency* in 2008, which tracked over 23,000 prison releasees, found that "private prison inmates had a greater hazard of recidivism in all eight models tested, six of which were statistically significant."[16]

Thus, while an effect of the private prison industry is that prisoners are subjected to higher levels of violence due to the way private prison companies cut staffing costs to generate profit; the private prison industry benefits from keeping prisoners behind bars. Those same prisoners are more likely to reoffend following their release—resulting in greater societal costs in terms of a recurring cycle of crime and incarceration that negatively impacts public safety.

Institutionalizing For-Profit Imprisonment

Perhaps the most deleterious effect of the private prison industry is that it has successfully legitimized the concept of for-profit incarceration. While people might question the notion of a privatized police force that benefits financially when people are arrested, allowing companies to profit from people's imprisonment has become an accepted and normalized part of our nation's criminal justice system.

Private prison companies and the ancillary businesses that support them do not operate in a vacuum, of course, nor are they solely responsible for crafting an industry that profits from incarceration. They certainly contribute to that state of affairs, though—sometimes literally. As with many other industries, private prison companies make campaign contributions to lawmakers and engage in political influence-peddling through lobbyists.

CCA, the nation's largest private prison company, spent $1 million in both 2009 and 2010 on direct lobbying expenses on the federal level alone. The company and its Political Action Committee gave an additional

15. "Recidivism: An Analysis of Public and Private State Prison Releases in Florida," a joint study conducted by Florida State University, the Florida Dept. of Corrections and the Correctional Privatization Committee, Dec. 2003 (www.dc.state.fl.us/pub/recidivismFSU/index.html).

16 Andrew Spivak, "Inmate Recidivism as a Measure of Private Prison Performance." Also see Andrew Spivak, "Private Prisons Don't Make Better Prisoners," *Prison Legal News* (Dec 2009) 11.

$812,000 in federal and state political donations in 2009, and more than $722,000 in 2010.[17] And that is just one company among many that comprise the prison industrial complex. Through such spending, the private prison industry is able to influence and obtain the support of legislators to further its goals of spending more money on prisons and expanding privatization in the criminal justice system.

Private prison companies also wield influence by hiring former public officials, mainly from corrections and law enforcement agencies, who use their connections to grease the political wheels that drive the private prison industry machine. CCA's employees and board members include a former director of Ohio's prison system, the former chief of facility operations for the New York City Department of Corrections, two former directors of the Federal Bureau of Prisons, a former deputy assistant secretary of defense for the U.S. Department of Defense, a former U.S. Senator, and Thurgood Marshall Jr.—son of the late U.S. Supreme Court Justice, who served as Secretary to the Cabinet in the Clinton administration.[18]

The private prison industry has further enlisted supposedly-impartial research allies to produce studies that laud the benefits of privatization. For example, the Reason Foundation, a Los Angeles-based libertarian think-tank that promotes privatization of government services, has received funding from private prison companies—which it neglects to mention in its research.[19]

Discredited former University of Florida professor Charles Thomas, who operated an academic project that studied the private prison industry, also produced research favorable to private prison companies. It was subsequently discovered that Thomas owned stock in the companies he was studying, sat on the board of Prison Realty Trust (a CCA spin-off), and had been paid $3 million by Prison Realty/CCA. Thomas retired from his University position after those conflicts became known; the Florida Commission on Ethics fined him $20,000.[20]

17. Data from www.opensecrets.org (www.opensecrets.org/lobby/clientsum. php?id=D000021940&year=2011); CCA Political Contributions Report, Jan. 1, 2009–Dec. 31, 2009 (http://phx.corporate-ir.net/External.File?item=UGFyZW50SU Q9NjA5MjN8Q2hpbGRJRDotMXxUeXBlPTM=&t=1); CCA Political Contributions Report, Jan. 1, 2010–Dec. 31, 2010 (http://phx.corporate-ir.net/External.File?item=U GFyZW50SUQ9OTkxMzB8Q2hpbGRJRDotMXxUeXBlPTM=&t=1).

18. CCA website, "About CCA" (www.cca.com/about).

19. "Carrying the Torch of Freedom," Reason donor list 2009; "Report on prison privatization plagued with conflicts of interest, faulty data, political connections," Private Corrections Institute press release, May 21, 2010.

20. Ken Kopczynski, *Private Capitol Punishment*; and "University Professor Shills

Additionally, members of the prison industrial complex have formed their own industry trade group, the Association of Private Correctional & Treatment Organizations. APCTO and CCA jointly funded a Vanderbilt University study that, not surprisingly, found benefits from prison privatization.

More disturbingly, private prison companies have been accused of promoting harsh sentencing laws that result in more people going to prison for longer periods of time—which, of course, benefits the prison industrial complex. For example, in the 1990s and early 2000s, CCA executives John Rees and Brad Wiggins served on the Criminal Justice Task Force of the American Legislative Exchange Council (ALEC). ALEC is a powerful free-market organization that describes itself as a "public-private partnership" between state lawmakers and private-sector businesses. ALEC claims almost 2,000 lawmakers as members—one-third of the nation's state legislators—and over 250 private companies and foundation members, including Wal-Mart, ExxonMobil, Phillip Morris, and the National Rifle Association.

ALEC produces model laws that are introduced by legislative members in their home states. The organization's Criminal Justice Task Force (which has since been folded into the Public Safety and Elections Task Force) has drafted tough-on-crime model legislation for mandatory minimum laws, truth-in-sentencing statutes, three-strike laws, and habitual offender laws—all of which result in longer prison terms that directly contribute to over-incarceration and prison overcrowding.[21]

ALEC has further promoted model legislation to benefit the private prison industry, including the Private Correctional Facilities Act, which permits state governments to contract with private prison companies. CCA senior director of business development, Laurie Shanblum, served as a member of ALEC's Public Safety and Elections Task Force, and in 2010 CCA was tied to ALEC model legislation introduced in Arizona that would increase immigrant detention.[22] CCA operates three facilities in Arizona that house ICE detainees.

CCA has denied that it influences legislation that results in increased incarceration. However, why would a private prison company participate

for Private Prison Industry," *Prison Legal News* (Feb 1999) 19; and "Prison Realty Board Member Settles Ethics Complaints," *Prison Legal News* (Sept 1999) 12.

21. See www.alecexposed.org/wiki/What_is_ALEC%3F

22 Beau Hodai, "Private Prison Companies Behind the Scenes of Arizona's Immigration Law," *Prison Legal News*, (Nov. 2010) 1; "Prison economics help drive Ariz. immigration law," National Public Radio, Oct. 28, 2010.

in ALEC's public safety task force except to influence criminal justice policy? The nation's second-largest private prison operator, GEO Group, has also been a member of ALEC.

By currying political favor through lobbying and substantial campaign contributions, and by funding academics who produce supposedly independent private prison studies, hiring former public officials, creating its own industry trade group, and influencing criminal justice policymaking though participation in ALEC, the private prison industry has achieved legitimacy and ensured that profit trumps public policy when it comes to our nation's criminal justice priorities.

Conclusion

This, then, is the egregious legacy of the prison industrial complex. While private prisons firms are only a small part of the overall corrections system in the United States, they have managed to hinder much-needed criminal justice reform—particularly in the areas of sentencing and prison release policies—by supplying additional bed space for overcrowded public prisons.

Prisoners held in for-profit facilities are exposed to higher levels of violence due to the private prison industry's business model of cutting staffing costs, which results in higher turnover rates, understaffing and instability, and inmates released from private prisons have higher recidivism rates, thus endangering public safety.

But the most harmful effect of the private prison industry is that they have made imprisonment-for-profit politically and socially acceptable, thereby creating an insidious business that benefits from incarceration while instilling the notion that justice literally is for sale and crime does in fact pay—for private prison companies and their shareholders.

Hopefully, at some point in the future we will look back on this time when private prisons were considered sensible and wonder how such a socially destructive concept was allowed to exist. For now, though, we must deal with the harsh realities of for-profit prisons and their role in the prison industrial complex, including their many flaws and harmful effects on prisoners, our justice system, and society as a whole.

6

Why It Pays to Imprison
Unmasking the Prison Industrial Complex

ANDREW KRINKS

IN A FEBRUARY 2010 special feature spotlighting nine of the region's most promising and innovative new entrepreneurs, Nashville, Tennessee's *City Paper* celebrated the entrepreneurial acumen of the owner of Prisoner Transportation Services of America (PTS), "a prisoner extradition company that transports inmates for state and local agencies." Taking advantage of a key niche in the marketplace, PTS proved not only to possess "a lot of room for growth," but even showed signs of being "recession-proof," which, as the editors of *The City Paper* note, surely proves the company was "doing something right" in an economic climate in which showing any profit whatsoever was nearly unprecedented. Just how much growth did the company experience? When PTS's owner bought the company in 2003, it "did less than $1 million in revenue . . . [but] has since grown 13-fold, doubling in 2008 alone."

As any free market economist knows, the key to successful entrepreneurialism lies less in being able to summon profit from scratch and more in identifying and narrowing in on those areas of the market that bear unique potential for profitability. In the case of PTS, the cue very well may have been taken from the climate surrounding recent discussion of U.S. immigration policy. With widespread and growing resentment at an ever-increasing influx of illegal immigrants coming across the U.S. border, the company's owner was right to expect continued growth. As *The City Paper* explains, "Crackdowns against illegal immigration are helping to grow a new line of business for PTS—sending planes full of deportees back to their home countries and continents."[1]

But PTS isn't the only company making a celebrated profit off criminalization and incarceration. Corrections Corporation of America (CCA) was recently named one of America's "Best Big Companies," and was listed as the "Best of the Best" in the "Business Services and Supplies" category by *Forbes* magazine.[2] It is no surprise to learn, then, that CCA—the fourth largest corrections system in the nation with approximately 75,000 offenders and detainees warehoused in over sixty facilities nationwide—joined the New York Stock Exchange in 1994, making it a major competitor on the world economic stage.[3] Illustrative of a burgeoning phenomenon, companies like CCA and PTS represent the heart and soul of what is called the "prison industrial complex," the multi-faceted network of businesses and corporations that keep a growing number of state and local correctional facilities operating by offering their services on a for-profit basis. And clearly, there is serious profit to be made in a country like the United States where the number of incarcerated men and women—over two million in recent years, nearly 25 percent of the world's inmates—far surpasses every other country on the globe.[4]

If there was ever any doubt, we can now be sure: it pays to imprison. The question is: *why?*

In a world where crackdowns against illegal immigration and disproportionately high incarceration rates serve as the means by which entire industries achieve economic success, a world in which such business practice is deemed most exemplary and exceptional, it is imperative that we learn to dig beneath the numbers themselves in search of the concrete realities such figures actually signify. What unacknowledged presuppositions, forces, and structures, we ought to ask, are at work beneath the surface of the prison industrial complex that guarantee the companies that comprise it such success? If it pays to imprison, then what is the *human* cost, and what might that cost tell us about the fundamental nature of those systems and structures—those institutions, principalities, and powers—out of which the numbers arise in the first place?

1. "The 2010 Entrepreneurs of the Year," *The City Paper*, Nashville, TN, February 22, 2010.

2. http://www.correctionscorp.com/cca-history/.

3. Preston Shipp, "What Has Happened Since 1973?" See above.

4. "World Prison Population List, 8th Ed.," International Centre for Prison Studies, http://www.prisonstudies.org/images/downloads/wppl-8th_41.pdf.

Digging critically beneath the surface in this way constitutes what might be understood as a sort of deconstruction: a *de*-construction of the ideological and linguistic *constructs* by which institutions like the prison industrial complex form their identity. And since it is largely through constructs—through deceptive masks that obscure reality and personify praiseworthiness—that institutional powers live and move and have their being, the work of *de*-constructing and *un*-masking those institutions that reap their profit by way of systematic dehumanization is an indispensible one. Indeed, such has been the vocation of a long line of prophets, idol-crashers, and holy fools: those men and women bold enough to proclaim that what the powers call sane may actually be insane, that what the principalities call "justice" may in fact be injustice in disguise, that what the institutions call "doing something right" may indeed be the very embodiment of evil.[5]

In short, I will argue that the criminal justice system and its prison industrial complex, together, constitute an institution that fosters not justice but estrangement; a principality in the business not of correction but transformation, commodification, and violence; and a power that so inverts language that its very way of being becomes a perversion of that which its own core vocabulary—"justice" and "correction"—purports to evoke.

Assertions like these are far from popular in a society that celebrates the supposed genius of companies like PTS and CCA. As Will Campbell once said, "It is never good news to say to those who stake their lives on the political order and its distinctions that God frees the prisoners."[6] But the good news of liberation has, indeed, been proclaimed (Luke 4:14–30). The Christian's task is simply to live as though it were actually true—and it is. Which means the most faithful response to those systems and structures that know only how to imprison and deport, dehumanize and diminish, may very well be to live as though the very presuppositions upon which they stand were nothing more than a set of illusions. And yet, as the concrete walls, iron cages, and barbed wire fences of our many prisons make clear, illusions often serve as catalysts for some of the most specious forms of violence. Therefore, the first and most important step in moving beyond any such illusion is to learn the nature of the illusion itself—to learn so as to unlearn, to unlearn so as to foster something new.

---

5. Isaiah 5:20: "Ah, you who call evil good / and good evil, / who put darkness for light / and light for darkness, / who put bitter for sweet / and sweet for bitter!" (All scripture citations, unless otherwise noted, are from the NRSV.)

6. Campbell, *Writings on Reconciliation and Resistance*, 21.

The Institutionalization of Estrangement

If it is true—if it is "righteous" and "just"—that we no longer regard any-one from the point of view by which their misdeeds are counted against them (2 Cor 5:16–20), then what are we to make of a so-called justice system that regards a person's misdeeds as punishable by death? And if it is true that to grace strangers and enemies with love and welcome is to be more deeply rooted in the spirit of the living God than to abide by those laws that establish and uphold borders (Lev 19:33–34; Deut 10:17–19; Matt 5:43–48; Luke 10:25–37), then what can be said of an industry that thrives off laws and policies that ensure estrangement?

According to the writers of Hebrew scripture, there is no such thing as justice apart from community. As Old Testament scholar Bruce Birch explains, the Hebrew word for justice, *mišpat*, a word used frequently throughout Hebrew scripture, particularly in the writings of the prophets, "relates to the claim to life and participation by all persons in the struc-tures and dealings of the community, and especially to equity in the legal system."[7] Often paired with justice, the Hebrew word for righteousness, *ṣedaqah*, "a more personal term, refers to the expectations in relationship for intentions and actions that make for wholeness in that relationship."[8] Life, participation, equity, wholeness—if the God of Israel desires any-thing, it is that human beings learn to interact with one another in ways that foster the flourishing of the whole community—including even those who exist outside of it.

Thus, whenever a Hebrew prophet, claiming to speak on God's behalf, arrives on the scene and begins to shout, it is because the indispensible communality of God's covenant with God's people has been compromised. As James Mays puts it, "Where someone cries out for justice, all hear in that word a claim that something has gone wrong in the relation between a society and its members."[9] Raining down curses and omens upon Israel for their perversion of justice,[10] for their mistreatment of the poor, the orphan, and the widow,[11] and for their misdirected worship,[12] the prophets are not upset because the letter of the law has been breached in some su-

---

7. Birch, *Let Justice Roll Down*, 259.

8. Ibid., 259–60.

9. Mays, "Justice: Perspectives from the Prophetic Tradition," 146.

10. See Amos 5:7; 6:12b

11. See Isaiah 1:16–17; 3:15; 10:1–2; Jeremiah 22:13–17; Amos 2:6–7; 8:4–6

12. See Amos 5:21–24; Hosea 4:12; 6:6

perficial sense, but because the people of Israel, if they are to be anything, are to be a *people*, meaning they are to be concerned, ultimately, with one another's livelihood. The prophets' call for justice, therefore, is a call upon the people to repent of their demonic and destructive disposition toward the fostering of estrangement, the fragmentation of community.

The irony of the criminal justice system, then, is that to be made prisoner, to be served "justice," is to be made stranger, alien, other—systematically cut off from relationship and community. In today's prison system, estrangement, for some, means spending twenty-three hours a day in a cramped, windowless cell, deprived of all human touch or interaction, for months, years, or decades on end. For others in prison, estrangement is the perpetual realization that, in a matter of months or years, one will lie on a stretcher to be poisoned with chemicals, drowned in a sea of concrete and barbed wire, with few, if any, who will stand by to weep or mourn at such a loss. If the God of Israel is a god who loves and executes justice (Psalm 99:4), a god who lovingly creates each human in order that she might flourish in relationship and community with others, then an institution that so systematically deprives even the most sinful and broken human beings of community, love, and livelihood is surely a godless one.

Thus, the good news that Christ, echoing the prophet Isaiah, proclaims at the synagogue (Luke 4:16–19), and which Paul later elucidates (2 Cor 5:16–20), is that since all humans have been liberated, redeemed, and reconciled to God, and thus to one another, estrangement is not the final word. Jesus proclaims freedom for the prisoners, then, because prison is the very institutionalization of estrangement, of the refusal to give life and restore community even in response to wrongs committed, of counting a person's misdeeds against them, even to the point of death. Thus, as Will Campbell and others bear witness, to follow Christ is to live and move and have our being in contradiction—in resistance—to those systems and structures that foster and institutionalize estrangement, not least of which are the criminal justice system and its prison industrial complex. For as Campbell says, "there is no such thing as 'prisoner' where the gospel is concerned."[13]

Transformation, Commodification, and Violence

The road from the courtroom to the prison cell, much like the road to Damascus, is a path that promises the complete transformation of those

13. Campbell, *Writings on Reconciliation and Resistance*, 29.

who pass along it. Like Jacob, Simon, Saul, and others in the biblical tradition, men and women convicted of crimes and sentenced to time in prison are given, by the sovereign power to which they are subject, a brand new name and identity. In other words, my friend Morris is no longer "Morris" and my friend Donna is no longer "Donna"; they are #126121 and #301924, prisoners of the state of Tennessee. Thus, despite the parallels, the difference between the renaming authority of God and that of the state should be obvious. In the biblical tradition, to be re-named is to be redeemed, gifted with new life. In the criminal justice system, however, to be renamed is to be deemed unredeemable, deprived of identity, deprived of the possibility of a productive livelihood.[14] In one kingdom, a new name is a sign of belovedness; in the other, a new name is a sign of nothingness. In response to wrongdoing, one gives life, while the other takes it away; in response to sin, one forgives and restores, while the other diminishes and destroys.

The transformation from free world citizen to prisoner of the state, furthermore, constitutes a phenomenon that philosopher Giorgio Agamben calls "the politicization of bare life."[15] Identified anew in terms of their subjection to a sovereign who literally "decides on the value or the nonvalue of life as such," a power who determines both one's every move and one's very future, the life of men and women in prison is life that has been re-conceptualized as "life unworthy of being lived." First employed by National Socialist lawyers and doctors in 1920s and '30s Germany, "life unworthy of being lived" was the term used to describe persons "devoid of value," the "incurably lost": those who were physically and mentally ill beyond repair, and thus deemed incapable of contributing anything worthwhile to society. As Agamben explains, however, the ethos that undergirded National Socialism's self-styled humanitarian euthanasia program eventually translated into the ethos that guided the genocide of millions of Jews and others who did not fit the standards of legitimate human life in Nazi Germany.[16] Thus, while the parallels between the policies of the American criminal justice system and National Socialism are certainly limited, the fact remains that sovereign state power is power that is capable of deciding upon the value or nonvalue of human life, of trans-

---

14. The near insurmountable challenge of obtaining sustainable employment and housing as an ex-convict is, in many ways, the punishment that keeps on punishing for as long as an ex-convict lives. For further information see Devah Pager, *Marked: Race, Crime, and Finding Work in an Era of Mass Incarceration.*

15. Agamben, *Homo Sacer: Sovereign Power and Bare Life*, 4.

16. Ibid., 136–43.

forming human beings into that which is less than human, and therefore capable of being justifiably done away with.

But the powers of human transformation are not limited to the state or the criminal justice system alone. According to the French philosopher Michel Foucault, to grasp the full breadth and depth of its influence, power must be defined *beyond* the concepts of prohibition and repression. If it is to be effective in the work it sets out to do, Foucault argues, power must act in more compelling and productive ways than through the use of brute, juridical force alone. "What makes power hold good," he writes, "what makes it accepted, is simply the fact that it doesn't only weigh on us as a force that says no, but that it traverses and produces things, it induces pleasure, forms knowledge, produces discourse."[17] And indeed, if the praises sung by *Forbes* and *The City Paper* offer any insight, the private prison industry has more than succeeded in making repressive power highly compelling. But beneath its compelling veneer, the total effects of politico-economic power on the men and women living inside the walls of the industry's prisons are anything but laudable.

To start, it must be understood that essential to every industry is its raw material: some expendable element, steady in supply, that is capable of being exploited on a large scale and transformed into a commodity that will reap a profit. From forests to petroleum fields, corn crops to coal mines, raw materials literally make the industrial world go round, producing goods that create jobs and bolster economies the world over. But the prison industrial complex utilizes an element quite unlike those of other industries.

In the eyes of companies that own and operate correctional facilities on a for-profit basis—companies that function, like any other company, on the basis of their "bottom line"—an empty prison bed literally represents a loss in profit, which is why, for companies like CCA and PTS, higher incarceration rates equal higher profit. Indeed, without a reliably steady supply of prisoners, there would be no private prison industry to begin with. So integral are high incarceration rates to the private prison industry that, as a special report by National Public Radio in October 2010 reveals, officials of CCA recently went so far as to help draft what would eventually become the state of Arizona's infamous tough-on-immigration bill, SB 1070. In the wake of the bill's eventual signing into law, the company's president made explicitly clear his intentions for the future of the business: "I can only believe the opportunities at the federal level are going

17. Foucault, "Truth and Power," in *The Foucault Reader*, 60–61.

to continue apace as a result of what's happening. Those people coming across the border and getting caught are going to have to be detained," he said, which can only mean one thing: "there's going to be enhanced opportunities for what we do."[18]

Clearly, once again, it pays to imprison. But in order to reap a profit off imprisonment, human beings must first be transformed into the expendable raw materials of the industry. And in order for something to be conceived of as a raw material it must first be reduced or diminished from whatever it was prior to a lifeless entity to be utilized in the "free" exchange that takes place in the market.[19] Indeed, businesses that comprise the prison industrial complex cannot, by their very nature, conceive of prisoners in any other way: the very profitability of each company depends upon such a dehumanizing reduction. Thus, if the criminal justice system can be said to transform human beings into that which is less than human, then the prison industrial complex is a force that functions by transforming that which is already less than human into something even less: profit-reaping raw material, a statistic on an end-of-year business report, a number shouted from the floor of the New York Stock Exchange, and, perhaps most ironically, a success story celebrated by the likes of *Forbes* and *The City Paper*.

And yet, despite the contemporaneity of the private prison industry, the problem of systematic exploitation and commodification is anything but new. Even ancient Israel could not resist the opportunity for profit that God's gifts possessed for those keen enough to exploit them. For the wealthy of Israel, the primary means of exploitation was the land itself: where it once served to support the people, the land eventually grew to serve an elite few at the expense of many. But before long, exploitation was no longer limited to the land alone. As James Mays explains, Israel's gradual shift in socioeconomic orientation included not only "the shift of the primary social good, land, from the function of support to that of capital," but also "the reorientation of social goals from personal values to economic profit," which included the "subordination of judicial process to

---

18. Sullivan, "Prison Economics Help Drive Arizona Immigration Law."

19. There is a notable irony to the fact that the *free* market here thrives off the explicit, systematic confinement of others—the *un-*freedom of millions of human beings. Such arrangements inevitably lead us to reconsider what, exactly, true freedom consists of. For a helpful discussion on the notion of "freedom" within free market economics, see Cavanaugh, *Being Consumed: Economics and Christian Desire*, especially pp. 1–32.

the interests of the entrepreneur."[20] In other words, writes Mays, "Justice was being commercialized."[21]

Little has changed in three thousand years. As the prison industrial complex of today demonstrates, when human beings are so dehumanized and diminished as to be subordinated to the role of raw material, justice itself becomes subordinated to the interests of a handful of politically influential business leaders. Listed, in effect, among entities like paper, gold, or oil, justice itself becomes a commodity to be bought, sold, and traded on the market. The irony, then, is that by transforming humans into raw materials and justice into a commodity, the criminal justice system and its prison industrial complex set in motion another significant transformation: the transformation of justice into injustice.

The fundamental business of the prison industrial complex, then, is not the business of correction, but the business of human diminishment, of transformation and commodification. And if one is in the business of transforming human beings into raw materials, of transforming justice into a commodity, then one is fundamentally in the business of *violence*. For the fact of the matter is, anywhere human beings are systematically diminished, reduced, made invisible, their dignity rendered irrelevant or nonexistent, then, regardless of whether anyone has been inflicted with physical harm or not, violence has been carried out. Indeed, human diminishment itself, more than just a form of violence, is in fact the very ground out of which *all* violence grows. For whether it be the more explicit violence of assault, murder, or warfare, or the more subtle violence of taking away a person's dignity, of reducing complex individuals into flat, objective numbers, it all begins with diminishment, with the moment at which it becomes possible to think of others in terms less than human.

Thus, when a person enters prison for the crime of trespassing the law, the means of their apparent "correction" is violence—not violence as explicit as the kind for which they may be in prison, but a more subtle, systematized, and slow-working form of violence. It is also important to recognize, however, that prisoners themselves are by no means the only victims of violence and diminishment in the criminal justice system and its prison industrial complex. Indeed, it is often the case that those whose job it is to imprison others are so dehumanized by their actions that they, too, are made victim in the process, though perhaps in a less recognizable

20. Mays, "Justice: Perspectives from the Prophetic Tradition," 148.
21. Ibid., 153.

way.[22] Therefore, from the initial victims of crime, to those imprisoned for acts of crime, to those charged with carrying out their punishment, the prison system makes victims of all parties involved.

It is for these reasons that a "justice" system that operates on the basis of violence and human diminishment can never truly be just, for true justice does not diminish or do away with human beings, no matter how criminal their actions may be. True justice undertakes the difficult work of restoration, reconciliation, and resurrection; true justice makes things right by remembering that all human beings are beloved by God. True justice acts with the understanding that human beings are made, at their most fundamental level, for community, that, indeed, the fracturing of community itself is one of the primary catalysts of crime and poverty in the first place. True justice, therefore, *re*-members those who have been *dis*-membered from community.[23]

Thus, in the end, while good things—restoration, job-training, education, and so on—certainly do take place in the midst of correctional institutions owned and operated by companies that comprise the prison industrial complex, it would be a mistake to concede that such things comprise the heart and soul of the industry. On the contrary, the heart of the industry would cease its beating if its fundamental mission were truly the restoration of individuals, for the restoration of individuals cannot come about as a result of the systematic diminishment of individuals. Indeed, if we can be certain of one thing, it is that the spirit that makes true restoration possible is not the same spirit that makes its profit off the diminishment and objectification of human beings, for authentic restoration does not even compute to a system whose bottom line (increased profit) excludes the possibility of engaging its raw materials (prisoners) as dignified, God-beloved persons. Authentic restoration is not the product of a system that can only operate as a diminishing force; authentic restoration is a seed that subverts such systems. And the fact that such seeds find their way inside prisons at all is a source of great hope. "The light shines in the darkness, and the darkness did not overcome it."[24]

22. Stringfellow, *An Ethic for Christians and Other Aliens in a Strange Land*, 131.

23. Dark, *The Sacredness of Questioning Everything*, 122.

24. John 1:5

Language as the House of Being

The German philosopher Martin Heidegger writes, "language is the house of Being." To be human, he suggests, is to dwell in the house of language, to *be* by way of words.[25] Indeed, so integral is language to concrete, lived human experience that it is even possible to assert with the French philosopher and theologian Jean-Luc Marion that "language constitutes us more carnally than our flesh."[26] But just as a tree is known by its fruit, so one's language does not necessarily represent the concrete reality one inhabits or embodies. And as the criminal justice system and its prison industrial complex demonstrate, it is all too possible to speak an uninhabited, disembodied language, to build with one's words "a house where nobody lives,"[27] to create a body with nobody in it. But so long as they are taken at their word, institutions like the criminal justice system and its prison industrial complex are free to create whatever reality they choose.

William Stringfellow argues that one of the primary stratagems employed by the demonic principalities and powers for the sake of their own self-perpetuation is the use of contorted language. From inverted definitions, to jargon, to euphemism, to doublespeak—the language of the demonic powers is fundamentally the language of manipulation.[28] Consider, for instance, the word "justice." If one is to take the criminal justice system at its word, then "justice" signifies not the establishment of a community sustained by participation, equity, and wholeness, but the violently systematic estrangement of already-broken human beings, the isolation, alienation, and execution of offenders of the law. And yet, because they carry the sovereign power and authority of the state and the law, the criminal justice system makes "justice" to mean whatever it wants it to mean. Indeed, for the criminal justice system, to even utter the word is to bind the bodies of human beings in captivity—a captivity that actually has very little to do with the true spirit of justice. Likewise, if one is to take the prison industrial complex at its word, then "correction" signifies not the act of righting wrongs, of restoring to wholeness the order that is displaced by an act of crime, as well as the disorder that long existed in the life of the person who committed it, but the transformation of humans into raw materials, the transformation of justice into a commodity. And

25. Heidegger, "Letter on Humanism," in *Basic Writings*, 217.

26. Marion, *God Without Being*, 141.

27. Tom Waits, "House Where Nobody Lives" (1999).

28. Stringfellow, *An Ethic for Christians and Other Aliens in a Strange Land*, 100–101.

yet, because they operate under the edifice of economic progress, so long as they simply utter the word, the compelling power of profit thrives.

If language is, indeed, the house of our being, if it constitutes us more carnally than our flesh, then manipulatively contorted language leaves us unable to *be*—to *be with* other human beings—in any truly just, restorative, or redemptive posture. And if the language we speak builds a house, then the language the criminal justice system speaks builds a prison; likewise, if the words we utter constitute our very bodies, then the words spoken by the prison industrial complex constitute a broken, maimed, and bruised body—a malleable body shaped not for living and flourishing, but for profit-making.

The question that must be asked, then, is how "just," how "corrective," can an institution be if it depends upon the transformation of men and women into raw materials, the transformation of human subjects into sub-human objects, the transformation of the realm of law into a marketplace wherein concern for justice is eclipsed by concern for profit? If such realities truly represent justice and correction—if the institutions themselves are truly willing to use such words to describe their actual function in society—then we are confronted with the very inversion of language, which is, itself, the perversion of the very body that speaks it. Thus, perhaps what truly needs correcting—even more than those men and women who have offended the law—are the very systems and structures that claim the execution of "correction" and "justice" as their first and only purpose.

So, if the language of the criminal justice system and its prison industrial complex exemplify the inversion of language, then what do words well-employed look like? Peculiar as it may seem, the purest example of faithful speech at our disposal is the very "speech" of God, namely the utterance, the evocation of the "word made flesh," Jesus of Nazareth.[29] In the Christian tradition, when God speaks, it is an embodied speech, a speech in which what is evoked is made manifest in flesh and blood. And indeed, to take into full account what this divine embodiment of language—Jesus—looks like is to encounter a way of being that welcomes strangers, loves enemies, and challenges the pretenses of empires, that proclaims good news to the poor and freedom for the prisoners. If Jesus is what the divine embodiment of speech looks like, then what, we might ask, ought our language look like? And how might it take flesh?

Walter Brueggemann writes that "the evocation of an alternative reality consists at least in part in the battle for language and the legitimization

---

29. John 1:1–14

of a new rhetoric."[30] And as both the Hebrew prophets and Jesus bear witness, the language most capable of breaking through the demonic jargon—the cold and lifeless speech of the principalities and powers—is the language of poetry. Poetry—from the Greek *poiesis*, meaning "making" or "creating"—is, at its root, the language of openness to that which is other, language that creates new contexts in which to imagine new possibilities for being human. In contrast to the lifeless language of the principalities and powers—what David Dark calls "the death sentences that generate a sort of verbal totalitarianism"[31]—the poetic word is that word which opens otherwise unimaginable spaces, spaces in which what was once dead receives new life. Awakening a new imagination, poetry summons us to see the world, and those in it, with new eyes. As the language of depths, poetry possesses the power to plunge beneath the pseudo-realities propounded by the principalities and powers, and there, to illuminate, evoke, and embody an alternative reality.

Indeed, one can almost hear the poet-prophet intone:

> *You who turn justice into a prison cell*
> *and confuse righteousness with retribution;*
> *you who deprive the poor of justice in the courtroom*
> *and deny freedom to those who have been slaves all their lives;*
> *you who earn your keeps by sending the alien packing,*
> *by stuffing your law-breakers into cramped warehouses,*
> *by taking away names only to replace them with numbers—*
> *your claims to just authority disgust me;*
> *I hate your pretensions of righteousness.*
>
> *The words of your mouth*
> *are the words of a tongue struck dumb—*
> *a tongue that keeps on talking, but makes no sound*
> *other than the sound of Babel.*
> *Woe to you, for the day will soon come*
> *when true justice will roll down like a river*
> *and wash your hollow house of mirrors away.*

---

30. Brueggemann, *The Prophetic Imagination*, 18.

31. Dark, *The Sacredness of Questioning Everything*, 122.

To Be What Our Words Evoke: A Conclusion

It has been said, "an enemy is someone whose story you have not heard."[32] To listen to an enemy's story is to risk the possibility of glimpsing his humanity, which might even lead to the eradication of the very concept of "enemy" altogether. And since having an enemy to loathe and fear helps fuel much of what passes as politics in our world, it follows that there is not a whole lot of storytelling or listening going on. For indeed, it is a great deal easier to keep enemies than to submit ourselves to the vulnerability of standing in someone else's shoes for even a moment. To make ourselves vulnerable to the ways in which other people (enemies, prisoners, "illegal aliens") live—to the dark and messy complexity of their often tragic histories and contexts—is to submit ourselves to a death of sorts: the death of what Cornel West calls our "tacit assumptions and unarticulated presuppositions,"[33] our limited worldviews, our solipsistic prejudices about the ways of the world.

Will Campbell writes that "one who understands the nature of tragedy can never take sides."[34] The social, economic, political, spiritual, historical, and geographical factors that give rise to such things as crime (and tragedy) are such that a black-and-white system of retributive punishment—a form of "taking of sides"—will never be effective in restoring or bringing life to either the victims or the perpetrators of crime. Indeed, since the factors that give rise to crime (and illegal immigration) are infinitely complex, it follows that our responses ought to be more complex, more nuanced, which means being vulnerable, flexible, and open to the uncertainty that comes with failure.

One might easily argue that the whole of these observations too easily overlooks the fact that prisoners are, in many case, people who have committed gravely serious offenses with real-life victims who continue to live in the shadow of the crimes committed against them. Indeed, one ought not emphasize the forgiveness and restoration of people in prison in such a way that the depth of suffering endured by the victims of crime goes unacknowledged. There can be neither justice nor reconciliation without some form of accountability. As Wendy Farley urges: "Forgiveness is not

32. Quoted in Žižek, *Violence: Six Sideways Reflections*, 46.

33. Cornel West, quoted in Taylor, *Examined Life: Excursions with Contemporary Thinkers*, 3.

34. Campbell, *Brother to a Dragonfly*, 225–26.

the first word to the afflicted; if it comes at all, it comes very late . . . An antidote to humiliation must first be offered."[35]

There is no question, therefore, that prisons are full of people guilty of all sorts of wrongdoing. But the world outside our many prisons is full of people guilty of all manner of wrongdoing, as well: "If you, O Lord, kept a record of sins, O Lord, who could stand?"[36] In the end, to struggle for forgiveness and restoration over condemnation and retribution is not to suggest that there is no such thing as crime, that murder, rape, abuse, exploitation, theft, and other grievous acts are not committed on a daily basis. Rather, it is to suggest, first of all, that no one is without sin, that, as Aleksandr Solzhenitsyn writes, "the line dividing good and evil cuts through the heart of every human being."[37] As Elder Zosimas in Dostoevsky's *The Brothers Karamazov* articulates so well:

> Remember especially, that you cannot be the judge of anyone. For there can be no judge of a criminal on earth until the judge knows that he, too, is a criminal, exactly the same as the one who stands before him, and that he is perhaps most guilty of all for the crime of the one standing before him. When he understands this, then he will be able to judge. However mad that may seem, it is true. For if I myself were righteous, perhaps there would be no criminal standing before me now.[38]

To struggle for forgiveness and restoration over condemnation and retribution, then, is to embody the reality articulated by the apostle Paul that, having been reconciled to God through Christ, our trespasses are no longer counted against us (2 Cor 5:19), which means we are freed to relate to one another beyond that which would otherwise separate us.

Thus, as far as the gospel is concerned, it no longer makes any sense to repay one wrongdoing with another. By the power of God made flesh in the man who asks God to forgive even his own executioners (Luke 23:32–34) one may seek to disarm wrongdoing by committing oneself to the long, hard work of blessing, forgiveness, and acquittal (Rom 12:14–21; 1 Peter 3:8–22). If such is the power of God at work in the world, then we would do well to reflect critically and at length upon the fact that the

35. Farley, "Evil," 17.

36. Psalm 130:3 (NIV).

37. Solzhenitsyn, *The Gulag Archipelago*, Volume 1: *An Experiment in Literary Investigation*, 168.

38. Dostoevsky, *The Brothers Karamazov*, 320–21.

"justice" systems of the world claim to make things right by returning violence for violence, by repaying wrongdoing with still more wrongdoing.

In the end, the wisdom of those who visit men and women in prison—who pray and break bread with, who teach and learn and laugh with, who are, indeed, "reconciled" with—is that they possess the foolishness by which to proclaim a deeper truth within a context that does not know what to do with such truth: the truth that each man and woman behind those prison walls is not primarily a number, a "criminal," or a raw material, but a name, a face, and a beloved child of God. Indeed, it is often the case that we don't *actually* learn this truth in all its confounding fullness until we are willing to walk through the prison walls ourselves and learn it from those who know it best, those who live and breathe it through their daily prayers on behalf of those who are supposed to be their enemies: their prosecutors, their victims and victims' families, and the prison guards who manage their every move. For until we actually learn what it means to *be* reconciled with those made invisible and all but nonexistent by the criminal justice system and its prison industrial complex—until we come close enough to listen, to allow "Morris" and "Donna" to eclipse #126121 and #301924—then our words will remain but noisy gongs and clanging cymbals (1 Cor 13:1).

William Stringfellow writes, "there comes a moment when words must either become incarnated or the words, even if literally true, are rendered false."[39] And as the lifeless language of the criminal justice system and its prison industrial complex demonstrate, disembodied words are more than just disembodied—they are deadly. Which means that, for those who seek to follow the word-made-flesh, the most faithful, most subversive thing one can do when confronted with such powers is to *be* what our words (justice, liberation, reconciliation) evoke, to embody the life that stirs within them—to live and move and have our being as if there were, in fact, no such thing as "prisoner."

---

39. Stringfellow, *An Ethic for Christians and Other Aliens in a Strange Land*, 21.

7

Why I Am a Prison Abolitionist[1]

LEE GRIFFITH

E VER WONDER WHAT SOME self-ascribed religious "conservatives" are seeking to conserve? Often championing long sentences and the rigid punishment of offenders, this retributive crowd tends to forget that, as people of faith, "our story" has often been that of the prisoner. Our history is not just about the imprisoned, it comes from the prison. Obedience to the principalities, in other words, has not been one of our traditional values. Start with scripture. Our forbears were the ones locked up, rather than the ones locking others up. In liberation struggles of the modern era, our identity is with those who have occasionally sought to overburden and clog the system of oppression by filling the prison cells with disobedient people who refused cooperation with injustice. With Gandhi in India under British rule, with Mandela in South Africa under apartheid, going to prison was not a mark of shame but of honor. King spoke of filling the prison cell with dignity.

But several factors argue against any notion that prisoners might offer an antidote to our proclivity for social conservatism and obedience. First, the political context in twenty-first century America is not one of radical or revolutionary struggle. We live in an imperial state with a politics that has been variously described as conservative, neoliberal, or even

1. This essay is adapted from Lee Griffith's "Peacemaking and Prison Abolition," in *God is Subversive: Talking Peace in a Time of Empire*. Reprinted by permission of the publisher, all rights reserved.

"friendly fascist."[2] Second, we live in a society of *mass* imprisonment, with a prison infrastructure that is in much better shape than the infrastructures of our transportation, education, or health care systems. If there are any illusions of launching a nonviolent movement of noncooperation that could overburden the prison system, the state is prepared with prisons aplenty. Third, and perhaps most obvious, the people in America's prisons today do not necessarily offer a paradigm for healthy disobedience. Once incarcerated, most prisoners will obey when they are forced to do so, and many will build up powerful reservoirs of rage and resentment.[3]

Along with confinement, the key to eliciting obedience from prisoners is perpetual surveillance. In the late eighteenth century, Jeremy Bentham, the father of utilitarianism, proposed a model prison that he called "Panopticon" *(opticon,* seeing—*pan,* everything). Bentham arranged tiers of cells in a circular pattern around a central tower. From within the tower, a single guard could observe any of the hundreds of prisoners arrayed around him, but Bentham included a series of blinds that would prevent prisoners from knowing if they were being observed at any particular moment. Through surveillance that was theoretically perpetual, the goal was for the prisoner to internalize the policing function, to become his or her own prison guard.[4] If the lives of lawbreakers can be reformed by placing them under the gaze of authorities who never rest or blink, perhaps such scrutiny can serve to improve the character of the rest of us as well. Through security cameras in shopping malls and on busy city streets,

2. Gross, *Friendly Fascism.*

3. The classic study on the psychological toll of these totalitarian institutions was conducted by Philip Zimbardo, "The Psychological Power and Pathology of Imprisonment," *Society* 9.6 (April 1972) 4–8. Zimbardo traces the toll on both the keepers and the kept. If the harsh and punitive environment of the prison invades the minds and spirits of the prisoners, the same must be said of prison guards.

4. The way in which the Panopticon was supposed to foster the internalization of surveillance and control is traced in greater detail by Michel Foucault, *Discipline and Punish: The Birth of the Prison,* 195–228. It should be noted that, if prisoners are subjected to perpetual surveillance, the prison itself is hidden from public view. While older prisons were located in or near large cities, newer prisons are located in areas that are "virtually uninhabited," the description that also applies to the locales deemed suitable for the storage of toxic waste. Is this concealment a way for society to deny its punitive nature? More likely, it is an intentional effort to render these perpetually observed prisoners invisible to the larger society. Philip Slater noted that, although our society claims to prize community and family values, the "problem people" are removed from visibility—the emotionally disturbed to psychiatric hospitals, the elderly to nursing homes, the poor to urban slums and rural hollows. Slater, *The Pursuit of Loneliness,* 15.

through monitoring of Internet and phone communications, through air-port watch lists and body scans, the penal ideology of perpetual surveil-lance has seeped through the prison walls.[5]

The prison is not a recent innovation, nor is Bentham's model the first or last proposal for prison reform. Indeed, the prison is such a magnet for reform that one cannot help but wonder if there is something about the institution that cannot be fixed. In one form or another—as a cage, as a house of detention, as a pit in the ground into which people were thrown—the prison has been around for as long as the state itself, which is to say, for five or six thousand years. During much of that time, the deten-tion area was merely designed to hold people until the real punishments could be inflicted, punishments that might include forfeiture of property, exile, mutilation, or execution.[6] The idea that imprisonment should *be* the punishment was the product of reform. In the eighteenth and nineteenth centuries, well-meaning reformers like John Howard and Elizabeth Fry in England and Quakers and Protestant evangelicals in America proposed that, rather than hanging offenders or whipping them in the public square, lawbreakers should be sentenced to imprisonment. And what would pris-oners be doing while serving their sentences? The recommendation of the Christian reformers was that the prisoners ought to be doing penance. Impose a regimen of silence, place each prisoner in an individual cell ("cell" being a monastic term referring to the rooms of monks and nuns), give each prisoner a Bible, and watch the wonderful transformation take place. In the silent halls of the first penitentiary in Philadelphia, prisoners were slowly driven mad.[7] It was time for another reform, and in keeping with the values of capitalist societies, the next reform focused on work. Perhaps what the prisoners lacked was not penance but a sufficient ap-preciation for hard labor. In the nineteenth century in Reading Gaol in England, prisoners spent their days moving huge piles of rocks from one

5. Foucault noted "the way in which a form of punitive system . . . covers the en-tirety of a society." Michel Foucault, *Power/Knowledge*, 68.

6. This is not to suggest that imprisonment was always of short duration in ancient societies. As a prisoner of war, King Jehoiachin spent 37 years in a Babylonian prison (2 Kgs 25:27; Jer 52:31). Although pretrial detention was the most common use for the prison, Ezra 7:26 cites imprisonment along with execution, banishment, and confisca-tion of property as possible penalties for violation of the law.

7. Rothman, *The Discovery of the Asylum*, 79–88. While the penitentiary had been intended as an alternative to corporal punishment, American prisons quickly became the setting for physical abuse. The torture included beatings, suspensions from ceil-ings and walls with chains, and "water cribs" to simulate drowning. See Rothman, *Conscience and Convenience*, 20.

section of the prison yard to another and then moving them back again. In America, the Auburn and Elmira Reformatories emphasized work that would be productive, including farming and manufacturing. To avoid the impression of slavery, however, subsequent reforms have urged that the compulsory work should be understood as "job training," and that prisoners should also receive education and "treatment" with counseling and psychotropic medications.[8] Prison reform is the persistent quest to find the magic formula that will reform the prisoners into the very image of no one so much as the reformers themselves.

I am a prison abolitionist, therefore, because I believe in the biblical calls to peace and freedom. Along with the police and juridical system, penal institutions are part of the domestic military. I am a prison abolitionist because I believe that any form of militarism is irreconcilable with biblical nonviolence. I am also a prison abolitionist because I believe that a society that locks up one percent of its population is not free. The prison is a totalitarian institution, and a society that is engaged in the expansion and enhancement of totalitarian institutions is not free.

I am a prison abolitionist because I believe that justice should be about peacemaking and reconciliation.[9] Justice should be about mediation and conflict resolution. Justice should lead us to determine the actual harm that a victim has suffered and to strive for restoration—insofar as possible, restoring the well-being of those who have suffered harm, and restoring the offender to community.[10]

8. Angela Davis notes that the development and reform of prisons in the United States has been influenced, not only by European models and precedents, but also by the American experience of slavery. When the 13th Amendment to the US Constitution was passed in 1865, it abolished slavery "except as punishment for a crime . . ." Davis observes that, in the years following the Civil War, one way to deal with former slaves was to return them to enslavement in the prison. Davis, *The Angela Y. Davis Reader*, 96–97.

9. Peacemaking and reconciliation belong together. If reconciliation is discounted, it is too easy to adopt the cynical view that peace is achieved when all potential adversaries have been consigned to the graveyard or the prison. When weapons are regarded as "peacemakers," which is what Samuel Colt called his revolvers, then there can be no coherent differentiation between warmaking and peacemaking. Colt's appellation for his revolvers is cited by Bellesiles, *Arming America*, 430. During the Reagan Administration, the MX missile was also dubbed "the Peacemaker."

10. In the biblical view, God's justice is always expressed as the will to restore—to restore community and to restore the covenant between community and God. This is why, as Jacques Ellul notes, God's judgment is always followed by pardon. In pursuit of restoration, God's justice is neither distributive nor retributive but substitutive justice. Ellul, *The Theological Foundation of Law*, 43, 88.

Prisons serve none of these purposes. Close to one-third of all prisoners are doing time for drug offenses and it is not clear that anyone has suffered harm as a result of these crimes, with the possible exception of the offenders themselves and their loved ones. Even in the cases of other crimes that result in actual harm to clearly identifiable victims, the prosecution of these cases is not depicted as the victim versus the accused defendant, but rather as the U.S. versus the accused, or the Commonwealth of Pennsylvania versus the accused. How did this develop that the state is now depicted as the victim of all crime and the people who have suffered actual harm are regarded as less relevant? The idea that the state is the victim of all crime can be traced back to some mystical, theological notions attached to the monarchy in medieval Europe, especially in England. Through some tortured theologizing that we need not trace here, the monarch's divine right to rule was grounded in a belief that the monarch actually had two bodies.[11] First, there was the commonplace, physical body of whatever mortal happened to wear the crown, but then there was a second, mystical body that was coextensive with the realm. A crime that was committed anywhere within the realm was an offense against the king or queen, and whatever debt was incurred by the offender was owed to the monarch. Later, this idea of the monarch's two bodies would have unfortunate consequences for a few kings when some discontented subjects asserted that, in defense of the realm and of the monarchy, they needed to get rid of the particular mortal who happened to be wearing the crown. At any rate, it was from this strange medieval brew of politics and theology that the idea emerged that what offenders owe is a debt to society, not a debt to individuals who have suffered actual harm.[12]

11. The premier commentary on the history and theology of this notion is by Ernst H. Kantorowicz, *The King's Two Bodies*.

12. In early English law, prior to the medieval developments in political theology, when notice was taken of the victim of a crime, it did not necessarily mean that the actual victim would be compensated. The rank of both the offender and the victim determined the nature of the penalty that could be imposed and the identity of the person to whom compensation was paid. Under the laws of Ethelbert, if a female slave was raped, compensation was paid, not to the woman, but to the slaveholder, with greater penalties imposed if she was the slave of a nobleman rather than a commoner. If a freeman raped the slave of a commoner, the penalty was five shillings compensation to the owner. If a slave was found guilty of a similar crime, the slave was castrated. Rank also entered into the determination of the nature of the ordeals that were imposed to arrive at a finding of innocence or guilt. For those of lesser rank, the ordeal might entail immersing ones arm in boiling water or walking across red-hot plowshares, and if there were no blisters after three days, innocence was proven. Priests, on the other hand, were simply required to swear an oath to their innocence and successfully

Back in 1985, I visited a Chemung County Court Judge in his chambers in Elmira, New York. The only reason I was able to secure an appointment with the man was because I was serving as Campus Minister at Elmira College at the time, and apparently the position of "minister" carried favorable connotations (quite undeserved in my case, I must confess). I phoned, and the secretary said, "Oh yes, Reverend, we can get an appointment for you." So, I went in to see the Judge, who immediately inquired, "Reverend, what can we do for you?" "Well," I explained, "All I'd like you to do is to let me take the place of a prisoner over Thanksgiving. I go in to get locked up on Wednesday evening and you let the prisoner go to spend Thanksgiving and the weekend with family and friends. Sunday evening, he comes back and I go home." The Judge asked, "Oh, is *that* all." And I said, "Well, not exactly. I'd like to do it at Christmas, too." The Judge's questions (all polite, seeing as how I'm a Reverend) started with the practical. How do we pick this prisoner? Since I had been volunteering inside the jail with a literacy program, perhaps we could choose one of my students, or it could be anyone who the judge might suggest. "And what happens if this prisoner doesn't check back into the motel on Sunday night?" Well, I explained patiently, I would be taking the place of the prisoner, so I would be kept locked up until the prisoner returned or until the sentence was served, with time off for good behavior if I deserved it. The Judge objected that there was no legal precedent for him to take such an action. In fact, I noted, the U.S. system of jurisprudence is based on the English system, and in seventeenth century England, Quakers did exactly what I was proposing. If a prisoner had special needs, a Quaker would take the place of a prisoner for days or weeks or months.[13] If prisoners are paying a debt to society, it should not matter if someone helps them to pay it, the same as it does not matter to the bank if I give my neighbor some money to help her to pay for her mortgage. Well, the good Judge got a little testier near the end of our visit. The prisoners *he* sentenced were not going to be getting any help paying their debt to society. But thanks for stopping by, Reverend.

The phrase "paying a debt to society" is a fundamental acknowledgment that the very definition of what constitutes a crime is fully divorced

---

swallow a piece of consecrated bread in order to prove that they were not guilty of the charges against them. Hibbert, *Roots of Evil*, 4–7.

13. In April 1659, 164 Friends appeared in Parliament to ask that they be allowed to take the place of other Quakers who were suffering in prison. This particular proposal for a large-scale prisoner exchange was denied. Donald F. Durnbaugh, *Every Need Supplied*, 201.

from any evaluation of what (if any) harm has been caused to real people or to genuine human communities. Actions are crimes or not based on the changing whims of legislative bodies.[14] Since the Harris Act of 1914, the U.S. federal government has been involved in policing drug trafficking based on its power to tax interstate commerce. Prior to that, drug laws were under the purview of state and local governments, and enforcement efforts would ebb and flow with perceived threats to class and race.[15] So in the late 1800s, the perceived threat in the Northwest was the opium-smoking Chinese immigrants, and in the Southwest it was the peyote-addled Natives and the coca-using Hispanics (never mind how a popular cola beverage got its name), and in the South and the urban areas of the North, it was the black people driven wild by cannabis. The racism and classism of the war on drugs has not changed. Drug raids are conducted in South Central L.A., not on Wall Street. Nor has there been any change in the perception that the drug threat comes from "outside." The drug lords are Colombian or Mexican or Afghan—that is, the *illegal* drug lords. The *legal* drug lords are the perfectly respectable CEOs of the alcohol, tobacco, and pharmaceutical companies that continue to feed our Prozac nation. What has changed, beginning with the Nixon Administration in the late 1960s and growing to quite hysterical proportions, is that the federal government has become the driving force in drug criminalization. If state and local governments wish to qualify for federal funds, they need to join the "war on drugs." Is it an explosion of drug use and drug-related harm that has filled the prisons, or is it an explosion of criminalization, media hype, and vastly expanded policing that has created a society of mass incarceration?

Of course, penologists and those who are in charge of the American prison system do not believe that they are propagating racism, classism, or totalitarianism. What they believe they are doing is either rehabilitating prisoners or deterring crime, exacting just retribution, or at times, combinations of all three. Rehabilitation, deterrence, and retribution are the dominant ideological justifications for the prison system today.

14. On the definition of poverty as a crime in nineteenth century England, see Sabina Virgo, "The Criminalization of Poverty," in *Criminal Injustice*, 47–60. It is not unusual that crime is simply equated with what the prevailing governmental authorities regard as sin or heresy. In seventeenth century Massachusetts, blasphemy, adultery, and failure to observe the Sabbath were identified as crimes. Quakers were outlawed because their particular expression of faith tended to undermine authority. The preferred punishment for Quakers was banishment, but in 1659 and 1661, exiled Quakers who dared to return to Massachusetts were executed. Lawrence M. Friedman, *Crime and Punishment in American History*, 32–36.

15. Parenti, *Lockdown America*, 9.

Of the three, rehabilitation has been in eclipse. Some proponents of law and order fret that educating, training, or counseling prisoners is equivalent to coddling them, but some penologists still maintain that the rehabilitation model offers the best hope for lowering recidivism rates among offenders. I believe that there are at least three reasons why prisons are not viable tools of rehabilitation.

First, most cultures have rituals designed to label, shame, and stigmatize offenders, and in modern cultures, prosecution and imprisonment serve that ritualistic function.[16] Institutions that are designed to stigmatize and segregate offenders are ill-suited to facilitate their reintegration into community. Prisons shatter family relationships and mark prisoners with a modern-day scarlet letter that makes them much less likely to be able to form friendships and find employment after their release.[17]

Second, very little of the preventable loss of life and wealth in our society is caused by the people sitting in prison. Over 60 percent of American corporations have been found guilty of criminal violations,[18] but you can't imprison a corporation, and it's big news indeed when a corporate CEO is unfortunate enough to darken a prison cell. Since far more lives are lost to accidents than to murder, and far more private and public wealth is lost to laziness and incompetence than to burglary, I fail to understand why prisoners need rehabilitation any more than you or I do.

Third, the idea of rehabilitation suggests that offenders have abandoned societal values and that, through remedial work, they can be taught to embrace those values once again. The idea is flawed from the outset. Many offenders are affirming societal values, not rebelling against them.

16. The classic psychological study on rituals of stigmatization is by Tannenbaum, "The Dramatization of Evil," 214–15.

17. The political leaders who preach "traditional family values" pay little heed to the manner in which 2.2 million families have been torn apart by prisons. In New York State, offenders from New York City or Long Island are often sentenced to terms in Elmira or Attica, while upstate offenders are frequently sentenced to prisons near New York City, thus making family visits more expensive and less likely. In an era of mass incarceration, the prison is a major contributor to the creation of single-parent households (or far too often, no-parent households). Mauer, *Race to Incarcerate*, 185. The laudable desire to protect children from harms like sexual predation does not extend so far as to protect them from the punitive impulses of the juridical system. In some states, 13-year old children are routinely tried as adults. As the movement towards "quality of life policing" seeks to apprehend graffiti artists and window breakers, even younger children are being labeled as "gang members." Parenti, *Lockdown America*, 66, 70–72.

18. The percentage has likely increased since this statistic was first cited by DeWolf, *Crime and Justice in America*, 12.

Thieves and perpetrators of fraud are affirming the value of greed in a hyper-capitalist society, and they are merely using different methods to get their piece of the pie. Gangs are affirming the territoriality of a nation that builds a fence along the southern border. Perpetrators of crimes against women are affirming the culture of sexism. Drug users are embracing the self-numbing escapism that others find through TV or Internet or consumerism. Most absurd of all is the notion that murderers and other violent assailants are rejecting America's supposed valuing of human life. Oh yes, when there's an Oklahoma City bombing or a Columbine or Virginia Tech shooting, politicians shove their way to the front of the camera to proclaim, "We've just got to stop this violence in America," while they're spending half a million dollars a minute bombing Iraqis. I am a prison abolitionist because I don't believe that prisoners or anyone else should be rehabilitated or habituated to the values of the American Empire.

Along with rehabilitation, a second presumed justification for the prison system lies in the ideology of deterrence. Simply stated, deterrence theory holds that punishment prevents crime. If the theory of deterrence were consistently applied, however, the harshest penalties should be meted out for crimes with the highest rates of recidivism—crimes like shoplifting—while there would be little deterrence value in punishing crimes with low rates of repeat offense—crimes like murder. While random stranger-on-stranger murders and serial killings grab all the headlines, these are very rare compared to the murders of family members, neighbors, and acquaintances.[19] It is this more prevalent murder of "loved ones," which is often an impulsive, circumstantial crime of passion and rage, that is least likely to be repeated or deterred.

Does deterrence work? Look for a moment at Tyburn Hill in eighteenth century London. Historical data indicates that Tyburn was one of the locales where the good citizens of London were most likely to be victimized by pickpockets. For the successful plying of their trade, pickpockets need crowded areas with people bumping into one another. They need spectacles that distract people, and the citizens of London gathered on Tyburn Hill for an interesting spectacle indeed—public hangings. The snapping of necks provided the perfect distraction for the lifting of wallet or purse. Since such pilfering was a capital crime in eighteenth century England, some of those being hanged were certainly pickpockets.[20] As

19. Wright, *Great American Crime Myth*, 24.

20. In 1940, Malcolm X made reference to the pickpockets of Tyburn Hill when his debating team from Norfolk Correctional Facility debated the team from MIT on the proposition, "The Death Penalty is Ineffective as a Deterrent." Arguing in the

Karl Menninger observed two centuries later, the thing that punishment deters is not crime but getting caught.[21]

Does deterrence work? Although U.S. courts typically impose harsher penalties than their European counterparts, crime rates in the United States exceed those in Europe for almost every category of offense. In some U.S. jurisdictions, the sentence for murder might be life in prison without parole or even execution, but for each year of the past three decades, U.S. homicide rates have been between five and ten times greater than those in Europe.[22] Between 1985 and 1995, the number of drug offenders in prison grew by 605 percent, and yet in 1997, Barry McCaffrey, who was then director of the Office of National Drug Control Policy, reported that "if measured solely in terms of price and purity, cocaine, heroin, and marijuana prove to be more available than they were a decade ago."[23]

But my problem with the idea of deterrence has less to do with its lack of effectiveness than with its fundamental lack of fairness and its disregard for human dignity. There are actually two theories of deterrence, specific and general. Specific deterrence contends that the individual being punished will be dissuaded from future offense. With general deterrence, individual punishment is intended to set an example that will deter the criminality within the rest of us. Like a George Bush war, preemption is the goal of both specific and general deterrence. The punishment is not intended to fit some crime that has been committed; it must fit some potential or imaginary crime in the future. With such a rationale for punishment, we move *Through the Looking-Glass:*

> The Queen said, "Here is the King's messenger. He is in prison now being punished and the trial does not even begin until next Wednesday, and of course, the crime comes last of all."
>
> "But suppose he never commits the crime?" asked Alice.
>
> "That would be all the better, wouldn't it?" the Queen responded.
>
> Alice felt there was no denying that. "Of course it would be all the better," she said, "but it wouldn't be all the better his being punished."
>
> "You are wrong," said the Queen. "Were you ever punished?"

affirmative, the team from Norfolk won the debate. Cited by Linebaugh, *The London Hanged*, xxii.

21. Menninger, *The Crime of Punishment*, viii.

22. Lazare, "Stars and Bars," 30.

23. The statistic and the McCaffrey quotation are cited by Mauer, *Race to Incarcerate*, 191.

"Only for faults," said Alice.

"And you were all the better for it I know," the Queen said triumphantly.

"Yes, but I had done the things I was punished for," said Alice. "That makes all the difference."

"But if you hadn't done them," the Queen said, "that would have been better still, better, better and better!"[24]

With deterrence theory, people are regarded as mere means towards the achievement of the supposed higher goal of reducing crime. I am a prison abolitionist because I believe that people should never be treated as mere tools. By the standards of deterrence, the worst role model imaginable is Jesus of Nazareth. "But I say to you that listen, Love your enemies, do good to those who hate you, bless those who curse you, pray for those who abuse you" (Luke 6:27–28).

The ideology of retribution is not concerned with whether prisoners are rehabilitated or crime is deterred. The very essence of justice, say the advocates of retribution, is that people should get what they deserve. If people act in a way that deserves to be punished, withholding punishment is a denial of justice.[25] "Eye for eye, tooth for tooth" (Exod 21:24;

24. Numerous commentaries on deterrence theory quote this passage from Lewis Carroll's *Through the Looking-Glass*. See, for example, Knopp et al., *Instead of Prisons*, 111.

25. Consistent advocates of retribution might contend that God acted unjustly by marking Cain for protection (Gen 4:13–15). Indeed, the qualities of mercy and grace are obstacles to the pursuit of retributive "justice." But one of the problems with retributive theory is that there is no objective set of criteria for determining what we each deserve. How is it determined that gay people "deserve" execution in Saudi Arabia and human rights in the Netherlands? One would need to believe in a literal transmigration of souls to argue that a child born into a wealthy family somehow "deserves" a better start in life than a child born in the slums of Port-au-Prince. Likewise, there are no objective criteria for determining what offenders deserve. Many U.S. states have enacted "three strikes, you're out" legislation allowing (or even mandating) sentences of life in prison without the possibility of parole for offenders convicted of three felonies. After California passed a "three strikes, you're out" law, Governor Pete Wilson began arguing in favor of a "two strikes, you're out" bill. Angela Davis comments, "Soon we will hear calls for 'one strike, you're out.' Following this mathematical regression, we can imagine that at some point the hardcore anticrime advocates will be arguing that to stop the crime wave, we can't wait until even one crime is committed." Davis notes that, since certain populations have already been criminalized, there can be no doubt that those who will be targeted before the first strike will be black or brown and poor. Davis, *The Angela Y. Davis Reader*, 66. Actually, some prominent public figures have already proposed variations of "no strikes, you're out." Dr. Arnold Hutschnecker, President Nixon's physician, proposed that psychological testing be administered to all schoolchildren at the age of six so that those with violent tendencies could be sent to

Lev 24:20; Deut 19:21). This *lex talionis* passage from the Hebrew Bible is often read as a call for revenge, but even without the radical redefinition of *lex talionis* by Jesus (Matt 5:38–39), its function in ancient Israel was to place limits on retaliation. Neither retribution nor restitution may exceed the scale of the actual injury that was suffered in an offense. If you steal my sheep, I get my sheep back and maybe one of yours as well (Deut 22:1–13). Crime is a disruption of covenant, and the answer to crime is a restoration of fairness and covenant.

Tell me what is wrong with this scenario. You break into my house and steal a hundred dollars. As a result, I get nothing, but you get a year in jail, a thousand dollar fine, the loss of your job and maybe your family as well. That is not an eye for an eye. That is mean-spirited vengeance, and vengeance is a downward spiral. Most prisoners will get out someday, and some will be getting out with an eye to exacting retribution for what's been done to them. "Turn the other cheek" is a way of saying that retaliation and vengeance must stop with me. The judicial system says to the offender, retaliation must stop with you. You must be of better moral character than the judicial system itself.

With retribution, all of the focus is on the offenders rather than on the victims and survivors of crime. Hundreds of billions of dollars are spent on apprehending, prosecuting, and punishing offenders, while very little is spent on addressing the needs of the victims of crime. Prisons increase the suffering of offenders while doing nothing to diminish the suffering of victims. I am a prison abolitionist because I believe that any system that has the net effect of increasing suffering does not deserve the title "justice."

I am a prison abolitionist because, if harm reduction is the goal, it is not possible to limit the focus to the people who have broken laws. When it comes to actual harm, the largest portion of it by far has not been produced by the people sitting in prisons. Murderers would have to go on a horrible killing spree to match the death toll of the war in Iraq, a death toll that by some estimates runs into the hundreds of thousands. Burglars would have to be very busy indeed to match the dispossession of millions of Iraqi refugees. Each year on this planet, millions of people die from malnutrition and preventable disease, yet the neglect and dispossession that cause these deaths are not regarded as criminal offenses. It cannot be called "justice" to ignore the immense but perfectly legal harm that is produced by people with political power and social respect, harm in which we are all complicit.

---

special camps for treatment. Mitford, *Kind and Usual Punishment*, 56.

I must acknowledge too that I am a prison abolitionist because of the experiences I've had as both a victim of crime and a prisoner. When I was at Jonah House in Baltimore in 1976, two men with a gun broke into the house and twenty minutes of sheer terror followed. As the violence and the robbery unfolded, I was not wishing that I could call upon the police and their firepower; I was wishing that there were fewer guns in the world, not more. In the days that followed, as I experienced my own small version of post-traumatic stress (paranoia, startled reaction to noises, depression, anxiety), the knowledge that I live in a punitive society did not leave me feeling safer. But along with being a victim of crime, I am also a criminal. As I've been sent to jail on more than a dozen occasions, I've become aware that the qualities of the people I meet on the inside are like nothing so much as the qualities of the people I meet on the outside. Both inside and out, I have met people of remarkable kindness as well as people who have succumbed to hatred and rage.

If I seem to be touting my stance as a prison abolitionist, it is actually a confession of my own irrelevance. The abolitionist position is really quite peripheral to the contemporary debates in criminology and penology in America. No doubt, abolitionists are doing significant work with bail projects, mediation efforts, and programs that strive for restoration and reconciliation. But the prison will not collapse based on the sincerity of the work or the cogency of the arguments of contemporary abolitionists. What portends the fall of the prison is the gospel.

Biblical perspectives on prisons were persistently shaped by Israel's own experience of captivity and by the historical identification with those held in bondage.[26] This is not to deny that there were prisons in Israel, but they were few in number and they were often built at the behest of occupying powers.[27] In the accounts of biblical witnesses, prisoners are not

26. Several scholarly works of recent vintage explore biblical perspectives on prisons. For example, biblical insights pervade the critique of American imperialism and the prison system by Mark Lewis Taylor, *The Executed God*.

27. The first mention of imprisonment in Scripture is that of Joseph in Egypt in Genesis 39. An example of the influence of colonizing powers on the utilization of imprisonment in Judah and Israel is provided in the account of the instructions to Ezra by Persian King Artaxerxes in Ezra 7:25–6. While Israel's unease with the prison was certainly influenced by its own history of captivity, an added factor that contributed to the paucity of prisons in Israel and Judah was the relative lack of garrisons and fortresses that were the standard locales for prisons. There was no distinction between soldiers and police, and the standing army was a fairly late development in Israel's history. When Jeremiah was arrested, he had to be thrown into a makeshift prison in the house of Jonathan the secretary (Jer 37:15). Later under Roman occupation, the prison was still a military institution. When Paul was arrested in Jerusalem (Acts 21:

presented as dangerous criminals. With a keen awareness that the wealthy could purchase the enactment of statutes (Isa 10:1–2) and bribe their way to acquittal (Amos 5:12; Mic 7:3), biblical witnesses counted prisoners among the oppressed (Ps 146:5–9; Lam 3:34–6). Messianic hope looked forward to the day when one would come to set the prisoners free (Isa 61:1–2; Zech 9:9–12).

The proclamation of freedom for the prisoners had roots in the Jubilee and Sabbath Year calls to forgive debts, redistribute land, and liberate slaves in remembrance of God's liberation of the Hebrew people from slavery in Egypt (Lev 25:1–10; Deut 15). In the social and juridical structures of ancient Israel, the kinsperson who was responsible for ransoming a relative who had been taken prisoner or driven into slavery through indebtedness was called the "*go'el*."[28] But what would happen to the slaves who were bereft of family ties or those who were so heavily indebted that no *go'el* could possibly ransom them? The Jubilee Year proclaimed that, for those who were destitute and without any hope of ransom, God would serve as *Go'el*. God had already paid the ransom price by liberating all of the Hebrew slaves from Egypt. To deny jubilary liberty to the captives was a serious affront to God because it was cheating the *Go'el* out of the ransom that had already been paid (Jer 34:15–7). When Israel failed in this work of liberating slaves and prisoners, the prophet recalled the people to their role as Suffering Servant: "to open the eyes that are blind, to bring out the prisoners from the dungeon, from the prison those who sit in darkness" (Isa 42:7).

This Hebrew Bible theme of liberty for the captives resonates throughout the New Testament. Believers are admonished to refrain from reliance on unjust courts that have no concern for reconciliation (1 Cor 6:1).[29] Believers are called upon to care for prisoners and to visit them (Matt 25:31–46). This call to "visit" (Greek, *episkeptomai*) carries a sense that is greater than just socializing. Biblical visitation is repeatedly associated with liberation and redemption (see, for example, Luke 1:68). In the book of Acts, captivity is renounced in the accounts of the miraculous de-

---

33–4), he was detained in the "barracks" of the Fortress Antonia. See Rapske, *The Book of Acts and Paul in Roman Custody*, 137–40.

28. See Sloan, *The Favorable Year of the Lord*, 6–7.

29. William F. Orr and James Arthur Walther maintain that a concern for reconciliation was one of the motivations that led Paul to admonish believers not to rely on the courts of the state. "The Christian mediator should have in view the reconciliation of the parties that they might get rightly related to the forgiving and loving God by forgiving one another." Orr and Walther, *1 Corinthians*, 197.

liverance from prison of Peter (12:1–11) and of Paul and Silas (16:25–34). But the boldest reassertion of the liberation theme is as the very outset of the ministry of Jesus when he proclaims liberty for the captives (Luke 4:18–9). The amnesties that are declared when kings are enthroned and prime ministers inaugurated are cynical affairs, with prisons being emptied only to be filled again with freshly designated offenders of the new regime. In contrast, the amnesty proclaimed by Jesus has eschatological rather than mere political significance, which is to say, it applies in a final sense for all time and all people. We must learn to hear this proclamation of freedom for the prisoners as *good* news.

The biblical renunciation of the prison is not simply the rejection of an institution that has failed to achieve its stated goal. Our modern ideologies of deterrence, rehabilitation, and retribution matter not at all to the biblical depiction of the prison. In the biblical presentation of it, the prison is not an apparatus that may be managed in a more or less efficient manner. The prison is a principality that holds us in its power, and that is the power of death.[30] The biblical association of prisons with the spirit of death may have originated with the practice of holding prisoners captive in pits and cisterns (see Jer 38:6). These pits are like graves, like entrances to Sheol and the underworld, and the prisoner is like one given over to death (Pss 69:1–2, 15, 33; 107:10).[31] While Satan was once depicted as serving as a type of prosecuting attorney in the heavenly law court (Job 1:6–12; Zech 3:1), under the influences of apocalypticism, Satan becomes the lord of the underworld of death, and he is identified as the one who casts people into prison (Luke 22:31–3; Rev 2:10). The biblical identification of the prison with the spirit and power of death demythologizes all of our contemporary theorizing about incarceration. The problem is not that the prison fails to forestall the reign of violence and chaos; the problem is that the prison is identical in spirit to the very violence that it claims to combat. Jesus' proclamation of liberty for the captives is a renunciation of death itself; it is a harbinger of resurrection.

For people of faith, all talk of prisoners must begin and end with the recognition that Christianity was born inside the prison, born as a promise of life in the midst of death. Our foremothers and forefathers were prisoners, and our sisters and brothers still are. All of the apostles were jailbirds, and as Karl Barth noted, the first true Christian community was

30. On imprisonment as a manifestation of the power of death, see Barth, *Introduction to the Psalms*, 51.

31. Keel, *The Symbolism of the Biblical World*, 69–73.

made up entirely of criminals, that is, the three criminals on the crosses at Golgotha.[32] For people of faith, all talk of prisoners must begin and end with Jesus of Nazareth, the prisoner at the center of the gospel.

32. Barth, "The Criminals with Him," in *Deliverance to the Captives*, 77–78. Barth is certainly correct in his forthright and rather startling identification of Jesus as a criminal. Northrop Frye writes, "Christianity is founded on a prophet who was put to death as a blasphemer and a social menace, hence any persecuting Christian is assuming that Pilate and Caiaphas were right in principle, and should merely have selected a different victim. The significance of the life of Jesus is . . . that of being the one figure in history whom no organized human society could put up with. The society that rejected him represented all societies: those responsible for his death were not the Romans or the Jews or whoever happened to be around at the time, but the whole of mankind down to ourselves and doubtless far beyond. 'It is expedient that one man die for the people,' said Caiaphas (John 18:14), and there has never been a human society that has not agreed with him." Frye, *The Great Code*, 132–33. It follows from this that, as Rowan Williams observes, the trial narratives of the Gospels put all of us on trial. Williams, *Christ on Trial*, 92.

A Demonic Principality

WHAT DO YOU NEED to know about the prison-industrial complex? It's demonic.

Admittedly the term "demonic" is long out of academic vogue. Perhaps it's too "old school," too reminiscent of medieval mythology. Maybe it's just too "low brow" for today's educated folks. Will Campbell and his Committee of Southern Churchmen colleagues, however, often found the term a vital biblical concept insofar as it describes a delusion and confusion. A demonic viewpoint entices us to see as good, to name as desirable, and to teach as laudatory that which is actually fallen, divisive, and deadly. The demonic, therefore, fouls our vocabulary and perverts our logic. It bedevils our worldview so that we see retribution as justice, or understand human impoverishment as correction. At the end of the day, "demonic" describes a faith (perhaps a possession) in the power of Death to achieve our desired outcomes.

The original collection of essays in the 1972 issue of *Katallagete* drove this point home. In his "Prison" essay, for example, James Douglass described the prison-industrial complex as "the primary weapon in the State's domestic war."

> That war begins with the studied manipulation of public opinion against "crime in the streets" to support the sharp build-up of tactical police squads to control insurgency in ghetto areas

and counter-culture communities. Riot-control and conspiracy laws are passed as a formal declaration of war against internal enemies: black people who won't wait and young people who won't conform. Once the law-makers have declared war, the police and the courts wage it with dedication. The purpose of the penal system in that war is to force the State's enemies to their knees. What the American bombing plane is to Indochinese peasants [in Vietnam], the threat and use of the penal system is at home to poor, mostly black, Americans: a technique to force subject peoples to remain in colonial roles for an imperialist power. . . . Our prisons are techniques for America's violent control of her rebellious poor, and in recent days, increasing numbers of young political resisters. To claim any further purpose for these institutions is, I believe, to dignify them beyond reality. From the experience I have had both within them as a prisoner and visiting others in them, I believe that their clear purpose is raw power in the service of a ruling class.

Drawing upon the work of Jacques Ellul, Douglass charts how a seemingly wise emphasis on controlling outcomes devolves into a demonic possession. A principality like the nation-state, or a power like the Pentagon, for example, "is an almost total withdrawal from the real world into a technological game room, a computerized self, whose automated thunder won't work on Vietnamese peasants. But although impotent in their power, the great danger of policy-makers is that their volcanic frustrations will pitch them into the ultimate act of effectiveness, global self-destruction: destroying the world to save it." According to the principalities and powers, our best, wisest means to "liberate" is to employ deadly force to command, control, and dominate. "Efficiency" and "effectiveness" means doing whatever is necessary—even to the point of killing—to achieve your idea of the right and good. This ethic honed in Vietnam is, Douglass argues, the logic that informs the life and work of the prison in the U.S.[1]

Likewise, in "The Draft Resister in Prison," David Miller illustrates how absurd the principle is. He notes that every warden will give "lip service to the goals of rehabilitation," but inmates actually encounter an institution "wholly lacking in socially redeeming value. The end products of our correctional systems are men and women humiliated, embittered, scarred, institutionalized, and often broken. Only infrequently do inmates come out of prison 'better people' and it is always in spite of tremendous odds, at great personal cost, and never to the credit of the correctional

1. Douglass, "Prison," 51–54.

process."[2] A corrections policy that cheapens and belittles human life is built on the same logic as a foreign policy that seeks to save a village by destroying it.

In his 1972 *Katallagete* essay "One Meaning of Prison in America," Norm Barnett agreed. As an employee of a maximum security institution, he saw the dominant ethic of the system: "'Let's re-structure,' 'Let's rehabilitate,' 'Let's prosocialate' psycho-social blasphemies of progressive penology. Under the blinding sear of the operating room lights of white-coated, tie-suited hosts of Mackflecknoes psychologiste, sociologiste, voc. specialiste, ed. specialiste, o.j. technologiste, etc., etc. . . ." The prison imposes an effective therapeutic regimen to kill the old and remake the person according to our desired image. "Since the program is not relevant at all to him, since it is nearly forced on him," Barrett has found, "he hates it. But, nearly to a man, he follows it. And that's where it gets interesting. It becomes a deadly serious game of wits. He hustles the PROGRAM, the PROGRAM attempts to remake him. It is a war."[3]

Ironically, those of us who *sound* most faithful to Christianity may be some of the more "possessed" by this ethic. As Harmon Wray discovered in his own work in prisons, "While most Christian faith communities [progressive and conservative] claim to believe in such values as fairness, peace, equality, justice, reconciliation, and forgiveness, too often their leaders and members tacitly or aggressively support a criminal justice system that routinely violates all these basic spiritual and ethical principles in massive and immensely damaging ways."[4] Our God-talk suggests our sincere desire to honor the loving, merciful, sovereign God. Despite our rhetoric, however, when push comes to shove our hearts and minds just aren't in it. Our faith ultimately resides in the power of Death. As Arthur McGill has argued, for most of us "Death is Lord."[5] We profess our credo when we order our lives according to death's so-called efficient power, rather than according to God's vulnerability and forgiveness. Death is our ethic. Death is our politics. Death is divine.[6]

Although the corrections system pledges balance, equity, justice, and security, the prison industrial complex uses the power of Death to impoverish, denigrate, and dehumanize. Prisons make "outcast or surplus

2. Miller, "The Draft Resister in Prison," 37–40.

3. Barnett, "One Meaning of Prison in America," 55–56.

4. Wray, "Models of Criminal Justice Ministry and Resistance," 10.

5. McGill, *Death and Life: An American Theology*, 44–45.

6. Ibid., 39.

people," and "render them more or less invisible."[7] For the nation-state, William Stringfellow explains, prisons are "the banishment or abandonment of human beings to loneliness, isolation, ostracism, impoverishment, unemployability, separation—all of which are forms of social death—[prisons have] become so dehumanizing that the victims suffer few illusions about their consignment to death or to these moral equivalents of death by American society."[8]

Many of the incarcerated corroborate Stringfellow's indictment; so let's not let Stringfellow alone describe the power of Death that defines prisons. Consider Donna McCoy's "Destination Home," what she describes as "an analogy of what the state has done to me."

> I am writing in hopes that you will look inside yourself and understand I am your responsibility.
> To the state, I am a slave, purchased by the blood of one who rests in a grave.
> To the public I am dead, R.I.P. hung over my head.
> When my mastah' first viewed my scars, he showed no concern,
> His hatred of my skin I quickly discerned.
> I work for three sometimes two hots and a cot,
> I receive incentives if I am capable of serving at the mastah's table.
> I am housed with women from all cultures and races, a menagerie of empty faces.
> Infamous, stripped of my name, branded a number, taught how to play the prison game.
> As a tool to conform, I am required to wear a uniform.
> Our hopes and our dreams hung on a tree as a prerequisite to our being free.
> I traveled on a journey that included mental illness, dysfunction, substance abuse, and poverty.
> My community destroyed, my incarceration began before the age of three.

7. Stringfellow, *The Politics of Spirituality*, 83. Former editor of the *San Francisco Chronicle*, Peter Sussman, has argued that the prison-industrial complex has worked aggressively and intentionally to restrict access to, and censor information about, correctional institutions. Simultaneously, journalism has embraced a more sensationalist, entertainment-oriented tactic, which shunts aside investigative reporting about prisons and panders to social anxieties about crime and criminals. Consequently, most Americans know precious little about their corrections systems, and prefer to keep it that way. See Sussman, "Media on Prisons," 258–78.

8. Stringfellow, *An Ethic for Christians*, 69.

Insofar as prisons are a demonic institution using the power of Death to silence and diminish, it is an act of resistance to hear those whom the principalities and powers are attenuating and terminating. So read the following essays from those in the system, and see if the institution described isn't demonic. If it is, break from its possession, and pursue the reconciling life of community.

Richard C. Goode

8

Security and Rehabilitation and God in a Godless World

A. PUCHALSKI

FEW PEOPLE ARE FAMILIAR with the psychological structure of a maximum security prison with its disciplined thoroughness. Fewer still can begin to comprehend the effects of certain aspects of contemporary prison life or that it might actually be more harsh and brutal than that practiced in our early American prison system with its physical punishment. And only those closely associated with our prison system are aware of the absoluteness of power wielded by prison officials to exact obedience from the wards entrusted to their care by the courts. It is a system that represents absolute totalitarianism, with no power or control in the hands of any convict faction, but rather in the hands of our keepers.

The most painful condition imposed upon a man in prison is the loss of liberty. Life becomes frustrating in the extreme. Not only do the walls serve as a grim, constant reminder of the restrictions and isolation that a man is subjected to, they literally serve as a barrier that separates the world of the living—from that of the dead. The numberless hours that hang like overripe fruit on a tree, by-passed by the harvester to decay and waste, magnify the loss and frustration.

Your great, big, wonderful world suddenly shrinks to a mere few acres of space where every movement and action is controlled by the puppeteer who seldom loosens the rein to permit too much freedom of movement. The months pass by agonizingly slow and the nagging fact that your confinement represents a deliberate rejection by society stings deeply. The isolation is complete, for the frightening realization soon dawns upon you that not only did society confine you to a prison—but within it as well.

With the stabbing pain of each deprivation imposed, a man oft times wonders just where he is going to find strength to persevere. Some don't. The bareness of the cell in which you're confined: your home, the absence of even a single piece of furniture that you might call your own, the traditional striped trousers and uniformity of dress—the overwhelming loss of identity, is stifling. Such is prison life.

Prisons have been built with only one thought in mind: Security. The comfort and welfare of the inmate who would be required to inhabit the dungeons were for the most part ignored. This is evidenced by the Bastille-like structure erected in the 1790s at my prison, which provides a cell measuring five by nine feet, or forty-five square feet of space per man. Here, we are required to spend on the average sixteen hours of every day—for the most part, vegetating.

But there is a far greater ugliness than that which meets the eye of the observer in the grayness of the walls that separate the two worlds. It is an invisible ugliness with far more reaching consequences than any achieved in the medieval Star Chambers—brutalization; dehumanization of men; an ugly system implemented for the sole purpose of manifesting that absoluteness of power to force men to their knees in submission—in the interest of security.

It is painfully stressed by the administration of our prisons that decision-making is no longer a function of a convict and that his most basic needs can only be attended to . . . by the grace of his benevolent keepers. This, then, is the beginning of our psychological annihilation; the suppression of independent thought; the reliance on our keepers to resolve all decisions for us. Serf-like dependency.

Dehumanization begins with the complete indifference of the keepers towards their charges. In addition to the strict administrative policy forbidding "fraternizing" with inmates, far too many prison guards treat their positions as nothing more than jobs and refuse to extend themselves to help an inmate in trouble. Their attitudes are basically one of contempt and that of master to slave, disregarding even our basic human rights. This attitude changes somewhat to a paternalistic one when dealing with informers.

While lack of any meaningful communication between keeper and kept is the greatest obstacle preventing understanding and therefore negating any program instituted to assist in the inmate's rehabilitation, it is but one of a series of policies deliberately imposed to accomplish a servile attitude in the inmates.

Fear produces submission; thus, if we brutalize a man, strip him of self-worth, denigrate him not only in his own eyes, but the eyes of his peers, we create an automaton: a *model convict*. But also of importance, only then can a rigid, uniform society be molded for easier control.

To accomplish this goal every inmate upon arrival at our prison has his head shaved bald. He is dressed in a denim, sack-cloth uniform without regard for fitting and cast into a cell, the size of which I mentioned earlier; furnished with a cot, cast-iron toilet, and a solitary chair. He is also issued one bar of soap, a roll of tissue paper and a scrub brush. He is reminded in no uncertain terms that the soap and tissue must last him a full month between issues—at which time he can receive more if he asks the officer for another issue. Dependence is emphasized.

During this quarantine or *conditioning* period that usually lasts two weeks, the inmate will seldom leave his cell, exercise, mingle socially with other convicts or participate in the inmate functions. His entire world centers around that nine-by-five cubicle and the occasional click of the guard's key in the lock which will give him a few minutes of freedom that comes when he is called out for interviews and physical exams. After spending an average of twenty-two hours a day in his cell, it isn't difficult to understand why the man starts becoming withdrawn in his manner. The system leaves very little room for resistance.

Few social contacts with the world beyond the prison walls are fostered, even to the extent that we are permitted to write only ten letters a month. Outside groups are frowned upon when they visit the prison—such contact only serves to remind those in the world of the condemned of freedom and loved ones, and to the visitor, the conditions of our environment. It serves to undermine the dehumanizing process and cannot be tolerated.

With the passing of time it is inevitable that most men succumb to the system and integrate themselves into the sub-culture of prison life. In doing so, civilized behavior and moral responsibility are shed and replaced with prison standards considered socially acceptable. Love and kindness are looked upon as weaknesses and *might* becomes *right*. Sexual perversion is an acceptable behavior, and the tough guy is admired with envy. It is a society where the weak are sacrificed to the strong to maintain the status quo, always with the approval of the prison administrators who know that by placating the tough guy and trouble-maker their own jobs become easier.

Despite, or perhaps I should say in spite of, the all-out campaign by prison officials to suppress autonomy in our inmate society and to control every movement, a sub-culture does exist. It is a culture that excludes all but convicts and is as orderly in structure as any free-world community. It lacks a duly elected governing body to represent it, but this is due only because of the prison officials' stubborn refusal to recognize any degree of independence. Nevertheless, there is a *de facto* recognition by the inmate population of certain *leaders* amongst them, men who are usually considered anti-administration by both the prison officials and inmates. Resistance to authority is sufficient to qualify a man for candidacy.

In the midst of what would to a layman's eyes be interpreted as a confused mass, there is organization. True, just as the prison officials' every effort is directed at dehumanization, the convicts' is structured to oppose, undermine, and compromise—thus, in that respect the convict culture is one that is diametrically opposed to the principles free society lives by. It is easy then to understand that a man spending a considerable period of time in such an environment suffers irreparable psychological damage and is hardly qualified to re-enter the society that once declared him an outcast.

Little time and effort are expended in teaching the inmate a vocational trade. The sad fact is that no vocational program exists at most prisons in America to which a man could apply himself. In terms of education, until recently when some college programs commenced, acquiring a primary education was a dubious endeavor. What alternatives are left for those who come to prison alone and whose families have deserted them or are unable to send them a few dollars every month?

As in any free community, ours too, offers diverse vocations to be pursued: gambling, narcotic peddling, predatory money-lending, and strong-arming, just to mention a few. And it shouldn't sound strange that the men pursue these vocations with as much determination as their free-world counterparts. They have no other method of providing for the basic necessities like toothpaste, soap, and tobacco. While it is true that approximately half the population at my prison, or six hundred men, are assigned to work in the State Shops and earn fifty cents a day, the average inmate makes, at best, fourteen dollars a month. This is hardly sufficient to provide for the things he needs. Consequently, he chooses one of the above-mentioned *professions* and pushes any thought of rehabilitation to the back of his mind. Where his initial misadventure with the law might have been an unfortunate incident, it now becomes one of *choice*.

It would appear at first glance that the convict's subversion of the ugly dehumanizing system is successful and therefore, few men become ensnared in its web. To the contrary, for while in some respects that might be true, the sub-culture, permeated with anti-social attitudes is far from conducive to rehabilitation. At best, it serves the interests of the long-term, incorrigible who has long ago lost all hope of release, while at the same time it destroys all positive attitudes in the younger convict, the first offender who could ordinarily still be salvaged. It is here that society is failing most miserably.

When viewed in retrospect, little hope can be held out for our penal system and the methods employed to deal with criminal offenders. An entirely new concept must be implemented, one with less emphasis on brain-washing a man into submission. Rehabilitation that must depend on the lash is soon discarded the moment the man takes his first step through the prison doors and into the free world.

There is a solution which, if properly executed, can have a marked effect on the present day crime problem. Success or failure will depend on the cooperation of those handling "custody," and the sociologists who at present have made little headway in explaining away the crime epidemic that is sweeping our country.

The first and major step is to destroy the "no fraternizing" policy so stringently enforced in our penal system today. Unless keeper and kept can establish a common bond through which they might relate to one another, the authority of the badge will continue to draw resentment. Group therapy sessions (voluntary, of course) where both sides are permitted to speak out freely not only opens the door to understanding, but permits the inmate to vent frustrations otherwise considered offensive and that could net him a disciplinary report.

It is equally important to remove restrictive policy that prevents outside groups from entering the prison and mingling with the inmate body. To this extent "custody" must be prepared to revamp its policies and thoughts. Security-minded officials who refuse to modify their thinking to conform with the new school of thought must be replaced with more open-minded men and women.

There is absolutely no sense in isolating men, 90 percent of whom will be returning to the communities they left. Nor is it wise in denying them some social contact that will keep them abreast of current events during their period of incarceration. At present we are nothing but social misfits who find it impossible to fit ourselves into what have now become strange surroundings.

Can such programs be commenced in prisons considered the country's eyesores; in prisons built over one hundred and fifty years ago to accommodate six hundred men and which presently house twelve hundred? Hardly, unless the archaic living conditions are brought up to date, and not until the present apathetic administration with its old school of "thought methodists" are replaced with something more conducive to rehabilitation. Until then, American prisons will continue to serve as nothing more than a convict factory—turning out *educated* criminals.

Now for some thoughts on a dimension of prison life seldom discussed or written about: few people concern themselves with a convict's spiritual needs. To most, he is an outcast to be hidden away in dungeons, called prisons, supposedly to repent of his sins. There he is stripped of his name and given a number, subjected to the vilest indignities devised by man, and quite often, long after he has paid his debt to society, he must still carry his moral cross of crucifixion with the stigma of being called an ex-con.

The attitude is an old, familiar one and is understandable where a gullible and apathetic public is concerned—until the finger of accusation begins to single out the clergy: "the shepherds of the flock."

At such times I can't help but recall from my childhood memory, a verse of Scripture from the Book of Matthew: "I was in prison, and ye came unto me." Suddenly my mind races over twenty years of my adult life which have been spent behind various prison walls, and I discover that I can count those visits on the fingers of one hand! It almost sounds absurd that a society would confine a man to many years in prison for the purpose of teaching him to repent of his waywardness—and simultaneously neglect to provide the necessary facilities and programs to attain that goal.

When one contemplates the role of the clergy and their failure in responding to the needs of the incarcerated felon, it isn't difficult to come away impressed that they are forbidden from entering our prisons and making contact with its inhabitants. Of course that is not so, but then, where are those who Jesus commanded: "Go ye therefore and teach . . ."? To whom did he preach these words? For whose benefit?

Are a young drug addict of nineteen, a burglar of twenty-two, a murderer of fifty, too old for redemption? Or are we like lepers, too unclean to be approached? Perhaps we should raise our eyes to Calvary and look at His two companions in death for the answer.

Many men arriving at prison are hurt not only physically but spiritually, although most would conceal their spiritual hurt. To do otherwise would only subject them to the scorn and ridicule of their fellow inmates. Others spend lonely weeks and months in county jails hoping beyond hope for a visit from their pastors and other community church groups of which many had been members prior to their incarceration. They seek a familiar face, a kind word to lift their spirits when the world is crumbling around them. But no one comes, or is concerned enough to suffer the uncomfortable feeling of approaching—much less entering—a prison. How uncomfortable then must it be for those who languish within its confines.

Forsaken by family and friends, rejected by the society they so wronged, we wander like lost sheep until finally, for lack of adequate religious guidance we become mired in lust and perversion that so abounds in prisons—originally the principal cause of our incarceration. This is a sad reflection indeed on those entrusted to preach from the pulpits the lesson of brotherly love. Is it any wonder why so many men reject the outstretched hand and look upon it with suspicion when finally it is extended?

This is not to say that men in prison are without some religious representation. To the contrary, Catholic and Protestant services are scheduled for every Sunday; Bible classes and religious tracts are available in abundance; religious medals and rosaries are yours for the asking. Salvation of the Spirit is the theme—but little, if anything is said of our *physical* needs.

The call for religious revival reverberates every Sunday from pulpits, to fall on deafened ears of men who cannot identify with impersonal voices gushing what has now become meaningless rhetoric. Regrettable is the fact that most preachers are completely unaware that the greatest wealth of revival material are the inmates—if only they would descend from their ivory towers and approach them on a man-to-man basis. Religion in prison has become a cold and emotionless ritual that should leave no doubt in anyone's mind as to the reason for low attendance.

Of what practical value is a Bible to me (except to roll cigarettes when I run out of paper?) when I need someone from my home town to keep me informed about my ailing children? Or how can the Sermon on the Mount help a youngster who is on the verge of committing suicide and cannot find someone to trust and who might be in a position to help him? But who is first on the scene to administer the last rites at death?

Part 3: A Demonic Principality

It seems almost unnatural that our clergymen, evangelists, and Christian teachers should segregate themselves from their flocks. It is here, in prison, that most men are vulnerable to religious indoctrination. It would be very foolish to believe that a twenty year-old youth could be so callous as not to have remorse for the crime he committed. Or that even the hard core convict has no use for kind words. It was this type of attitude initially that had created the existing communication gap and unless something is done to bridge it, many men, particularly the younger set, will continue falling by the wayside.

Most members of the clergy seem to feel that quoting Scripture from memory and spouting off a lot of silly numbers ends their obligation to their fellow man. Seldom do I hear anyone refer to spiritual guidance as an integral part of a man's rehabilitation. Little, if any emphasis is placed on religious guidance for men being released from prison. And few Christians are willing to come forward to embrace an ex-convict in true Christian fellowship—without the "Jesus Saves" overtone. How often are ex-cons invited to participate in church socials?

During my many years of incarceration I have spent what would amount to at least four years in solitary confinement. At such times my only companion was a Bible which I have read and re-read. How great were the emotional conflicts that arose to challenge my distorted social and spiritual values! Many were the tears I shed in frustration and shame in those solitary cells where I groveled in confusion and youthful ignorance, to emerge time and again full of cynicism. I must admit that the Bible served its purpose—it occupied my time even if it didn't do a damned thing for spirit or empty stomach. I wasn't converted; I didn't see the light, and it has only served to further shake my belief in God. One can hardly expect our youth to practice love and kindness in an environment that is shunned by those who preach it.

Convicts are not heathens and atheists who denounce any need or the existence of a Supreme Being. We are people, human beings—your husbands, sons, and brothers; alienated perhaps from our Maker, and now as it would appear, from our fellow man; adrift in a wilderness of confusion. We are not the caricatures portrayed on Hollywood movie screen—mental defectives incapable of loving, to be treated like wild beasts without souls. We are mere victims of our foolish follies, separated from our free brethren by no more than the grace of God, "for all have sinned . . ."

Few people are aware of the harsh and oppressive conditions of prison life and adopt the negative attitude of letting someone else worry about our needs—our social leprosy is too ugly for them to bear. But if our incarceration is to be at all meaningful to us as a lesson in deterrence, it must consist of more than the lash, cruelty, and cold indifference. There must be a contact established with our communities, especially the religious groups, to allay our many fears of the unknown that will surely confront us upon our return to society. After many years of living strict, regimented lives in an environment where decision-making is almost non-existent, transacting a small purchase, even ordering from a menu in a restaurant, can create uncertainty and prove complex to many men.

There must also be material as well as spiritual support, since both are interrelated. Responsible community businessmen must be ready— nay, eager—to extend their Christian fellowship to us with offers of employment. But of greater importance, they must be ready to enter our prisons, to observe first hand the conditions we live under, to familiarize themselves with their less fortunate brethren and to study their needs. In essence, to disseminate that Christian fellowship.

To establish such a relationship, to close the communication gap that is growing ever wider, the clergy is responsible for laying the foundation and must accept the burden of taking us into their folds and forget the traditional excuse that we are not in their parish. Is it not written that "For where two or three are gathered . . ." Is a lost lamb no longer part of the flock from which it has strayed, and will not the shepherd leave the hundred and search for the one? Or are these mere flowery words, to be read on Sundays and quickly forgotten?

It is difficult to welcome the prodigal son home with open arms. Too frequently people forget that no man is perfect and to err is human, even unto seventy times seven. And yet, it is the errant, not the righteous, who need guidance. Christianity acknowledges human failure, can man do less than accept this precept in dealing with his brother? Would he deny to those in most need of redemption the right to stand in the shadow of the Cross? How long will our brothers, so blessed with plenty, require us to suffer the cold, begging for spiritual alms?

Society must stop viewing the convict as some denizen, and prison as a place where lawbreakers are housed until their time is up. Punishment without rehabilitation is futile and serves no constructive purpose. And rehabilitation is more than a Sunday church service with a preacher extolling his charges to virtue while he waves a fire brand of hell and damnation for evildoers—then disappears until the following Sunday.

Religion is an integral part of that rehabilitation process which begins not when a man is released, but the day he is delivered to the prison. It is then that he is most apt to respond to practical spiritual overtures, founded not so much on Scripture-quoting, but on Christian fellowship, if he is to comprehend the error of his ways. Only this way will he feel secure in the knowledge that while society is ready to punish evildoers, it is equally prepared to forgive and not harbor resentments.

Are our "souls" the only concern of the clergy? Are they not also an integral part of our personality, our "human-beingness?" Is the quality of a convict's soul less worthy and deserving of salvation than that of another Christian? Are not our physical needs to maintain health in body and mind equally as great?

I urge you to keep your Bibles, tracts, medals, and organ music. Instead, give us of yourselves, your time, and help just as He gave of himself to the sick and poor and needy. Come out from behind your cloaks of hypocritical self-righteousness and wallow a while with us thieves, pimps, drug addicts, and murderers.

If religious training is in fact an integral part of rehabilitation and our Christian brothers continue keeping themselves aloof from these men in prison, then let me be the first to proclaim that GOD IS DEAD!

9

The Incarcerated Village

SHELLY A. BREEDEN

Part One

The Life of the Villagers

IN THIS INCARCERATED VILLAGE, my life is simple. I am a number. To most of the world this is all I will ever be, a few digits, like the bar code on a cereal box—a meaningless existence. They will not know that I am an artist and a poet. They will never see me cry. They will never know my laughter. They will not appreciate me as "daughter," "sister," "friend," or "mother" because the title and bar code imprinted on me is all they think they need to know. In their world that makes me a bad person, a villain, a monster, and there is nothing more to me than that. Society does not care who and what I really am, and for that reason the penal system has *carte blanche* to use, abuse, or mistreat me at will if they so wish. Because our culture does not hold these government agencies accountable for their actions, and does not demand that humans be treated humanely, we allow these proceedings to be the acceptable practice and, in doing so, millions of incarcerated people suffer the consequences of society's blind eye. Society can go to sleep at night knowing that I am getting what I deserve. Some days, I agree with them. My grief and guilt allow me to justify the authority figures' actions.

I am currently 34 years old, and serving concurrent sentences; one of twenty-five years at 100 percent for second degree murder, and the other of twelve years at 30 percent for conspiracy to commit second degree murder. I have been incarcerated for almost thirteen years, and must serve nine more years before I will be released. I am, however, lucky. I will only be 43 when I am released. Many others, who have lengthy sentences like mine, are much older when they are released. Still others will die while confined.

Twice I have filed for clemency, but each time I have been denied. The first denial was because I had not served 45 percent of my time in calendar years/days. Apparently, rehabilitation can be judged by the amount of time one serves in prison, not by what one does while they are in the custody of the state. The second denial was due to the seriousness of my crime. A less serious conviction would have provided regular parole hearings, and would not have required applications for clemency. I believe that my situation is typical for a woman with my felony type.

I was only 21 when incarcerated. It was the prime of my life, and I had my whole life to try new things. Now 34, I am outdated. Not outdated because of my age, but because the world I knew is gone. Technology, for example, has passed me by. I have never used a cell phone, or a DVD player. I did not have a computer before being incarcerated, and I have never surfed the Internet. I have never driven a car, nor enjoyed a Big Mac. I suppose we all take things for granted until they are lost to us. As excited as I am to experience all the "new to me" technologies and advances, I am equally terrified that I have done too much time and cannot survive in the "free world." "What ifs" fill my nightmares. Think about it. If I live to my release date, I will have served exactly half my life in prison.

During incarceration my physical and mental health has declined. The quality of medical care is poor; many of us often go without medicine. Someone is always dropping the ball on getting what we need, if it is on formulary (the approved drug list). These medications range from over-the-counter products like Ibuprofen and analgesic rub to antibiotics and disease-specific treatment drugs. If a needed prescription is not on formulary, inmates have to do without medication/treatment, because getting approval for an alternative medication is too tedious for the staff members. They say they don't want to fight all the red tape. It is also a regular occurrence that they give one inmate another inmate's medication by mistake.

The daily life of an inmate is full of tribulations. Due to the budget cuts, people frequently walk away from the dining room still hungry. Inadequate clothing makes the weather hard to endure. Sleep deprivation is common. The third shift officers make a lot of noise and shine their flashlights in our faces. They also leave the pod lights on, so that it is bright in the cells all night. Although these are accepted practices, they function as forms of intimidation, abuse of authority, and cruelty. Complaints generate promises of change, but nothing changes. Inmates filing formal grievances or writing letters to the administration, run the risk of retaliation. Many officers and inmates boast a reputation of being rude, loud, profane, inconsiderate, aggressive, abrasive, belligerent, abusive, or cruel. But what can I do?

Although I long for opportunities, rehabilitation programs are largely unavailable. The system does offer a few classes providing tools to live and be better, yet those courses are often filled by "short timers" and parole violators so that they can take the certificates to the parole board. A large percentage of the inmate population will not get a chance at parole. For those I know who have a lengthy sentence that includes a parole hearing, their mandatory hearing seems to be a mere formality. Parole is often denied.

Those with drug addictions have behavioral patterns that are hard to break. Unfortunately, I see even those who succeed in the federally funded Therapeutic Community Program, return time and again. Society often calls these type offenses "victimless," but I wonder if the offender's family, children, and the community that pays for all the trials and therapies would agree that it is victimless.

For the incarcerated person life is a constant bombardment of hate and sorrow. One either learns to take it, or be broken by it. Between the loss of contact with family and friends, and the unreasonably stressful day-to-day, life is dark hopelessness. How do we make peace with that? I try to take the impact of each day in stride. I try not to take it as a personal attack. Unsure how others manage, I rely on the "family" that I have in here—the two or three people whom I have a sincere friendship and connection with. If I did not have these bonds, I don't believe that I would be able to survive. Granted, an "out date" is the proverbial light at the end of the tunnel, but there are so many uncertainties. People die from medical issues, old age, and accidents. I cannot focus on the year 2019. I have no guarantee I will see it.

Before prison, I had friends whom I believed were as close as family. Once locked up, however, I had no friends. They wholly abandoned me, without even a second thought. In an instant, I was completely and utterly alone. I felt like my entire life was in a train wreck, and I was the only survivor. As I grieved the loss of my friends, it seemed that in reality I was the only one who died in that train wreck. Their lives continued without issue or incident. When I reminisce about the "good old days," it is like a knife in my heart every time—a serrated reminder that none of them cared enough about me to stand by me. The pain of solitude is omnipresent.

Upon removal from the global village of society, a new world unfolds. One falls through the looking glass into new familial bonds and dynamics. In an all-female prison, other inmates become your mothers, daughters, and sisters. Some of those female inmates will take on more traditionally masculine characteristics, that is, they tend to fill the role of father figure, brother, or son. I believe this is due to a primal need for these roles to be cast. Our most primitive human instincts dictate that we are to be pack animals. We require emotional interaction but are expected by the institution and the judicial system to act as if we do not. Our biological family and our developed family are essentially mirror images, divided only by razor wire fences.

I should suffer the consequences of my actions or inactions. I take full responsibility for my culpability. I do not understand how the number of days I spend in this institution determines my rehabilitation status. I cannot comprehend how any of this benefits society. There is no reconciliation for my victim's family. I attempted to contact them on my own and offered, by any means, to assist in their healing, but it was either ill received or did additional harm. Neither of these were my intention.

My greatest concern is not for myself or the other inmates but for the future. I tell you these things so that you may truly see what makes me frightened for my children. This is what could happen to them, and what could happen to your children. The reality of its probability is becoming more and more evident.

Part Two

Our Children, The Future of the Incarcerated Village

I am a mother of three perfect children. Like any proud mother, I wanted the world for my children, but I made a terrible error in judgment. I allowed myself to be abused and dominated by someone else, because of my terror and weakness; it is for my inactions and my codefendant's actions that I am incarcerated. I fear that my mistake will cost my children their freedom and their lives. I live in a dead panic that my children are doomed.

I fear that my life may be a haunting specter of their future. Is it the utter cruelty of fate? Will they fall prey to the statistics? If my children are subjected to this life, will they break under the weight of someone's thumb? Will one of my children die because of a staff member's error? Will they spend months, years, or even decades of their lives in this regime? Will my children know this mind-numbing isolation?

You've heard it said that it takes a village to raise a child, but what if that village is incarcerated? The global village is bleeding into the incarcerated village at an alarming rate. More and more people like you, your family, friends, and neighbors are becoming people like me, like the people in this alternate tribe that I live in. To those who see the statistics, it is clear that the future is spiraling out of control and down a path that can only lead to darkness. But consider that every statistic is a human being. Every ID number and every percentage is someone's family member and friend. Every discarded individual is someone's child.

Though I write and call my children every week, I feel largely disconnected from them and the rest of my family. Out of sight is out of mind. Since they were very young when I was incarcerated (5 years old, 17 months old, and 2 months old) I worry if I did all I could to bond with them before I lost them. Did I spend every second I could trying to encourage them? Did I tell them I love them as often as I could?

In the rare visits I receive, I am allowed to sit with my children in the prison's visitation gallery. I can hug and kiss them once when they arrive and once when they leave. This interaction must be done in front of officers who watch on as if they are analyzing my affection for my children, appearing as if they will demand justification for it. I can't hold them. If you break the rules the officers will terminate your visit and possibly not allow you to visit for a specified amount of time in the future. My children and I both feel the stress of these stipulations. We are separated right in front of each other. How can you be with your babies and not offer them any comfort?

Especially now, with the limited contact I have, I wonder if I am doing enough, or of it even matters. I am not included in their lives. I am not told about school and social events until they are long over. No one asks my opinion on decisions that affect their lives. But I am all too easily blamed for any negative behavior. This is not how I wanted the phrase "you are just like your mother," used when someone was talking to my children. Now I have learned that my being in prison may have doomed them to live my existence.

I have missed all the big things from my two youngest children and most of the great events of my oldest. Missing teeth, Christmases, birthdays, Easters, first days of school, first snow, first hair cut, first steps, all memories I will never have. How I took for granted all the times I watched them sleep, laughed with them, held them close. What I wouldn't give to get that back. Life is so uncertain here, I feel paralyzed as a parent. Do I waste the few precious moments I have with them trying to cram in all the important things they should know, or do I just enjoy them and hope someone else teaches them the life lessons they will need to stay out of prison? If my family can afford it I will get to visit them face-to-face for two hours once a year. So precious are those fleeting moments. How best should I use them?

If I don't die while incarcerated, my children will be grown and on their own when I am released. Their lives will be full of their own responsibilities. No one will need me. If my children are condemned to be incarcerated, will they live through it? Will they be out when I am? Will there ever be a happy family holiday, or even a joyous moment, for us again beyond this cage?

Like most inmates, my family has taken the responsibility of raising my children, which means my entire family is suffering from my incarceration. Nevertheless, my children are not safe. Not just *my* children, but everyone's children are put at risk due to school programs being cut so that the state can find sufficient money to fund the Department of Correction. I see this televised every year when Tennessee's budget comes down to the wire. In this vicious cycle, children are set to their own means without the direction of educational and community programs. With no programs to occupy idle hands and encourage and guide them toward positive paths, children become vulnerable and more easily influenced by individuals in negative ways, and once having made a poor decision, that choice can lead straight from the school yard to a six-by-nine prison cell.

Consider the numbers. Recently published statistics place some 2,319,258 Americans in jail or prison at the start of 2008—one out of every 99.1 adults. Additionally, one in every thirty-two adults is in the system, on parole, or probation.[1] Further studies have found that in 2007, 1.7 million American children had an incarcerated parent. That translates to one in every forty-three children. The Washington Sentencing Project's

1. The Pew Center on the States, *One in 100: Behind Bars in America 2008* http://www.pewcenteronthestates.org/uploadedFiles/8015PCTS_Prison08_FINAL_2-1-1_FORWEB.pdf

"Incarcerated Parents and Their Children" found that one in every fifteen African American children of incarcerated parents will be incarcerated him/herself. For Hispanic children the rate is one in forty-two, and for Caucasian children the rate is one in 111.[2] According to Tennessee's former Commissioner of Correction, there is an average of two children per inmate and 70 percent of them will eventually be incarcerated for more than overnight or booking. Those children will likely do "real time" at some point in their respective lives.[3]

Here's what I know. The statistical probability is that 2 of my 3 children will end up imprisoned. This is a mother's worst nightmare, made all the more atrocious by my own experience with the system. The parent who has never been incarcerated can only imagine what their child suffers. I know what fate awaits them.

I know they will be punished because I am incarcerated. The courts will rush them through the system and stick them with a record regardless of guilt, innocence, or culpability. The system will justify it with the dismissive retort, "They have a felon parent; they must be a bad seed." I know that once inside the fences and razor wire they will be exposed to staff and inmates determined to dehumanize and abuse them. I know that their separation from family and abandonment from their friends will eat away at them like soul-sucking parasites. I know that their health, physically and mentally, will decline at a shocking rate. They will go hungry, suffer the weather, and many nights they will be sleep deprived. They will not be rehabilitated unless they fight for their education. I know they will not get a fair chance at parole. I don't know, however, if they will survive it. I did not raise them to be convicts. Who could have known if I should have made them tougher? My family has done the best they could to raise them well, but does it matter?

The statistics that suggest my children are doomed to this life are overwhelming, and the guilt consumes me. No one in my family was ever incarcerated prior to me. As time progresses, the correctional system grows. More children, in turn, are being exposed to this life. Is the judicial system determined to incarcerate all of society? Where does it end? Who will be responsible for offering our children a better way?

Tennessee law states that if a "parent has been confined in a correctional or detention facility of any type, by order of the court as a result

2. http://www.sentencingproject.org/doc/publications/publications/inc_incarceratedparents.pdf

3. *The Tennessean*, February 12, 2009.

of a criminal act, under a sentence of ten or more years, and the child is under eight years of age at the time the sentence is entered by the court" their parental rights can be taken away and they can't do anything about it.[4] An incarcerated parent is powerless against the system. Due to this law I have not seen my baby boy, who is now 14 years old, in nearly thirteen years. His father's parents have full custody and may have adopted him. They have no contact with my family. Not knowing if he is okay might be the most torturous thing I face everyday. I do not know how this has affected him. Does he stand a better chance of escaping this fate by not knowing me?

My children were especially devastated when my release was denied. I think it is a large part of why my oldest son has shut me out of his life. He can't stand being crushed every time he gets his hopes up that I will come home.

My oldest son is 17 years old. He lives with his father, who is different than the father of my two younger children. He has shut me and my parents out of his life. Sure, all teens get rebellious but, I haven't heard from him in over a year. I worry that he is in with a bad crowd, and I fear that he will make a decision that will ruin his life, or worse that he will allow others to make a decision that will ruin his life. He has even cut ties with his sister so that he has no connection to us. When I contacted state offices and the courts for assistance, they said there was "nothing they could do until he is arrested." How is this not discouraging?

My daughter is 12 years old. She resides with my mother. I pray with my whole soul that she does not fall into bad patterns. She is very intelligent and mature, but her teenage years are at hand. Will she rebel like her eldest sibling? She is in several church and school programs and is very committed to charity work at a local animal rescue. Will this be enough to keep her on a positive path to a successful future? Will she develop a crush on the wrong guy? Will she allow an abusive person to take control of her life? Will she fall victim to her own fears and insecurities? Will she be like me? I would give anything to make certain she has a better life.

When I cradled my babies in my arms, peered into their curious little eyes, and dreamed of their future this was not my dream. I dreamt of crawling and walking, learning to talk and read, dances and crushes, class projects and field trips, the world was theirs for the taking. When I worried over events that would happen in their lives, my fears were trivial

4. *24663 § 36-1-113, West's Tennessee Code Annotated, Title 36, Domestic Relations. *24667 (6).

compared to the ones I have now. My fears then were about chicken pox and broken hearts, not their freedom, not that their lives would be completely wrecked over a mistake, one mistake.

What were your mother's dreams and fears for you? What are your dreams and fears for your children?

This was not my mother's dream for me either. She and my father mourn for me constantly. My father was a police officer for over eighteen years. They both believed that because I didn't kill anyone, I would not go to prison for murder. It was completely unfathomable to them. Surely, the system would work. They were destroyed when I was sentenced. When I applied for clemency they got their hopes up—only to be crushed when the board denied my appeal. My sister still feels like a part of her was taken away. She grieves for the loss with no hope of healing.

As a whole, the judicial process is a river of disease. It branches out in creeks and streams, pumping devastation into the bodies of our friends, family, and community. It erodes everyone's spirits, and drowns all our hopes. It will carve out the path of our future, a path that is austerely bleak. How will we stop these rushing waters? Our children are standing in the path of this black swell. Will the global village be annihilated by the raging floodwaters that are sweeping our children into the hopeless valley of the incarcerated village? Who will come to their rescue?

Will we allow more and more of our children to be sacrificed to a life of incarceration and never rise up? Will no one shout, "No more!"? Will no one demand change, for the sake of these innocents? Where is the global outcry for justice? Can there be no crime and rehabilitation, must it all be punishment? Will there ever be a way to stop the vicious cycle from sweeping our children down into the whirlpool?

Will my children be stuck in the same limbo that I am in: never moving on, never growing, never healing? My children are suffering because of my incarceration, but the courts do not deem them as victims. Yet they suffer the most.

My children and my family should not have to pay the price for my mistakes. Since 1973 the inmate population has grown from 204,000 people to some 2.3 million. More than 1,100 individuals have been executed. Will my children fall into those statistics? Will yours? The projected vision of the future of this nation as one village is bleak. It takes a village to raise a child; we've chained and imprisoned our village. Who will raise our children now?

10

"What Prison Has Taught Me"

CRYSTAL STURGILL

How do I watch the image in the mirror grow older behind razor wire fences and bars? How do I get up every day and know that I will never leave? How do I cope when my family members die and I can't even go pay my final respects? I don't know the answers to those, or many other questions; I just know that I do it everyday.

My reason for being a lifetime resident of the Tennessee Prison for Women is a long one. At age 17, the State removed me from the home I grew up in. There I suffered abuses that I won't delve into here, but psychologically and physically I was left broken. I floated between foster care and staying with my extended family and friends, who tried to help me. While I was preparing for trial, some investigators counted some of the places I laid my head. I think they said I stayed at thirteen different homes between December 1996 and April 1997. Five months. Five months in which my downward spiral reached full speed.

The last place I stayed was with some people I had gone to grade school with. I was there two or three days before the crime that cost me my life took place. Fragmented memories make up that time for me now. One of the people I was with killed three people, I got the same time as the killer because of a felony murder law. I didn't care if the guy stole the car. I didn't help. I didn't know what he planned, and afterwards, when I ran, it was because I didn't know what else to do. I had just turned 18. My only dealings with the law had, until then, been the interviews with the state police before I was taken from my home.

I admit my poor choices, and know that no matter how many years of my life I forfeit, I will never make whole the people who are the true victims. I know I belong in prison. I don't argue my guilt, or even the fact that I believe the felony murder law was designed for a far different purpose than that which it is applied by today's criminal justice system.

I write to tell you what it is like to spend a day, a week, a month, a year, a decade in my shoes, wearing one of only four pairs of pants I am issued, with a stripe down my leg identifying me as a prisoner of the state of Tennessee. I write to give voice to all those who, like me, will never walk freely upon a street, will never go into the grocery store and decide what they want for dinner, will die alone and frightened in a world that will not allow their family to comfort them in even their last moments on earth.

When I was asked to write a submission for this book I asked several other people, people who have done more time than my thirteen years, if they would consider such an undertaking. They all told me "No." They said that telling "free world" people wouldn't make any difference. I believe that it can. If nothing else, it can give a better understanding of what life is like for the growing number of men and women who are living out their lives behind tall fences and locked doors.

When I came to prison I had just turned 19. The judge had announced that I was sentenced to three consecutive life sentences without the possibility of parole. After being transported by sheriff's deputies from jail to prison, I sat with my two codefendants and filled out the booking paperwork. It took all day. I only saw two inmates the whole day; one who came to issue our uniforms, and another who brought our lunch trays.

I had been strip searched frequently in jail, so, as much as anyone can be, I was accustomed to that type of humiliation. Then I was made to shower in front of the booking officer to make sure that I used the delousing shampoo that she gave me. I was given a pile of paperwork, rules, and medical procedures. It was overwhelming and scary, though I know the booking officer tried to make it as painless as possible. I was escorted by a guard to the segregation housing, where I had to stay until I had been medically cleared. I spent three days there and was only brought out of my cell to shower and have an hour of recreation, which one of the other inmates told me they had to provide. I only saw my own codefendants during that time. I guess for our own protection they just left us together.

When I entered general population I had no idea what to expect. I was moved into another room, this time with a roommate. My roommate was a woman who had been booked in on the same day as me. She had been here before. She told me not to worry, she would show me the ropes. I quickly found out that I was fortunate that my family supported me financially. Otherwise, I would have been left to my own devices. I didn't have to worry about having enough money to buy food, cigarettes, or personal products. I did, however, have to worry about people thinking I was a pushover. I learned the hard way that you can't loan anything to the other inmates, because they'll bum you dry. They will ask for anything and everything, with no care or intentions of paying you back. The best piece of advice I could give someone coming into prison is not to mistake kindness for weakness, and don't allow people who do make that mistake to define your actions.

Thankfully, I'm not in a really physically rough prison. I can say that I only know two people who have been sexually assaulted by another inmate, and a few more that have been sexually assaulted by an officer. There have been no violent outbursts that have resulted in any real and lasting injury while I have been here. That doesn't mean, however, that there aren't other outright tortures.

The looming guards, most of whom are male, frequently serve as an intimidating reminder that we are powerless to stop them from doing any-thing they want to us. They scream, bang doors, keep us awake sometimes at night, and go out of their way to make life as unbearable as possible. Not all the guards are bad, but the ones who are should simply be avoided. That isn't always possible. They have a way of seeking out the most eas-ily intimidated, but to go out of your way to avoid the confrontation is sometimes worth it.

As a woman who has issues with men anyway, like so many of the women I am surrounded by, when approached in an aggressive manner the fight or flight instinct kicks in. To fight would only be a losing battle. Chances are, you'd get the hell beaten out of you and you'd still wind up spending years in segregation. To allow your flight instincts to take over will only get you so far, since you are in prison and cannot leave. It is a situation with no inmate winners. Either the officers will have their way, or they will break you.

The petty rules are the ones that eat at you. Don't allow your t-shirt to show while in uniform. You can take only one shower a day. You can have anything that our approved vendors sell, but if the institution thinks you buy too much you'll have to throw it away. You can't call anyone who doesn't have a land line, and only ten numbers will be allowed for you to call. Only eight people can be on your visitation list, even if they are family.

This list of petty rules goes on and on. The staff always worries about the wrong thing. Overlook the fact that I can get high anytime I want and focus in on whether or not officers can see the tail of my t-shirt, or if my hat is store-bought or homemade.

This is the world I live in. The world where low-level officers can make up their own rules and enforce them at will. Most of us still have some hope of getting out; otherwise no one would be able to survive. This hope is the only reason that we don't rise up. The guards are easily outnumbered, and while some of them have guns they wouldn't be able to shoot us all. No, we will sit here, stewing in the venomous spite that brews inside us with each newly enforced petty rule, until one at a time we succumb to the system.

The most obvious harm done to us is that the system takes away the ability to choose. I don't set my own schedule. I don't choose my own meals. I don't make decisions about much of anything. There is no fretting over what to do. Do what you are told, and they say you are a model prisoner. What you really are is an automaton, spitting out the correct vague answers to the monotonous questions asked by officers and staff members who already know exactly what you should say. I do what is expected of me. In all these years, I have never had a "discipline" (i.e., never been caught breaking some petty rules). You might look at me and say that this is some proof that I have learned how to function, but the truth is that I have learned how not to function.

I have learned how to bend to the will of the system. I have learned to roll with the punches of the most brutish guards. I have learned to stifle the voice inside me that screams with each new injustice I am faced with. I have learned to stand and be berated, humiliated, and dehumanized. I have learned not to let emotion show; sometimes I'm not even sure if I feel real emotion anymore. After so many years of stuffing things down, holding them in, trying to subjugate myself, I am warped. That is a good way to describe me, warped by the system. The real me was lost a long time ago, maybe before I even got here.

I spent over eleven months in isolation, awaiting trial. I saw my family once a week through a window about twelve inches wide with two inch thick Plexiglas, so that it was like looking at a carnival mirror. The only real human contact was with my attorneys, who came by to see me as often as they could. I had never before been alone. I never lived on my own, and had never spent more than a day or so without seeing someone else. In jail that wasn't the case. I did see deputy sheriffs. They came around every few hours and let me use their lighters. I was allowed to smoke, but not allowed matches or a lighter—the first of the petty rules. I was lucky to have a small window that looked out to a concrete wall about six inches away. I had natural light to tell day from night, unless it was raining. This was my first experience of sensory deprivation; the lights were always on, though occasionally dimmed overnight. They glared at me with their fluorescent grins. In that solitude some may find peace or comfort, but I found my own little piece of insanity. My mind was stagnating. I was only allowed four books a week. I read and reread them two or three times before my week was up, and I would have my family bring four more. So much for the myths about well-stocked inmate libraries.

Isolation was psychologically more than I was able to withstand, and before long I had to be medicated. The pills helped. I slept most of the day, and I was able to convince the jail administrators that I should be allowed a walkman. This was some kind of outside contact; at the very least I could hear the news.

I don't know who the person was that started the lie about inmates lying around in plush cells watching cable TV all day. They were wrong. The Greene County jail was anything but plush and I didn't see a TV the entire time I was there. For several months I didn't even have a mattress to put over the metal "bed" that was bolted to the wall. It wasn't much of a bed, kind of like an old ship bed, just a piece of steel with a raised lip on the edge bolted to the concrete wall. There were no pillows, and I was given two wool army blankets to try and keep warm.

Ironically, life at the Tennessee Prison for Women did bring some level of stability. I could have a personal TV. My family was able to send me a few sets of either white or gray clothes, and, praise God, some real shoes. I had spent the past 11 months wearing what the jail called "deck shoes."

General population is what they call pretty much every inmate here. In GP there are stipulations that you must have a job. When I arrived, the inmates who didn't have a job were considered "unassigned," and they cleaned showers, picked up trash, and did any other jobs for six hours that the officers could think up. For all their work they were given six dollars on the fifteenth day of every month, pay day. With that six dollars they could buy soap, shampoo, toothpaste, a few razors, and, if lucky, maybe have enough left over to get some non-necessity.

They stopped giving those inmates six dollars several years ago. Now they say that if you are truly indigent and don't get six dollars from anywhere else in a month, they will provide some hygiene products. People who are unfortunate enough to have to go this route will tell you that what they get lasts about two weeks, and you cannot request more for a full month. Can you imagine what it is like to have to run a hustle for things like shampoo? The media makes it seem like inmates hustle for drugs and contraband, and some do. But more than anyone really knows, most are just people trying to get the things they cannot do without. How long can you go without bathing and washing your hair? Too many inmates can tell you the answer to that question.

I was in my senior year in high school before I was locked away. Because of my age, I was afforded the opportunity to go to school. I happily went to school. I had always wanted an education and I was glad to take my GED test. As it turned out, there wasn't a lot that the teacher could teach me, since the focus was on being able to pass the GED. School counted as a job for me, and I was paid seventeen cents an hour. After that, I took more classes. While in cosmetology I worked in the prison beauty shop. I got my state license and then took additional training to become an instructor. I was in that class for a couple years, and while there I reached "top out" pay of fifty cents per hour.

Since I left school, I have been lucky as far as jobs go. I have spent years working in an office setting, and I get paid the highest wages that the prison offers, $1.25 per hour. Not everyone gets that kind of job and I do what I can to make sure that I hold on to it. It has helped me become more comfortable, and I take pride in what I do. I like being able to support myself. I am no longer dependent on my family to take care of me. I have also learned some good skills, that if I ever get that chance at parole, I'll be able to hopefully use those skills to get a good job.

Mostly prison is what you make of it. You can rebel and fight the system, but with enough time you will eventually succumb. You have the opportunity while here to take some classes, and work the twelve step programs, because officials seem to think that those will fix whatever ails you. Hopefully, you will come out the other side a little better prepared to survive. You can use the time to become hardened, learn other ways to skirt the law, grow hatred for your captors and fellow inmates, and allow the system to make you all the things people assume about you. You can do what they tell you and lose your sense of self, learn to be dependent on the system, and lose the ability to make choices. It's up to you. You are the one who has to serve the sentence, and nobody can really tell you how it will be best for you. Don't worry, with the lengthy sentences that are handed down these days, you will probably have time to change your mind if you pick a path that doesn't work out for you. This is what prison has taught me, inmate #288306.

What will you allow prison to teach you? I can paint a picture of life for millions of Americans, but I have lost my voice. When I address problems in the system I am easily dismissed. I am a convicted murderer, a number, the nameless drone of the prison machine. You are not. You are John or Jane Voter. You are the future leaders of our country. You are the target audience for almost every product on the market, and your voice resonates clearly and effectively.

You have the power to change the system, to make it more effective, to institute new and innovative ideas in rehabilitation. My fervent prayer is that you will allow this work to open your eyes to the grave injustice being done to society by our justice system; that you will enact change within your lifetime. You will see a reformed system, one that contains more than just years behind bars, a system containing healing, rehabilitation, and the knowledge that you are doing a service to teach people who are eager and willing to learn. Most inmates would jump at the opportunity to expand their minds. They lack, however, the tools to do so. It is up to you whether they get the tools needed to become productive members of society. If you want criminals to learn their lesson about committing crimes then teach them how to live, not how to become dependent on the system. Open their minds. Open your hearts and remember that for most, the doors will once again be opened to allow these outcasts back into your community. The abilities and skills that they have when they get there are up to you.

11

Transformations
How Prison Changed Me

DONNA MCCOY

Until I was thirty, I had only seen one prison, and someone had to tell me what it was. To my young mind, prison was the place where the bad guys went for doing bad things. I thought prisons rehabilitated and restored offenders to society. I believed in the death penalty for those who took life. I even thought women weren't incarcerated, so I never imagined myself in prison.

Beware preconceptions.

Today, contrary to my preconceived notions, I have found that the reality of prison is a conglomeration of lost values formed out of sexual, physical, emotional, and psychological abuse. I've met women whose self-image is absolutely null and void. They go from being abused outside the razor wire to being abused on the inside. The penal system takes those already bedfellows with abuse and sucks the final bit of usefulness out of them, only to release them into the world expecting success—all from a person who has nothing left to stand on.

Prison was a huge detour off the path I had believed I would travel. While awaiting trial I stayed in the county jail, where I was housed in an open bay dorm designed to house fifty women. On any given weekend, however, it held a minimum of one hundred women. It was so crowded that women slept sitting at the tables in the common area, lying on the floor under face basins, or even in the showers. Discarded like last night's trash by frustrated family members and mental health professionals, most of the women sleeping on the floor didn't care where they slept—they were simply sleeping away the aftereffects of crack, crystal meth, alcohol, domestic violence, a police beating, or a lack of mental-health-stabilizing drugs, grateful to finally have rest from their own personal storms.

When it finally came time to appear on the auction block before the judge, we were awakened by a duty officer's yell. Some of us were still half-asleep, but the repeat offenders who knew the system were wide-eyed and ready to go. Altering their appearance to resemble someone's daughter, a favorite cashier at the fast food place, or the girl next door, the women I watched worked hard to earn their way to a sentence lighter than required by their offense. They carefully soaked the coating out of M&Ms for delicious lipstick and eye shadow and collected cigarette ashes to use as eye liner—all to receive the best price possible before the judge, the medical administrators, the DA, and the officers on the auction block.

Like slaves in ships leaving the harbor, heading for their various slave states, we were gathered into a cargo van and sent into the heart of the penal system.

Upon receiving a guilty verdict, and while awaiting sentencing, I was remanded to the custody of the state and returned to CCA's (Corrections Corporation of America) Silverdale facility in Hamilton County, Tennessee. Located all across America, CCA facilities are "for-profit" businesses that collect monies from federal, state, and local governments for housing offenders of the law. Upon my arrival, the Warden left orders that I spend the next nine months isolated in an eight feet by fifteen feet cell. He did not, however, provide any explanations. I was simply isolated from other felons and placed in a "fish bowl" cell directly in front of central control. I was on exhibition for CCA officials, grand juries, and state and local politicians. They were not true visitors, and I was no longer human. I was an exhibit of their tax dollars at work. This fish bowl, with eyes on me at all times, left a most unusual psychological scar. To this day, I retreat emotionally to the fetal position when anyone gazes at me for any duration without any verbal interaction. I also suffered from renewed abandonment issues. Constantly surveilled, I had no sense of time or days.

My first response to incarceration was fear. Roughly two months after being booked, photographed, and fingerprinted, I began to notice that I harbored an irrational fear of my surroundings. My body dried out from drugs and alcohol, but I did not quite achieve sobriety. Emotionally,

I tottered between anger and fright. For hours, I sat as still as a chameleon attempting to match shades with the puke colored walls in hopes of becoming invisible to an unseen foe. In the end, my fear was not of the officers, staff, or your run-of-the-mill felon. I was afraid of mental illness. I cannot attribute my fear to a single person, either by name or appearance. I recall no one person over another invoking fear in me. Rather, mental illness itself created my terror.

While at CCA, I spoke with various psychologists and even took a few psychotropic medications, but these measures deterred neither my psychological issues, nor my attempted suicide. In a single-cell environment, every bump and bang echoes with the eerie reverberation of a haunted house. After months of hearing unidentifiable noises through the night, cutting myself, listening to the screams of women suffering from mental illness, as well as my own screams at the brick walls and the officers and staff, I threatened a lawsuit. Who knew that a threatened lawsuit was the key to the Warden's ear?

The Warden reasoned, "You warranted isolation due to your actions prior to bonding out three months earlier. Specifically, you had $8,000 mailed into *my* facility." The Warden mistakenly saw these dollars as funds to bribe his lower middle class staff—his logic, not mine. I had not given a single thought to bribing my way out. He continued, "This act, in addition to more than six previous visits to segregation, is grounds for labeling you as a threat to staff and other offenders." He granted an administrative hearing on my segregation in thirty days. At that hearing, I was granted limited movement, but restricted to housing in the medical unit. The Warden never considered the threat I was to myself; he simply wanted me contained in a larger fishbowl. Thus, I gained a reputation as "incorrigible." Looking back, I wonder how big an increase to CCA's bottom line I grossed them.

Two experiences from this time in my life illustrate what the institution called "corrections" does.

The first came in my eighth month of administrative segregation, when I was allowed outside of the cell on average five minutes in twenty-four hours. My cell was a seven-by-ten-foot, one-man area. I had a toilet just above my head and a bed. There was a window in the front door that covered approximately half the doorframe (I imagine this was for those who wanted to look in). A second window allowed me to look out on the concrete recreation area. For five straight months my only view was concrete . . . I began to long for nature. I had limited contact with other inmates and officers. My visitors were screened and I could be denied or have a timed visit if a particular shift was short of staff persons.

During this time, I was allowed to go out of doors and feel the sun on my face on very few occasions. If there is any exaggeration in these numbers, it is due to the trauma associated with being caged as a wild animal. I awoke one morning at 5:00 a.m., as had been my usual habit for nearly forty years. I bathed, ate, and as uncustomary as tie and tails at a barbecue I was told I'd be allowed outside to the recreation area on this day. An hour after the scheduled eight o'clock "head count" of all offenders, the roving officer who worked in the same capacity of a gopher in other venues came to prepare me for the recreation area.

The recreation area was approximately 1600 to 1800 square feet of slab concrete. Block brick were the walls, with two reinforced steel doors on either end, one leading to the atrium between the men's and women's dorms, and the inside of the building facing central control. The other door led to freedom—green grass and paved roads. Freedom. Imagine being encased in a concrete tomb . . . and then attempt to imagine longing to spend time in this area. I did because it was very different, better than looking at eyes that stared blankly at you.

On the wall by the entrance into the building was a lone security box with speaker. If the officer needed to communicate with me or vice versa, this would be our one line of communication. Entombed in the rec area I never understood the reasoning for the additional security precautions. Most of the precautions befuddled me. First, I would be strip searched, allowed to put my clothes back on, fitted with an oversized belly chain, handcuffed, and shackled at the ankles. For some of the more humane officers this jailhouse jewelry was removed for ease of movement while I was on the yard. For many other officers, this was considered at the minimum a serious violation of policy and procedure, and at the maximum end of the spectrum an undeserving act of kindness toward a felon. This day I was fortunate to have a humane officer who removed the jailhouse jewelry at the entrance to the recreation area.

On my three previous treks outside, security warned if I were to sit, the expectation was I sit directly in front of the observation camera. If I walked laps, I had to make my presence viewable at the same intervals. (I learned to count my steps during this time; this proved to serve me well in prison where much of what I heard and saw I had to ignore). Most times, my jailer would not allow me to take anything outside with me, citing I had no one to talk with. The consequences for violating any of these would be continued lockdown without any consideration of time spent outdoors.

The first few hours I sat in the designated spot with eyes closed, using my senses to imagine my environment. I mused what grass looked like that time of year; were there any ponds, lakes, or flowers nearby? I could hear birds sing and wondered how they knew to stay outside the walls of the recreation area. An occasional beetle bug would work its way through the block brick and I would have a mental conversation of warning with the unsuspecting creatures. Strangely, I was afraid to speak the words in fear that the intercom might pick up my and the beetle's conversation and deem I was planning my escape.

At lunchtime, the same humane officer asked if I wanted to come in or eat outside for lunch. I asked if it would be okay I would like to stay outside always adding a "please" to every plea. The officer served me lunch, which I gladly shared with the instant picnic crashers—ants. The officer came and took my tray as her shift was nearing an end. She said she would make second shift aware that I had spent the day out of doors as she removed the tray and lunch debris from the recreation area. After she left, I began to walk the 1600 square feet. I was renewed by this officer's kindness. The doubts I felt about my sanity for talking with bugs and insects were now assuaged by the human touch this officer gave to her job of securing me. Today, I decided, was a good day.

This momentary euphoria came to a screeching halt as I noticed the back door leading to the outdoors and freedom was somehow open. I became anxious, scared, lost, and confused. I ran immediately to the safe spot in clear view of the observation camera. I couldn't seem to make a decision as to what to do. As a daughter of a schizophrenic mother, a single mother to a man-child, and a mid-level supervisor with a major corporation, I had made many spur of the moment decisions. However, at this moment I was so stricken with panic, I simply froze. Emotions ran through my psyche as a dry brush fire. Conditioned by my environment, none of my thoughts even remotely sounded my ESCAPE YOU IDIOT! alarm. Ironically, none of my inclinations were to inform my jailer either.

I prayed that the perimeter officer assigned to secure the compound's (CCA) boundaries would note the door standing ajar. Instantaneously, I felt ill. I needed to regurgitate, urinate, and defecate. If I didn't alert someone, I would be found standing in a puddle of my own body waste. Another section of time blew by. Then after what seemed like an eternity, I hit the buzzer alerting central control I had a need. The voice that shot back at me I recognized, from the distinctive accent, as one of the female officers who worked second shift. She snarled at me what did I want. She went into a tirade about I better not be calling to complain about being outside because I had several chances on first shift to come inside. My dilemma was now heightened by her irritability, my stomach cramped, and I felt faint. I steadied myself on the wall and explained the back door was standing ajar. She screamed back "you better not move" and as a rush behind her words I heard the escape alarm sound. Within seconds, six S.O.R.T. team officers in full gear with shields, facemasks, and tasers blaring came in the back door. The front door also came open and there stood the second shift captain with an officer and an officer with camera in tow.

I was confused and scared. I was interrogated as to how I worked the door open. I told the truth . . . I didn't do it. It just came open. The S.O.R.T. officers investigated the door and saw no signs of tampering. I was told because I did not notify anyone and try to come in I would be placed on recreation restriction until further notice. I felt an injustice done to me. After I had processed all possible scenarios, I did notify the central control officer.

I broke. I cried out as a banshee, "WHY DIDN'T I RUN?" When escorted back to my cell, I broke down safety razors to expose the blade. I would cut myself for being too stupid to run. My anger and hurt ran deep. I was awaiting sentencing for felonious murder so I was not a saint, but I did not deserve to be treated so arbitrarily badly.

The anger and frustration from this experience has since left me, but the Stockholm fear is still so very real.

The second experience, which reveals the nature of this prison institution, covers my first fourteen months at CCA, when I learned how to "jail." "Jailing" is a process akin to predatory survival. You stalk victims for money, usually someone who is weak, and you go in for the kill by strong-arming the victim by way of sexual aggression or false promises of protection. Sometimes the weaker females voluntarily come to you looking for protection and comfort. Denial is the absolute worst part of "jailing"—denial that you are doing evil to yourself and others. I knew I had done a terrible thing to wind up in jail, but no one in jail treated either my crime of murder, or my fast-taught jailing actions, as the awful acts against my neighbor and society that they truly were. Administration, medical staff, the DA, offenders, and officers all seemed to want me to learn "the box." I, however, simply wanted and needed space to figure out where I went wrong—and to cry.

These were confusing times for me. I never knew the good from bad in myself or others. I couldn't understand why no one in charge of house-sitting offenders did anything to stop this process of declining morals. At times, I would feel so disgusted with my actions and the savagery of it all that I either fought or arranged to get caught holding contraband—tobacco or pills—in order to garner a much-needed "vacation" from general population: segregation from other offenders for a period of ten days a trip.

Broken by fear, I behaved helter-skelter. Like any trapped being, I regressed and cried out to my Pa. I had no assurance that he would come to my rescue, but I played on my status as his "muff," the little jester that brought the world laughter. Pa had once loved her and would surely come to her rescue, I thought. And he did! I cried to him about my fear of imminent death. I told him of the horror stories, of having to fight to make it, of being surrounded by people who suffered from my mom's malady. But when he took one look at me, a derogatory chuckle escaped his lips. My mind began to race. Why the smirk? Why no kiss? Why no hug? After what had to be the longest pregnant pause in history, Pa spoke: "You look like a gangster. There's no way you're in any danger of being harmed."

I was crushed on so many levels. And yet, my Pa's sarcasm was like drops of water on my forehead: he chastised me to rethink all I knew prior to coming to prison. "Donna, you are now a part of a culture considered deviants of society, unfit for normal society," he said. "Truth, honesty, and morality will not be on the agenda anytime in the near future." To stave off another such call from his transformed little girl, he added: "Don't worry, the officers will lie as well." These conversations helped me realize how society, and more importantly my family, would view me as a liar, a misfit, and a gangster. They were right, to a point. I had worked so hard to appear a normal inmate that I became lost. Emotionally broken, now severed from society, I was sinking fast into a terrible abyss.

It was my turn on the auction block. Listening to terms unfamiliar to me—about me—I came to know the confusion of my ancestors on the block. After five days of being berated by people speaking a language as foreign to me as Slovak in a court of law, I realized I had made a mistake. No one looked directly at me, not even my court-appointed attorney. I was a piece of meat on the slave block with no value other than the sweat of my brow. I'm not sure how I expected restitution to transpire: not one member of the entire cast of characters sought justice—not even me.

When one first enters prison, the manicured lawns, flowers, and trees lull one into a sense of peace. Even those who come only to visit breathe a sigh of relief that their loved one is in such an environment. Rather than the open bay design, housing units are two-man cells. The changes one experiences in the county jails are base. In the county's open bay dorm, you are aware that your surroundings are foreign. The desire to free oneself is constant and matches the extreme nature of the environment that one desires. I've heard of bears freeing themselves from the hunter's snare by chewing off a limb. This same desire is great in the county jail. This desire for freedom lends itself to camaraderie among the oppressed—something akin to slave stories. In the county jail, one witnesses persons from differing tribes and backgrounds striving toward the same goal. Prisons, on the other hand, are *designed* to resemble community. However, this design contradicts the reality: backstabbing, rapes, attempted murders, and the surrendering of one's right to privacy.

When I arrived at the Tennessee Prison for Women, everything seemed designed to reflect conditional peace. I longed for freedom and sought it now through all legal means available to me. I realized early on, however, that the Department of Correction's desire is to warehouse offenders with as little effort and monies toward rehabilitation as possible. I had to find my way to freedom on my own. This is reminiscent of the slave-master relationship. The authorities are willing to provide sunlight, food, clothing, and community as long as one satisfies ascribed conditions. A sameness forms one's daily routine: food, clothing, and accepted relationships. The individual must satisfy this sameness to receive reward. Whether by choice or osmosis, the sameness creeps into your mind and spirit. From the "fun house mirrors" to the required uniforms and undershirts, to scheduled callout, to the same seasonal rotation of menus, everything works to change how one sees oneself. Life becomes a blur of interchangeable folk.

The change to one's physical image in prison is subtle at first. Before incarceration, I prided myself on remaining fit and healthy. Even at my lowest moments, I exercised and watched what I ate, and even without much choice in my diet, I didn't think any differently. But in prison, you are kept from viewing yourself. You are told what to wear, when to come and go. From the stereotypical single-design uniforms, to the "fun house mirrors" that reflect only what members of society and the Department of Correction wish you to be, you begin to view yourself differently. Try spending eight hours, over 365 days, for five years—for a total of 14,600 hours—just looking at your image in a fun house mirror. This distortion is one of many ways that prison reinforces the less-than-human-but-more-than-animal treatment one experiences at the hands of other offenders, staff, officers, and administrators.

Major changes to an individual can also be noted in attitude and the willingness to accept the personal sacrifices that come with being incarcerated. Some offenders will tell of the feeling that comes with being loaded into a cargo ship destined for the abyss. The single requirement is a willingness to relinquish all natural relationships as mother, wife, lover, and friend, and adopt a corrections persona, in hopes that, by following the proscribed program, one is enabled to reclaim life as one once hoped it would be. Still others will tell of dying to dreams deferred; retirement plans that included travel abroad or cross-country trips with grandchildren exploring the wonders of America; or sharing a childhood memory so that it would live on through one's descendants. Still others cite the need to carve out a path that entails neither yesterday's dreams, nor today's fears, but a new hope that could not be achieved except in a controlled, disciplined society. In prison, the transformation is physically and psychologically in direct correlation to the mental effects of stone, razor wire, and the privileged, prying eyes. All of these traits encapsulate different phases of the "Morpheme" that individuals experience through their journey in the prison catacombs.

I had the first opportunity to view myself in a glass mirror after ten years of incarceration. The devastation of my appearance wipes from my memory the actual location of the mirror. Yet, seared into my memory is the grotesque body I now possess. My physical self was transformed from a lean tadpole into a toad. Through the lack of structured exercise and forbidden running, a steady diet of starches, soybeans, and various animal inners, and a regimen of various steroids to aid in breathing poorly ventilated air (which cause an environmental lung disease), I have become a toad. Ten years of avoiding Plexiglas funhouse mirrors altogether and adjusting to the scratched, filmy, and distorted images of my daily reflection, I have lost touch with my appearance. Looking into that first mirror, I was like a baby kitten looking for the first time at my reflection, determined to discover who or what was mimicking my movements so perfectly.

Michel Foucault describes prison as a schematic of buildings and personages used to erect mental razor wire, which controls the offender's will and conforms it to societal norms. A major part of controlling is indoctrination. The role of the officers and staff is to give the aura of government-ordained authority. They become the eyes that aid in developing an abnormal sense of paranoia—creating the "I can't get free because someone is watching me" phenomenon. They threaten or cajole you to do things that your mind rebels against—like cavity searches, or flashlights in your eyes at 3:00 a.m., demanding that you roll over while you sleep so they'll know you're a live body. Prisons are designed to enable a new form of torture, not correction. If offenders serve five years or more, they have to be debriefed as if coming home from a war zone or outer space. Psychiatrists justify the need for such debriefing as a means for minimizing the suicide rate. I wonder if it's because prison has worked so hard—and effectively—at removing all sense of humanity.

PART 4

By and with Death

IN 1972, WHEN WILL Campbell and the Committee of Southern Churchmen published their *Katallagete* issue on prisons, the U.S. Supreme
Court suspended capital punishment. Thus the original collection of *And
the Criminals With Him* essays lacked a discussion of the death penalty. By
1976, of course, the High Court reinstated executions, and to this point
in the 21st century the U.S. has executed over 1,100 fellow reconciled
humans.

Over the last 35 years we've often made the death penalty one of our
favorite, polarizing disputes. Candidates for elected office, for example,
make capital punishment a campaign pledge, promising to get people what
they're due (retribution and/or revenge). Criminal Justice experts analyze
it as a public policy (i.e., whether it effectively deters future offenses). The
three essayists here illustrate how such polemics can impoverish our communities by masking the real costs of executions. When it comes to capital
punishment, we're not talking about some "issue." A crime has shattered
lives and community relations as they ought to be. No matter how severe and well-intentioned our punitive reprisal, however, we can neither
erase the pain and loss, nor do some final *just* thing to delete the offense.
Community is found in our ongoing response to the offense, rather than
on some once-for-all, ultimate payback inflicted on the offender. Insofar
as both the victim and the offender are our siblings, our challenge is to

live beyond retribution, and love beyond revenge. Our commitment is to restore right relationships after the horrendous offense. Toward that end, we're not called to settle the score—as if our vengeful might could return life to some prelapsarian state. We're called to be reconciled—to incarnate the reconciliation that has already restored right relationships.

Even though the original '72 *Katallagete* issue did not include a discussion of capital punishment, since its reinstatement Will Campbell has offered wise, prophetic counsel. Harmon Wray, who worked with Will in the Southern Prison Ministries, captured Will's testimony in 1976 before a committee of the Tennessee legislature poised to vote for the resumption of the death penalty. "You may assume the power to take lives," Will warned the officials, "yet in the process lose your own souls. Your own hubris, the arrogance that *you* can set things right, may do you in."

> As I understand it, the state, by the very definition of the word, the state can do anything it wants to do and wills to do. That is the purpose of the state.
>
> As near as I can tell, the Bible is a book about who God is, who we are . . . and then again who God is no matter who we think we are.
>
> And what kind of God does this book talk about?
>
> The kind of God in the Bible is one who reserves certain things for himself. A jealous God.
>
> "Vengeance," for example, "is mine." "Render unto Caesar those things that are Caesar's," yes; "Render unto God those things that are God's," most certainly.
>
> Because God is that kind of God, it seems to me that it is far more the business of a preacher to be concerned with souls than it is to be concerned with lives.
>
> In the prophets . . . the prophet Amos, for example, when there was suffering and death in the northern kingdom, he was sent here not because there was suffering and death but because other of God's children were causing the suffering and death.
>
> So it is with the immortal souls of those who have the power to appoint to die, which is my concern more than with the lives of those who are appointed to die . . . because in my understanding of scriptures God has seen to that in the resurrection.
>
> We do not have the final word. We only have it in our power to appoint to die. Jesus was not concerned with the suffering and the death, but was concerned with the souls of his children, brothers and sisters, who were causing them to die.
>
> I would ask you to give very serious consideration to what you and I are about to do here because I am concerned with

your immortal souls, you who have within your power—but with our proxy—to appoint to die.

If you ask, "Who are you to come here preaching to us? We have preachers of our own," I can only say, sir, I am your brother and that is my testimony, my witness. May God have mercy on the souls of us all."[1]

Some years later, Will exposed society's idolatrous inclination toward Death.

Gary Gilmore, in 1977, was the first person to be executed after the Supreme Court ruled it permissible years earlier. Shortly before the state of Utah was to kill him by musketry, he twice tried to kill himself. And twice the state went to extraordinary measures to save his life. Somehow, that makes no sense to me. If it is in the best interest of society for a man to be dead, what difference does it make if he does it himself? Unless, of course, we get some depraved gratification from doing it ourselves. How then do we differ from the one we kill? Sure, there are the arguments about guilt and innocence, all based on Old Testament texts. But the death penalty was prescribed there for twenty-three offenses, including sassing your mamma and having a dangerous ox. All of them pale into lunacy when viewed in the hot light of the teachings of Christ.

Now they have killed Carla Faye Tucker in Texas. Moral leaders from around the world, including the Pope, Billy Graham, and many who support executions by the state, men such as Jerry Falwell and Pat Robertson, begged that she be spared. We call it the death *penalty*. If the Christian doctrine of an afterlife is true, is death really a penalty? I'm not sure what death is. I'm not sure what life is. I do know death is the enemy and life is of God, so we mortals had best be careful how we piddle with it.

I was once asked to debate the death penalty with a well-known scholar. He gave a lengthy and learned statement on why he favored it. I was embarrassed because I had prepared no remarks. So I said, "I just think it's tacky," and sat down. That led to confusion as to what "tacky" meant. Well, tacky means ugly, no style, no class. I didn't win the debate, but I do believe America as a nation has too much class, too much character, and too much style to go on sinking to the crude level of death practiced in executions. Do for the sake of our own soul, let's just cut it out.

1. Wray, "An Eye for an Eye," np.

The "ever-rolling stream" called time is both comforting and re-proving. Fifty-three years ago, August 6, 1945, I stood with my buddies on a cliff on the island of Saipan. After more that two years overseas, about the only recreation we had was watching the hefty bombers land on nearby Tinian Island. "I'll bet that's the one!" someone screamed. It was the *Enola Gay*, a plane we had seen many times. We had been told by way of an under-ling grapevine that something big had happened, something so extraordinary that the war would soon end and we would be going home. We knew nothing of the details and didn't care. We were cheering, pretending the cheap PX beer we sprayed on each other was champagne, slapping each other on the back, and throwing steel helmets and M1 rifles into the deep pearly waters of the Pacific Ocean. More than a hundred thousand of God's children lay in carnage—burned, mangled, eviscerated. Dead. And we cheered.

Thirty years later I was part of another vigil. This one out-side a Florida prison near where I had trained as a soldier. A single one of God's children was about to die inside the prison. A group of young men and women nearby cheered as lustily as we had done on Saipan that day. "That's it! That's Ole Sparky!" I heard as the lights inside the prison walls blinked from a power surge. "Fry the bastard! Fry the bastard! Bring on the barbecue sauce." Their callous chant was sickening. Then I felt a greater af-fliction: the sudden realization that I had once celebrated death as crudely as they were doing. How different, then, was I from the odious adolescents of central Florida? But for time. And grace. That bequest that trumps the chants of us all.[2]

So, what do you need to know about the prison system? It kills peo-ple. Social and economic death? Sure, but this principality uses its power to perform premeditated homicides.

Insofar as the institution actively offers up humans to Death, it is de-monic. Again, hear the essayists. Listen to those who live on death row, or who have experienced first-hand what transpires in the execution cham-ber. If at the end of this section you must still view capital punishment as a necessary corrections "program," "policy," or "protocol," then at least recall the Good Friday execution of the convict, Jesus of Nazareth. More importantly, remember that our story operates from the proposition that on Easter morning the executed Christ achieved—once and for all—the

2. Campbell, *Soul Among Lions*, 10–11, and 29–30.

death of Death. We may profess "Dying, Christ destroyed death," but every time we offer a neighbor up to Death our practice belies our confession.

Richard C. Goode

12

My Friend Steve

REVEREND STACY RECTOR

A s I GOT OUT of my car, the sting of the wind nearly took my breath. The temperature was hovering around twenty degrees, but the wind chill made it feeyl more like ten. I ducked my head to shield my face as I crossed the parking lot of Riverbend Maximum Security Institution in Nashville. My eyes watered. My ears and fingers throbbed. But even the wind was no match for the knot in the pit of my stomach and the chill that went through me as I entered the front doors of the prison, a chill that had little to do with the weather.

Today was Tuesday, February 3. Steve Henley was now spending a few hours with his family. This was his last visit with them before his execution scheduled for 1:00 a.m., February 4, 2009. As his spiritual advisor and friend for the last nine years, I had been allowed to visit him on deathwatch the past couple of days, always with glass between us. Steve was exhausted. You could see the resignation settling in his eyes. His fighting spirit was waning. It started when the officers took him to deathwatch two days before in the middle of the night. He recalled to me the quiet on the unit as his wrists and ankles were shackled for the walk across the yard to the cell where he would spend his last hours. As daunting as this walk would be, he was actually looking forward to his feet touching the grass again, something this old farmer had done only once or twice over the past twenty years.

A teary-eyed correctional officer approached him as he was leaving, saying, "My son died two years ago in a motorcycle accident. When you see him, will you tell him that his mama loves him?"

"Don't you worry, Officer," Steve replied. "I surely will." And with that the doors of Unit 2 clanged behind him for the last time.

He had been hopeful that he might get a stay. Up until then, no inmate in Tennessee in the modern era of the death penalty had been executed on his first "real" execution date. The courts always seemed to intervene that first time around. Tennessee had only executed four other inmates since 1960, so this whole process was still a bit foreign. And, at the time, the state was entangled in litigation about its lethal injection protocol, which had been deemed unconstitutional by a district court. I couldn't imagine the courts allowing the state to move forward with this execution before the Sixth Circuit Court of Appeals ruled. The decision was expected any day, so what would another few weeks matter. Steve had already been on death row for twenty-three years while the state had spent millions to secure a death sentence for him (far more than a sentence of life without parole). Why rush things now?

He was dreading this visit with his family. Unlike some of the other inmates on the row, Steve was very close to his family, and they never wavered in their support of him the whole time I knew him. He always talked about how much he loved their visits, but how depressed he was for days after.

"Sometimes I am not sure it is worth it," he would reflect. "It hurts me so for them to see me like this, and I know it is hard on them. Then when they leave, it tears me up."

I had met his parents and one of his sisters a few times throughout the years, but in the last few weeks, we had become close as we all tried to help each other figure out how to prepare for something like this.

"There is no manual to teach you how to get executed," Steve would say on those last visits before he was moved to deathwatch.

Steve's kids, a son and daughter, were adults with children of their own who called Steve "Gramps." His children's grief was profound. In these last days, his daughter had gotten a bad respiratory infection, and you could tell she felt terrible. They were reliving a lifetime of hurt as they now prepared for their father's death. Steve and their mom divorced when they were children, and as pre-teens, Steve had been convicted of a double murder and sentenced to death. Their mother remarried, and life was hard. Their whole lives they struggled to balance the shame of having a dad on death row with the love they felt for him. In recent years, their connection with him had strengthened as they re-discovered the loving daddy who had been kept from them all those years.

Both wanted to be present for the execution, though Steve tried to convince them not to. He did not want their last memories of him to be those of a helpless man strapped to a gurney. But they were determined. There was no talking them out of it. It was the last thing that they could do for him after feeling so helpless all their lives. They wanted their faces to be the very last ones he saw.

I told Steve that if he wanted me to, I would come to the prison that afternoon as his visit with his family was winding down, in case they needed me. I worried about Steve's son, who wrestled with his own personal demons, and what his reaction would be if the correctional officers put their hands on him to get him out of the visiting area.

I finally got through all the checkpoints, signed in the logbook that was kept outside of deathwatch, and entered the visitation room. The family sat in a circle to one side of the small room while two correctional officers sat in the far corner, staring at the wall. There were wads of tissue all over the seats and floor as the harsh fluorescent light draped everyone in a sallow pall. One of Steve's sisters was quietly weeping, not saying a word. The other was talkative—sharing memories and cutting up every now and then to try to lighten the mood. His kids were struggling to hold it together, and his father was sitting with his back against the wall, making little eye contact, face wet with tears. Mr. Henley looked up at me and patted the seat beside his, grateful for a distraction. I sat down. He started to kid around with me about my cooking and talked about his garden. Then he would get quiet and mutter, "This is awful," and look away, tears streaming down his weathered cheeks.

But most distressing was Steve's mother, a tiny woman who had already lost her youngest son, David, to murder while Steve was incarcerated. She was now curled up in the lap of her only other son, almost in fetal position, arms wrapped around his neck, head leaned against his broad chest, staring vacantly at the wall like she was trying to memorize how it felt to hold her boy.

Steve kept saying to her, "Mama, don't you worry about me. I am tough, just like my mama."

I kept glancing at the correctional officers out of the corner of my eye. They were stoic and never once glanced over at the scene. How could they? I wouldn't have looked either if I could have escaped it somehow. All the emotion they were swallowing was obvious as they held that stare. At least we could cry and embrace. They could not. They only stared at the wall.

Part 4: By and with Death

Finally, the officers stood and announced it was time to go. Steve gently set his mother on her feet and stood up. Though he still looked worn out, he had another look on his face now. It was the face of a man with something to say. He went around the room and held each person, looked into their eyes, and told them what each meant to him and what he wanted for each one. When he came to his son, Steve seemed to be looking into a mirror as he placed his hands on his son's shoulders. He told him that he wanted a different life for him, that he loved him, and was proud of him no matter what. He embraced his daughter and told her he loved her and that it would be all right.

As everyone sobbed and walked toward the door, Steve turned back and said, "Mama, Daddy, everybody, I just want you to know that I didn't do this. I didn't kill Fred and Edna." With that, his ruddy face reddened to crimson and the tears flowed. "You have got to know that."

"We know, Son." "We know, Daddy. We love you." The visit was over.

At 7:00 p.m. that evening, a service was held at a small church not far from the prison to remember all victims of violence and to resist the use of the death penalty. I invited Steve's family to attend, and shortly before the service started, his children and his sister arrived, along with a high school friend with whom Steve had recently reconnected. His parents were too exhausted and distressed to attend. Standing in the back of the sanctuary was Doc, an old truck driver from Sparta, Tennessee, who, for the past nine years drove to Nashville every other week to visit Steve.

Shortly after Doc began visiting Steve on death row, Doc's wife was diagnosed with terminal cancer. Steve supported Doc through her illness and death. Over the years, when I arrived at the prison for my visits with Steve, I would hope to see Doc's name in the logbook too. The three of us had a mini-reunion every time our visits coincided. We would tell stories, laugh, and talk theology, sports, and politics. A few months before Steve was to be executed, Doc had moved to Texas to live with his daughter. He had been diagnosed with macular degeneration, and he knew he had to get closer to family. Doc's departure was like a death for Steve. Though they wrote to one another, Steve sensed that this was just one of the many losses for which he was preparing. But Doc had made it. He drove from Texas over two days time to be there. He couldn't even get into the prison to visit Steve, but he came anyway.

The service started, the church was packed. Hymns were sung, and prayers prayed. I spoke and began to struggle as the emotion overcame me. In those moments, I thought of Fred and Edna Stafford, the elderly couple, who were shot and whose home was burned to the ground in Jackson County in 1985. I wept for the brutality of their murder, and the trauma that their family had been through for the last 23 years waiting for this execution. I wept as I recalled the broken voice of their sister-in-law when I called her to ask if I could come and see them—when she told me that they wanted nothing to do with any of this anymore, that they were too tired and needed it to end. I wept as my anger welled at this system that would put a family through 23 years of waiting and that would sentence a man to die based on the word of another man—a man who made a deal to save himself. I wept as I stared at the faces of Steve's family in the front row, tear-stained and pale. Mostly, I wept as I was confronted with the violence that had already claimed the lives of Fred and Edna Stafford and would soon claim the life of my friend, Steve Henley.

Honestly, it was the first time that I had truly cried. Steve was frustrated with me that I had not shown more emotion. I told the crowd, "Steve got onto me yesterday when he saw a tear roll down my face."

He said, "Girl, you are finally crying. If I could, I would come out from behind this glass and whip your rear end for waiting so long."

To be honest, I wanted to cry on several occasions, but I just couldn't. There was a part of me that had convinced myself that Steve would not be executed. Although I watched him saying goodbye to the people he loved, for me, it still wasn't real. None of this was real. That is the thing about the death penalty. When you are up close to it, you can't imagine it. You can't imagine that in our nation today, so many of us, friendly, church-going folk, who eat our Cheerios for breakfast, play catch with our kids, walk our dogs, and never forget Mother's Day could possibly stand by while a man's death is being planned down to the last detail to be carried out with our tax dollars, in our name.

But standing there in that pulpit, staring at all those faces, saying the words that I had written, realizing that the courts were not going to stop it, the Governor was not going to stop it, and that most Tennesseans would be in bed oblivious to it when it happened, suddenly, it hit me—the state was going to kill my friend, and there was nothing I could do about it.

I don't remember much about what I said. I do remember one of the musicians handing me a tissue as my nose dripped, and my skin glistened with a mixture of tears and sweat. I was able to finish and pull it back together. I had no choice. I wasn't done yet. I had to be at the prison again by 9:00 p.m. to sit with Steve until 11:00 p.m., when I would have to say goodbye too. I already had on my clerical shirt and collar. I collected my Bible and the communion kit. Several inmates had gotten word to me through their visitors to tell Steve that they were thinking of him. I was making mental notes. I also knew that Michael McCormick, the first man released from Tennessee's death row after he was found not guilty in a new trial, was driving up from Chattanooga to be there. Michael spent twenty years fighting his conviction and sentence. I knew Paul House, the second man released from death row in Tennessee, who now lived with his mother, Joyce, would be waiting for the word to come down. Steve always asked about Paul and his mother. The guys on the row had taken care of Paul when he first started showing symptoms of the multiple sclerosis that now confined him to a wheelchair. Some of them would carry him when he could no longer walk on his own. He had been released after nearly twenty-three years on death row when his conviction was thrown out based on new evidence. He and Steve came to death row just a few months apart.

I pulled up to the prison driveway and checked in with the correctional officer monitoring the entrance. I had never been this close to an execution before so I wasn't sure what to expect. Usually, at this point, I was out in the field beyond the prison where the others were now gathering to stand in the dangerously cold temperatures, candles clutched in numb fingers, witnessing to their belief in the power of life, even in the face of this act of death.

When I walked into the prison, the staff looked at me with a mixture of sadness and curiosity. I was shaking from the cold and my rattled nerves as I retraced my steps from earlier in the day. I ended up waiting in a locked holding area with one of the same correctional officers that had been with the family earlier.

As we stood there waiting for the door to unlock, he said with concern, "How are you doing?"

I replied, "I'm okay." That was probably all he really wanted to hear, but I went on, "What we saw today in that visiting room, I wouldn't wish that on anybody."

His demeanor changed a bit as he replied, "Except no one in their family was murdered." The door clicked open, and we walked through.

I didn't know how Steve would be holding up. He was often an anxious guy and suffered from high blood pressure for which he was medicated. Over the past few months, I had received so many calls from him, agitated and needing me to do this or that. I just didn't know what to expect from a man who had only a few hours to live. What would I do if he was coming unglued, when I myself was barely hanging on? But there he was, sitting quietly on his cot, eyes peering up at me from behind large, prison-issue, reading glasses, journal in his lap. He was so calm. He told me that he had even taken a nap just a short time before.

I was a bit taken aback at his composure.

"Steve, I don't know that I have ever seen you this relaxed."

He looked up at me with a puzzled expression, "Stacy, I can't explain it. I just feel so calm. I don't know."

"The peace that passes all understanding we hear about, maybe that's what it is, Steve." I said with a hopeful smile.

He smiled back and nodded as if that's what he was already thinking, "I guess that's it 'cause I don't know what else it would be. I am so tired, and I want to be done with it all."

"I know, Steve. I know."

We sat quietly for a few minutes while the 10:00 news blared from the television mounted on the wall outside the cell. There was footage showing the earlier service and the vigil going on outside.

"I sure wish those folks would go home and get out of this cold." Steve remarked, but I could tell that he was grateful to see a crowd, now numbering about eighty people.

I told him about the service and how moving it was and how many people were there. As we continued to sit, he said, "You know what, Stacy, I am a lucky man." This man, who was now less than three hours from execution after serving twenty-three years for a crime he always maintained he didn't commit, was calling himself lucky.

"Steve, what do you mean?"

"Well, even with all the bad that has happened to me, I know that there are folks in the free world that ain't never been loved the way I have. That makes me lucky."

My eyes welled as I said, "I am not sure you are lucky, my friend. But, you are loved."

As the clock ticked, I pulled out the Bible and read from Luke 23:

> One of the criminals who were hanged there kept deriding him and saying, 'Are you not the Messiah? Save yourself and us!' But the other rebuked him, saying, 'Do you not fear God since you are under the same sentence of condemnation? And we indeed have been condemned justly, for we are getting what we deserve for our deeds, but this man has done nothing wrong.' Then he said, "Jesus, remember me when you come into your

kingdom.' He replied, 'Truly I tell you, today you will be with me in paradise.'

We celebrated the Lord's Supper—a few saltine crackers and grape juice—blessed and broken and shared through steel bars as together the Crucified One joined us for a taste of God's Kingdom come among us, even and maybe especially in that place. And, in our meager sharing, we were provided with far more than either of us thought possible in such a desperate moment—for we both were loved and fed in ways that I am still struggling to understand.

Steve kept saying under his breath, "Jesus, remember me. Jesus, remember me," memorizing the words so that they would be fresh. We prayed, holding hands through the bars. It was approaching 11:00 p.m.

"Ma'am, it is time for you to go now." I heard the voice of the officer who was monitoring Steve say quietly. Someone was always there watching him to be sure he didn't hurt himself before the state could execute him. Steve told me earlier that the officers on deathwatch had been really good to him, and he was grateful. We stood and I leaned through the bars and gave him a kiss on the cheek.

He blushed and said, "Now don't you let this scar you, girl."

I smiled, "It won't because of your peace tonight—that's the reason that I will be okay. I wasn't sure I'd be okay before, but I am now. I love you my friend, and I will see you later, okay?"

"I love you too, and I will see you."

I would see Steve again at 1:00 a.m. strapped to a gurney, trying to smile and be light-hearted for his kids and sister just before the poison entered his veins. I saw him lying there arms outstretched, speaking his last words slowly and calmly, conveying his sorrow for the death of the Staffords and his hope that his death would bring the family some peace, but adding "I don't really believe that there is much that can help with that kind of pain when someone you love is taken from you."

All the anger and frustration that Steve had felt over the years at his situation seemed to be completely gone. He was a condemned man strapped to a table, and, at the same time, the most peaceful and dignified person in the room. Though when the blinds first opened, and I saw him like that, I felt like I had been punched in the face. I literally struggled to keep from clawing at my own skin, desperate to get out of there. Instead, I just sat, shaking my head.

Later, I spoke to several of the media witnesses who commented on the genuineness of his words and how unusually peaceful he seemed in those last minutes. Steve ended his statement with, "But I do want to say that tonight you are killing an innocent man."

The Warden said, "Proceed."

Steve raised his head just a bit, saying, "I feel it coming . . ."

Then, he slowly began to die as his sister and I shouted the Lord's Prayer to drown out the deep snoring sounds escaping from his mouth. "Our Father who art in heaven, hallowed be thy name . . ."

We shouted so that we couldn't hear him and so that he couldn't hear his son screaming and his daughter, vomiting in a garbage can. Fourteen agonizing minutes later, Steve Henley was declared dead, and we were led from the room.

I will never know what happened that July evening in 1985 on Pine Lick Road. I will never know if my friend Steve committed those crimes in a drug-induced haze; or in an outburst of misplaced rage after losing his family farm to creditors; or if he was with the wrong person at the wrong time and got caught up in something he couldn't stop; or, if as he always maintained, he truly had no idea what really happened that night when he dropped off his acquaintance, high on Dilaudid, in a field near the victims' home while he went to his grandmothers' house just down the way to check in with her about her doctor's appointment and to pick up a spare part for a sprayer. No one will ever know. But that isn't the issue really. The issue is how we sent a man to his death based primarily on the word of someone else—someone who had everything to lose, who made a deal, and walked away after only five years in prison to the protests of the victims' family. Is that justice? Is that the best we can do? Or is that just the price we pay and the risk we take in order to hold onto the death penalty? I don't know. But, here is what I do know. I know that we cannot undo the murder of another human being once it is done. There is no balancing the scales when a life has been brutally taken. But we can choose how to live in the wake of a murder, in the aftermath of violence, even when it is excruciatingly painful and hard. We can choose differently than those who choose to kill. The question is, "What do we choose?"

13

_____

The Diary of an Execution
Is Lethal Injection Really Painless?

WILLIAM R. STEVENS

Editor's note: What do you need to know about an execution? It's much more than what occurs in the death chamber. An execution is a relentless, often decades-long march of the condemned toward death. The final destination is known, but not the time of arrival. Thus, an execution's trauma is slow and repetitive.

Here is the power of Bill Stevens' diary. Instead of condensing the process and rushing to the conclusion, he guides us deliberately through the final five months of an execution. Please, don't get impatient and hurry through the journey. Bill is describing the system's belabored, premeditated homicide of a neighbor and friend. Take the time to listen. Get a feel for the institution's methodical pace. Appreciate the uncertainties of an impending execution, not merely the concluding facts. See the interminable, inexorable, torturous repetition of saying goodbye to loved ones. Understand the slow, gut-wrenching walk to death that we require.

> Writer's note: Several things should be mentioned before you read this article. First, in August 2008 I received a letter from a dear friend who is a teacher in Wales. She teaches the British equivalent of G.E.D. classes to a very rough and tumble bunch of young men whom she calls either "my lot" or "my boys." She told me these young men felt an execution by lethal injection was a painless and humane way not only to die, but also to execute someone.

I believe it is also true that just as these young men think—so do most people in this country. Most people think the execution is simply those few moments laying strapped onto a table, or sitting in a wooden chair. To some few, the execution is the seventy-two hours of "deathwatch," which is usually turned into a circus by the local media.

As I wrote a letter to these young men in Wales, I realized most people in this state, this country, probably felt the same way. It was due to that realization that I was prompted to write this article.

Second, this diary is a composite work of what I have personally witnessed during the pending executions of four men. Three of whom are now dead: two by lethal injection and one by the electric chair. And since one man is still going through this drama, no name will be given to the subject of this diary.

Third, as I began to plan this article, I had to wonder if this might not make all the "angry people" happy, and support their efforts to murder people they've never met. But I also had to consider all the people who haven't truly thought of the reality of an execution—the cost of an execution on a very personal level. What is really involved in all of it?

Lastly, it should also be understood that no matter how long a person is on death row, as long as he or she has an appeal in the courts, there is some level of hope for justice. Not until that final appeal is lost, and the State's attorney files for an actual execution date, does the reality of it all set in—and the execution begin.

On Thursday, September 11, 2008, the attorney for the State of Tennessee asked for an execution date for one of my friends. Yes, one of my friends. I've known this man since September 12, 2001. Throughout the next few weeks there was a lot of discussion and speculation about "the timing" and the current hold on all executions in Tennessee.

It wasn't until Monday, October 20, that it all became very real. I was out on a visit, when my friend came into the visiting area, and a local minister was waiting for him. The good reverend was there to bring my friend some troubling news. Earlier that day the Tennessee State Supreme Court had assigned Wednesday, February 4, 2009, as the date of his execution. As I was talking to my visitor, I noticed that my friend had turned white as a sheet, so I knew something bad had happened. Knowing me as they did, they called me over and told me what had happened.

The next day I started to understand how deeply this was affecting my friend. It was during a card game, in the middle of a hand, that my friend just stopped, and said to no one in particular, "I'm so tired of this, of living this way. I'm ready to go." Then he started to play again. Soon after that came a moment I think I will carry with me forever. In a voice that was so filled with pain and anguish, a voice so tortured and filled with grief, he said, "What am I going to do about my Mom?" No one at that table could speak.

On Sunday, October 26, my friend was again in the visiting area, with his son, his daughter, and his grandson. They all sat quietly in a corner, tears falling from their eyes, unable to comfort each other (visitation rule number one—no touching). As I sat in that room with my visitor, we could hear the quiet words from a father, trying in some way to bring comfort to his children. You could hear the desperation in his voice as if his very soul longed to reverse time and circumstance.

After this visit you could see how the pressure was affecting him. His temper grew short, and he had very little patience with anyone.

I want you to understand that in all this time, my friend had not once said a single word about losing his life. His every thought, his every worry, fear, all the stress and pressure, was for his family and friends who also had to deal with it . . .

Momma, goodbye
I must leave you now
The future awaits me
It is time to be born
Momma, goodbye
Please set me down
I must learn to stand
I must walk on my own
Momma, goodbye
Let go of my hand
I must go to school
My new friends await
Momma, goodbye
What troubles you so
Why are you crying
She is only a girl
Momma, goodbye
I must leave you now
My future awaits me
It is time for me to die

On Sunday, November 2, my friend is once again in the visiting area with his daughter. She is telling him about a website set up by one of those citizen-action groups, and all the good, decent, law abiding, Christian people who are calling for my friend's death . . . volunteering to push the button . . . wishing to watch it happen . . . desperately wanting to be a part of it. I would also mention that 99 percent of these fine citizens never heard of my friend until "the angry people" started the website.

On Tuesday, November 4, I actually looked my friend square in the eyes and asked him if he had committed the crime he was accused of. He locked eyes with me, and told me that he had no part in it. He then told me the circumstance of his arrest, and what led to his conviction. But this article is not about "his crime," or the legalities of his case. All I wish to say is that my friend has always maintained his innocence, but this was the first time he spoke to me about it.

On Sunday, November 9, my friend's parents came to visit him. This was their first visit since receiving his execution date. I didn't have a visit that day, but I did see his parents as they walked away from the unit. His mother was leaning against his father, his face was a mask of male strength as he tried to support his weeping wife, and guide her from this place of stone and steel. Out on the rec yard, an hour after his visit, my friend was still shaken and unable to concentrate on playing cards . . . (We, of course played through it without comment. We try to support each other at such trying times). I know full well that no words at such a time could ever ease a son's heart, and I have seen too many mothers sitting in this building with tears falling into their laps. This is where an execution starts, for both the men on death row and for their families. For three hours that afternoon, my friend sat in silence—except to bid his hand—and then, in silence, returned to his cell and closed the door.

> Return my love
> To my mother's breast . . . Grant to me
> A son's true rest
> Return my body
> To my father's knee . . . Let me die
> And set me free
> Allow my soul
> To pass God's gate . . . And trust in me
> For you to wait

On Monday, November 10, my friend was in a much better mood. As we played cards I asked, if he would need to go in at 3:00 p.m., which is when the guys who are expecting visits that evening go in to get a shower, and shave. You could hear the relief in his voice as he said, "No, not today." I guess that it was some small mercy that he wouldn't have to face the tears again, at least not tonight. I believe this is the heart of the matter. It is not only my friend who has to face this tortuous situation; it is his entire family, and everyone who cares about him. While dealing with this difficult situation, they have to see, and to hear, countless people laughing and cheering at every turn.

Suggested reading—John 8:1–11.

I think that the worst part of any execution is sitting alone in a dark cell, knowing it was your own choices in life that led you, and your family, to this place and time. Unless it would be knowing that you were in fact innocent—which has happened in this country and our state.

On this night, my friend did receive a visit from his minister. This time their discussion was—for lack of another word—a more positive talk. She was telling him of the approach that The Tennessee Coalition to Abolish State Killing was going to take as they tried to protest his execution. A website would inform people about the truth of his conviction, and many kind people wanted to provide funds so that he could telephone his family over the holiday season. It is a nice and very welcome blessing to know that in the middle of all this anger and vengeance some people can still react with true Christian love and charity.

On Sunday, November 16, my friend was forced to undergo his most difficult trial yet, a special visit with his mother, his three sisters, his daughter, and his minister. Along with his father they sat in silence, tears in every eye, as the good reverend described the process of the seventy-two hours of deathwatch, and the actual execution procedure. I couldn't help but watch the terrible, yet lovingly passionate description that was slowly crushing the heart of his mother. No one wanted her to witness her son's death, but how could she sit miles away and allow her little boy to die alone? His sisters, wanting to love and support their only brother, dying for a crime they know he did not commit; how could they not be there? How could he allow their last memory of him be such a nightmare? A family in tears, trying to love and support each other, as death drew ever closer.

I looked at my own visitor, and through my own emotion I said, "They just don't know. How could anyone want this?"

All the time this family was trying to deal with this terrible ordeal, fourteen other people were chatting away in the Visitor's Gallery. Three young children laughed and played together. Guards, nurses, and unit staff walked by seemingly without a thought or a care. This is the heart and soul of a painless execution. There would be no card playing on this day, no idle conversation, no silly distractions from reality. My friend just returned to his cell, and there he sat . . . alone . . . in silence . . . in the dark . . . as he faced his future . . . as he faced his past . . . as he tried to live with his memories. I know this to be true, simply because that is what I did also.

On Monday, November 17, I watched my friend go through the most "interesting" visit with his father. Now I understand that all parents want to protect their child, but what can they do when the danger is unavoidable, and coming towards you in slow motion? My friend's father showed up with a bag full of burgers and some root beer. They sat for two hours talking about the farm, fishing for catfish (fried up with hot cornbread). For two hours they discussed and debated "Ford versus John Deere," "rolls versus bales," and the Farm Bureau. I've known my friend for seven years, and I never realized that he was a farmer. They spoke of seven generations of their family living, and working, and dying on that land.

> My Daddy had to go away
> But they won't tell me why
> They said it was an angel's fault
> And all Mom does is cry
> I remember what my Daddy said
> As he left for work that day
> We were gonna get a bat and ball
> And go out back and play
> My Daddy always told me
> That I was his little man
> Now I must grow up alone . . . And I don't think I can

On Wednesday night, November 19, my friend and every man in Unit 2 received a Tomis Offender Sentence letter with the night's mail. This printed form is an official state notification that you have been sentenced to death; that you have no parole date, nor any possibility of release. That these official notices remind us of our sentences is bad enough—every 60 days or so—but I've got to wonder what my friend is thinking tonight. His letter has an added bonus. His will come with his execution date printed across the top of the page. Sometimes I wonder if this letter isn't just some sort of twisted punishment. Every couple of months "they" write, just to "remind us" that we are here waiting to die. This may not seem like much to anyone outside of this unit, but to a man who is dying little by little, day by day, this is rubbing salt into his many wounds.

On November 23, my friend had a visit with his daughter, and his granddaughter. (He later told me that this beautiful child is the mirror image of her mother at that age.) All through the visit my friend would stare at his daughter whenever he held his granddaughter. You could see his heart breaking as he traveled across the years, back to those times of happiness and promise.

Something occurred to me as I watched my friend interact with his granddaughter. Was he in some way committing his family to memory, and trying to leave them with some small piece of himself to carry throughout the years? As I watched this moment, I realized that his daughter also understood what he was trying to do. She had to witness this moment with both of her children. How much love and strength did this moment take for her to endure? What a remarkable woman she must be to share this final moment over and over again. And then it happened. At the end of the visit my friend touched his granddaughter's face. He stroked her long blonde hair. As he pulled her into a desperate embrace, he turned his eyes to his daughter. I know that at this moment, he was holding his little girl. His daughter, also traveling back to those happier times, put her hand on his arm, and I heard her quietly say, "I love you, Daddy."

Thursday, November 27, was Thanksgiving. I and my visitor were sitting with my friend and his daughter in the Visitor's Gallery. Through this type of situation, over the years many families will get to know each other. At times, two or three men and their families will sit and visit together. Personally, I think that we were drawn into this visit by both my friend and his daughter, because neither of them wanted to face this final Thanksgiving by themselves. So we sat together and passed the first hour. Slowly, the talk turned to past holidays and happier times. Then my friend's daughter started to tell a story that was most dear to her heart. In June of 1985, only one month prior to the crime that destroyed her family, she was only eleven years old, and as a special treat for Father's Day, her mother let her prepare his breakfast. As it turned out, this would be the only meal that a little girl would ever cook for her Daddy. As she spoke of it, she was eleven-years-old once again. Words like "Mommy" and "Daddy" were used throughout. Without warning, tears filled her eyes, and she spoke of losing her mother when she was sixteen.

Friday, November 28, was a cold, gray day. Very few men wanted to go outside on such a dreary day, so I was alone at the table with my friend.

We sat quietly for a while, until I noticed that a ladybug had landed on his hand and he had been sitting quietly just watching this little creature walking across his palm. Finally, he said, whether to me, or to the ladybug, I'm not quite sure, but he said, "Do you think they'll let me walk on the grass? I'd like to feel the grass again." What do you say to a man who has not felt anything but concrete since 1995? As he sat there thinking of these things, he got up and took the small insect to the side of the cage and blew her out of his hand and into the grass.

After a while I said, "They let Sedley [Alley] and Phillip [Workman] walk on the grass." (When one is talking about that final walk outside, a lot of discussion is not necessary.)

On Saturday, November 29, my friend did not go outside for afternoon rec. It was the first one he had missed other than on visitation days, so I came in early to check on him. He was in his cell, sitting at his desk, working on something, so I left him alone. Later that evening he had in his hand a coloring book, which he had drawn out in his own hand. It was even sewn at the seam. His only granddaughter wouldn't pass this final Christmas without a gift from her grandpa.

What would become of this little girl? How do you explain things like "justice" and "vengeance" to a child? I wondered if she knew what February could bring to her.

But it does bring me back to the original question: Is lethal injection really painless? I wonder what this little girl will think on February 5, when she wakes up without her grandpa.

Thursday, December 4—December seems to have struck my friend very hard. The month of November was filled with hours spent outside, watching the sky, tracking the jets as they crossed the small bit of blue that is ours. Even time spent with a ladybug, trying to understand how big—and small—life really is.

So far, my friend has not gone outside this month. He has not joined us for group meals in the pod, nor has he attended any of the group activities available to the level "A" residents. I can, in some way, understand what it must be like to face our last Christmas, to be haunted by the ghosts of past holidays, and trying to live with the dreams of "what could have been."

This, to my thinking, is the heart of an execution; hours upon hours of reflection and regret. This is also the basic point that doesn't seem to sink in with the "angry people." If you take some sense of justice, or some level of satisfaction, of even a measure of revenge from the long hours of loneliness, pain, and regret, why then would you want it to end?! Wouldn't justice—even revenge—be better served by a long life of this brand of slow torture and imprisonment? Whatever my friend is struggling with these past few days, it is not something he wants to share. Nor can I help him to deal with.

On Sunday, December 7, a very upset little girl came to visit her grandpa. Through tears, and in a voice she couldn't control, she told my friend about her week at school . . . how "her friends" told her about her grandpa's pending execution . . . how her classmates laughed at her pain and tears . . . how they took delight in telling her all about "his crime" and how he was such a terrible man who deserved to die.

The visiting room was silent. No one could speak, nor hide the fact that we heard every word. Then, in a soft voice that begged for some refuge, she asked her grandpa, "Did you really hurt those people?" My friend looked at her and said, "No." Then in a whisper she asked, "Are you gonna die?" What could he say? What could he do? He hung his head and said, "I don't know, maybe."

As he embraced his granddaughter, everyone tried to find something to talk about. I think I now understand why my friend is staying to himself, and why he is staying in his dark cell. Sometimes living in solitary confinement is a blessing. How do you "chat" with your friends after such an emotional outpouring? How do you listen to the petty complaints of your fellow inmates? How do you tell a little girl that an execution is painless?

Monday, December 8, brought my friend's parents back to the visiting room. I could see how tired and worn his mother looked. She didn't say much over the 90 minutes they spent together. She just sat quietly, holding her son's hand as he spoke to his father. My friend was sharing a bag of popcorn with his father and it was so sad to see how his mother's hands would shake without her son's hands to steady them. Most of this visit his mother sat silently, just looking at her son's hand.

Due to the holiday season, the courts are not looking at appeal motions that aren't "eleventh hour" situations, so my friend's family will spend their Christmas watching the calendar and counting the days until their only son's execution.

At the end of the visit I saw no tears as his mother touched his face, and then hugged her son . . . Her pain and grief had moved beyond tears, her broken heart lay in pieces, and she just waited for the courts, and the calendar, to decide her son's fate.

On Sunday, December 14, I received a visit from a friend who is a theology professor at Vanderbilt University. At my request, he had gone online to find the websites of the "angry people." I wanted to know what was being said and being shared in their chat-rooms. I still don't know. What I do know, however, is that I have never seen my friend (visitor) so upset, nor so disgusted by something in the five years I've known him. He couldn't believe this sort of vicious and hate-filled material would be allowed on a website.

I know from past executions that you can find, not only the prison address for writing to the condemned inmate, but you can also get the names, addresses, and telephone numbers for all of the inmate's family members. I found it very interesting trying to explain to an educated person, how so much anger and hatred could be allowed to exist, and encouraged to grow. As if in answer to my visitor's disbelief, my friend's daughter came into the visiting area and when she saw me she came over to us to talk to me. (It was my friend's daughter who told me how to find those websites.) As my visitor expressed his shock at the things he found, my friend's daughter started to tell us about all the hateful letters in the mail . . . all the nasty messages left on the answering machine. Then on the night of the tenth, someone removed the Christmas wreath from their mailbox and replaced it with a coil of rope. It should also be noted that none of these brave acts came with a signature, or a return address. When my friend came into the room, his daughter got up and said, "Goodbye," and we went on with our visit.

On Tuesday, December 16, my friend is once again called out for a short attorney visit, but on this day my friend comes out for our evening activity time. Over cards he tells us that all of his appeals have been rejected. Of course, his attorneys aren't worried, they plan to re-file everything in January, and re-file it all once again on February 2. Their strongest reassurance to my friend is that, so far, no one on Tennessee's death row has ever died on their first trip to deathwatch.

The attorney sits there like some great savior, spouting the most useless load of trash you could think of. What can my friend tell his family? How does he explain to them that his best hope is a dice-roll? How does he explain that this year for Christmas he was going to play the odds, and bet against the house?

At this point I think that I should remind you of one special little fact . . . if . . . if my friend does indeed receive a 90 or 120 day "stay" of his execution, and if, as my friend thinks, it will fail anyway, then they all go back to where things started on September 11. Then my friend will once again will have to drag his family through this nightmare one more time. This will be the price of my friend's life.

On Saturday, December 20, about 7:00 p.m., the "angry people" gathered in Centennial Park to hold a silent tribute to the victims of violent crime. This, in and of itself, is a beautiful tribute to lost loved ones. But this tribute is far from silent. At the memorial, the local police chief calls for harsher punishments and swifter payments. The local district attorney begins to explain why the very fabric of our national freedom depends upon executing my friend as soon as possible. Soon the spokeswoman for the "angry people" starts speaking for the victim's family of the crime my friend is accused of. I believe this would have been a lot easier for me had I not seen the following blunder made "live" on the news.

Just moments after her speech to demand "justice" for this victim's family, the reporter asked the spokeswoman, "What would you want to say to (name of the victim), if you could?" There, on live television, this spokesperson, so angry, so incensed, so filled with righteous indignation for this terrible crime, said, "Who?" Now one would think that before you got so angry and started demanding another's life that you would at least know the names of those victims that you claim to represent. To me the simple truth is that none of those "oh so angry people"—from the district attorneys to the judges, all the way up to the wives of politicians—none of these people seem to be able to see past, or understand anything beyond, their own anger, pain, hatred, or political grandstanding.

On Sunday, December 21, my friend receives a special visit—special in many ways, since this visit is from an old friend who goes back to his school days. One of the facts of prison life is that your friends tend to fall off as the years pass by. So, out of the blue, an old friend writes to my friend and gets a special visit. I found it very amusing to see my friend sitting in the corner with his feet up on a trashcan, talking and laughing. You could hear small bits about old cars, old girlfriends, hang outs and jobs that aren't there any more. I think my friend needed to lose himself for a while in another world, even if that world is long since gone. For a short time his attitude and demeanor was totally changed, buoyed by friendship and laughter. I know for a fact how much my friend needed this visit—and the time away from his reality. "I guess that we can forgo the question of 'Where have you been for the last twenty years?'"

Monday, December 22, finds my friend once again in the corner of the visiting room. His mother and father are with him, talking about the family's plans for Christmas. It breaks my heart to see his mother trying so hard to control her emotions. She sits so straight and stiff in the chair, her hands clasped so tightly in her lap as she so obviously fights for control. But this only underscores the real truth of this situation. For every moment of laughter or comfort, times of payment and pain will always follow. Yesterday, my friend left his visit laughing and talking with me and a couple other guys in our pod, but today, he will leave his mother's embrace and quietly return to his cell, alone. He will sit in the darkness until he can bear to face the approaching holiday.

On Thursday, December 25, Christmas Day, I received a visit in a very empty visiting room. It is a sad fact that most people on the row will spend their holidays alone. The fortunate ones will have phone calls to look forward to, but visits are few and far between. About thirty minutes into my visit, my friend's grandson slunk into the room, and threw himself into a chair against a wall. (Only a teenager can express such dejection and personal oppression.) When my friend came into the room, his grandson began his list of reasons for walking out of his home on Christmas Day. Apparently my friend's mother is getting frantic as February draws ever closer. She starts to cry for any number of reasons. She sits in silence for hours, just looking at old photos. She is absolutely inconsolable. Life in the family home is tense beyond belief. Despite the holiday decorations there is no holiday joy or spirit.

Sunday, December 28, finds us once again in the visiting area. This diary spends so much time in this room, because this is the only place that I can see how this execution is touching my friend's family, and also his friends on the street. One anti-capital punishment activist said, "in the end, an execution accomplishes nothing. Instead, the State's act of taking a life only causes another senseless death; it creates another grieving family; and it perpetrates another act of violence. The victim's family is now joined in their pain and grief by 'the criminal's family', all of whom have now lost a loved one to homicide." So, I watch as my friend's family sees the time slowly disappear. There is a certain comfort in knowing, or saying, that what you fear most is still "next year," but on this night, that comfort is now gone. "Next year" isn't even "next week," so no matter how it goes, the next time my friend sees his family, the distance becomes "next month."

I do understand that some people, possibly a lot of people, want to savor every moment of pain and suffering that my friend is going through, but I cannot begin to believe that they could find any satisfaction in the tears of his mother, or of a six year old little girl. Of course, I would expect that most of the "angry people" will simply turn away and try to ignore what they don't want to see. So here they sit, six people in silence. What is there to talk about after almost twenty-four years in solitary confinement? I think that the next five weeks will be very awkward, and very stressful.

Monday, December 29, is another evening of family visits for my friend. A sister who I have seen only once in seven years, has come to see her brother. Along with her is another small, blonde child. One of the sad realities of any prisoner's life is that many of us lose our families. Whether it is due to the crime, or to the distance, or just the many, many years of separation. As my friend faces his final days, however, his family slowly gathers to give comfort and support—not only to my friend, but to each other.

I want to be *very* clear about something. Neither I, nor my friend, nor anyone I know personally in Unit Two, has ever said anything in any way to belittle the pain and loss of "the victims" or their families. But this diary is not about people about whom I know nothing. This diary chronicles the final days of a friend and his family, as they face what is said to be "a painless execution." And allow me to be just as clear with one more fact, the pain, the tears, and the suffering of my friend, and of his loved ones, is just as real and significant—even if no one wants to acknowledge it.

I know that time is quickly running out for my friend. You can almost hear the seconds as they slip by. As I watch my friend saying "Goodbye" to another little girl, I wonder if anyone will care and try to do something, anything.

> *Note:* I write this next entry to honor the memory and the final request of Mr. Phillip Workman. His final request to his fellow inmates, both on death row and throughout R.M.S.I., was to pray for our Warden and his family. So, if you have any problem with this entry, take it up with Phillip.

Tuesday, December 30—I've got something to say, something *very* inappropriate and so very politically incorrect for an inmate to write about, particularly a death-row inmate. Will anyone, on either side of the argument, consider what this execution will do to the Warden? It is very easy for me, for all the men in Unit Two, to look upon the Warden in the same way that all the "angry people" look at us. This man is going to push a button and kill my friend, and it would be very easy for me to hate him for it. But the real truth at the bottom of all this is not something that we want to acknowledge, nor accept. That truth is simply this, no matter how "right wing conservative," no matter how "hard-lined" he may be in his outlook towards us, the Warden is the man who has to push that button. It is by his action that a human being will die. To date, our Warden has pushed that button four times. He has also had two heart attacks to go along with it. An execution provides plenty of stress for everyone involved.

I think that it is very important to "give the devil his due." Do not forget that the Warden will approve, or deny, a special visit for my friend on Saturday, January 31, for a final visit with his family. My friend's normal visitation time would be Sunday, February 1, from 8:00 a.m. until noon. However, at some time, early on that morning, my friend will be escorted to Building 8, and deathwatch. So, it is without a doubt, entirely up to the kindness of the Warden to give my friend and his family this last special visit.

The point is Phillip Workman was able to reach out with Christian charity to the man who would soon take his life. Phillip was grateful for those few acts of kindness by the Warden, acts that Phillip's family will cherish for a lifetime. We might also want to remember that neither Phillip Workman, Sedley Alley, nor Daryl Holton wasted their time—their final hours—hating a man for doing his job. On February 4, 2009, there will be plenty of pain for us all. Do we really need the hate?

Maybe we should ask the Warden's doctor how painless an execution really is.

Thursday, January 1, 2009—I believe that I was more correct about what the New Year would mean to my friend and his family than I care to admit. When I walked into the visiting room I see my friend sitting with his daughter. Her hands are in his hands, their heads almost touching, as they speak so softly to each other. No one wants to infringe on this moment, so four other visits are sitting together on the other side of the room. At the end of the visit my friend is rather upset, and as we waited to pass back into the pods he tells me, "You are right, I've got to write some letters." I sure don't envy the task in front of him, trying to express your love and gratitude, and your regret and sorrow to your family, all in a way to cover a lifetime of shame and pain.

On Friday, January 2, I received the answers to some rather touchy questions that I didn't really know how to ask. My friend sent someone up to my cell. He wanted to talk to me privately, so I used my position as staff-writer for the *Max Times* to get us into the pod's small holding room (passive room) for whatever my friend had in mind. He wanted help writing some letters to his family. He had written letters to his mother, his sisters, his daughter, and his granddaughter. These letters will be given to his family by a trusted friend in the event of his execution. Personally, I didn't think that it could get any worse than some of those moments out in the visiting area; until I started reading his letters. The words he found to give to his mother were beyond anything that I could have come up with. I know that my friend is "just a farmer" (his words, not mine), and I know that he is not an "educated man" (again, his words), but the words that he found to express his love and his sorrow should be in a book somewhere. So I told him, in all honesty, that I could not help him beyond correcting some of the spelling. I also told him that I had no intention of helping him change a single word in his beautiful letters. I also told him that I would no doubt be using some, quite possibly a lot of his exact words if I ever have to write those letters to my own dear mother, and my own sisters.

All of a sudden he asks me, "Do you believe in God?" My friend knows that I claim to be a Christian, that I attend various religious services, and that I "try" to conduct myself as I should. My friend also knows my many shortcomings. So the answer for me was easy. I said, "Yes." His next question, however, was much more difficult to answer. He simply asked me, "Why?" Then we spent the next two hours in the most sincere discussion about God, about sin, about forgiving others, and about the essence of grace. I'm not sure what struck me most, the depth of my friend's belief, the understanding of "just a farmer," or that I had been invited into this conversation at all. Most of the people, who "talk" about God—whether it is in this prison, out on the streets, in churches, or even on the radio and television—have no idea what it is like to face their own death. But my friend knows the day, the hour, and the cause of his death. I can honestly tell you that I have never been to a religious service that was more meaningful or moving. In less than five weeks my friend is going to face his God. I can't begin to wrap my mind around that, but it is some small comfort to know that he has this part of his life so well in hand.

I can remember all the hateful comments that were made about Philip Workman prior to his execution, when he spoke about his own belief and expressed his faith in his salvation. After everything that was said about Mr. Workman (much of it by the Christian community), I can understand why my friend has kept this part of his life private.

On January 7, the Warden came to give my friend the "opportunity" to choose the method of his death. You see, prior to January 2000, those people sentenced to "death" were to be killed by electrocution. My friend actually has to *ask*, or to request, or to choose to be put to death by lethal injection. It won't take long for the news of the warden's visit to spread through the unit, and once again a lot of discussion will take place as to who would opt for which method. Which method is really faster? Which is more dignified? Which is just easier to deal with in general? It should also be noted that the biggest factors in "the choice" to use lethal injection is not any questions of pain, or ease, or dignity. The biggest issue in front of my friend, in front of most condemned inmates, is how that choice will affect his family and loved ones. At 10:00 a.m. this morning, my friend made the choice for lethal injection, solely to spare his sisters as much trauma as he can. Soon my friend will "get" to choose his last meal. He will have to choose a minister. Who will share his final hours? Who will also watch him die, and then try to give comfort to his grieving family? Over the next four weeks my friend will receive many such visits from the warden. They will come to my friend and ask him to "help" plan his own execution . . .

Laid on a table
Strapped down so tight
All chances are over
You can't even fight
They hire a stranger
To slide needles in
If they botch it the first time
They just try it again
Trapped on the table
A fire in your chest
Drugged into a coma
They think you're at rest
Your mind in a panic
Your heart beats so fast
Your lungs are exploding
How long will it last
Finally, your heart
Lays dead in your chest
Such agony and torture
They say it was best

On Sunday, January 11, we are once again out in the visiting room and I am shocked at the appearance of my friend's parents. His mother is noticeably thinner; her nerves have her constantly fidgeting in her seat. She seems to jump at any noise and doesn't seem able to follow the conversation. His father looks like he hasn't slept in weeks. He is pale, lined, and weary beyond words. Their only son will die in less than twenty-three days, and they are powerless to help him.

Sometimes there are no words. Sometimes there is nothing to be done but to look away. So I talked to my visitor about her holiday and her travel plans. Later, watching this small woman trying to say "Goodbye" to her son was heart wrenching, at best. Her hug is more of a desperate clutching of her little body. She kisses her son and touches his cheek, and once again a grim-faced father, drawing upon some inner well of strength and love, leads a tearful mother away from this unit. I don't know how to describe this scene fully, but I've seen it often enough. It never gets any easier to witness.

Monday, January 12—This will not be a good day for my friend. At 5:00 p.m. his grandson comes to visit. From what I see and from the tone of their voices, it is a good visit for them both. After yesterday's visit he needs a break, but this is not going to happen. At 6:30 p.m. our visits end and as this young man tries to say "Goodbye" to his grandfather, he breaks down completely. Everything that he has been trying to hold in comes out. My friend has his grandson in his arms. This young man is sobbing his heart out and I can see that my friend is also about to lose control.

Sometimes you've got to give credit to the guards. There were four guards waiting to search us and to pass us back into the pods. My friend was holding up the guards, the visitors, and the other inmates. Much to my surprise they allowed this moment to play out without any interference. Not a word was said by anyone as we returned to our cells. No light has been turned on in my friend's cell since his return. I hate to think of what my friend, and his family, will have to go through over the next three weeks.

Wednesday, January 14—my friend is now down to three weeks. I decide to stop by his cell since I have not seen him since that last visit. He has been very busy. Most of his "stuff" is being sorted and placed in several piles on the floor of his cell. My friend is beginning the final phase, that of personal preparation. He has to figure out what to do with all the things he has gathered over the past twenty-four years, who gets what. Does it go to family, friends here in prison, or simply throw it away as "so much trash?"

It may please "the angry people" to know that, from what I have witnessed, from this point on my friend's mind will never be far from his pending execution. It should please "them" to know that he won't get another night's sleep. What little sleep he will get will be filled with bad dreams. His waking hours will be spent with his memories and regrets. He won't be able to concentrate on anything else. Soon, if he acts like the other men that I've seen go through this, he will start to skip meals. No peace. No rest. No comfort. Only twenty-one days remain.

Thursday, January 15—I was called out of my cell to report to the manager's office, which is never a good sign. This usually means trouble and inconvenience, but this time it is far worse. It is the prison chaplain waiting with a very serious look on his face, and the phone in his hand. My sister, through sobbing and tears, tells me of my mother's death. Where do I go for comfort? Who can I lean on at such a time? I simply return to my cell and wrap myself in the darkness.

At 1:00 p.m. whom do I find at my cell door, telling me to come outside for a while? My friend is going to die in less than three weeks, and he has it within him to try to support me. It amazes me that anyone would think that the world would be better off killing such a person. Prison is a place of pain and loss; it is a darkness beyond my ability to express. Soon it will be so much darker.

Monday, January 19, brings my friend's father for a visit. There will be no big meal for my friend tonight, no casual chat on the front porch. This visit is going to be very difficult for them both. This man is about to ask his only son what his final requests and wishes are.

I've said this before, and I'm quite sure that I'll say it again—until people stop the hatred long enough to listen. I just can't believe that any-one really wants this. I cannot believe that even "the angry people" can find joy and satisfaction in this elderly man's grief and breaking heart. There has to be some measure of Christian love and compassion for the innocent people like my friend's father, who will soon become a victim of crime, as surely as the original family.

I can hear small pieces of their conversation. The lawyers will soon bring papers to sign. His mother wants him to lie at her side in a new cem-etery. The father tries to describe the site. His stone will be flat. Something about "loving father and son." Tears fall from this man as he speaks, and I watch the real cost of a painless execution.

Tuesday, January 20, 10:30 a.m.—My friend is called out for an attor-ney visit. It takes about an hour, and his face is a mask as he returns to his cell. I have a pretty good idea about the subject of today's meeting. I think that it should be noted that most of the men in our housing pod have been very concerned about our friend as he tries to deal with the situation. We have all found some reason to stop at his door to speak to him and check on him. With only two weeks to go I don't have anything clever to say.

Part 4: By and with Death

Wednesday, January 21—With two weeks to go the Federal District Court in Nashville has ruled against my friend on all of his issues. There will be no going back from this point in his appeals, and there are only two courts that separate him from his death. As my friend told me about this latest development, or should I say this latest setback, I heard the helpless tone of his voice and there was only hopelessness in his sad eyes. My friend has only fourteen days to live.

Another bad sign, the local media has shown up today, seeking interviews to air during the big circus that they will make out of his execution. I can't imagine what this weekend's visits will be like for my friend and his family. I wonder which of his family members will find the love and strength to face this final visit, and the growing reality of what will be. It has also occurred to me that as often as I've stopped at his cell door I have not seen my friend in his bed, or asleep.

Monday, January 26—Tonight brought my friend's minister in to the visiting area. As a minister, she is trained and is used to dealing with pain, suffering, and death. I've seen her explain the execution procedures to his family without the first hint of emotion. She has been "a rock" all through this last five months. So I was surprised to see her lose control as she sat with my friend. (After so many years of their visiting together I guess I should say—her friend.) Along with this most welcome (for me) display of real emotion, yet one more person is brought to tears by this "painless execution." The desire for vengeance, or "justice," has now caused pain and suffering to a man of God, (well, a woman of God). However, you look at it, this "person" of God will cry out her pain *directly* to her God. I am very glad that I'm not the person, or the people, that God will turn his attention to for causing such pain to one of his children.

Tuesday, January 27—As I write these words, my friend is in the unit-manager's office with prison officials. The Warden will offer some the details of the execution, simply for my friend's peace of mind. Some matters he is to pass on to his family. My friend is to select his spiritual advisor, who will wait with him at his deathwatch cell as that final moment approaches, and until that moment when "they come for him." He must also decide who will witness his death. He is allowed six witnesses, family or friends. He is to decide who will visit him during this last seventy-two hours, and any last minute additions to his phone list. One of the special "treats" of an execution is that the inmate must assist in its planning. No, this is not a criticism, since both the inmate and his family are grateful for the ability to make certain choices. He will also make his decision about his last meal. My friend will do what the three men who were executed before him did, my friend will assure the Warden of his cooperation at the times of his movements. The simple truth is that he will go. It is up to him if he goes "the easy way," or if he opts for "a more difficult way." Either way, he will go.

Every man living in Unit Two knows that this meeting is taking place. The silence echoes in every cell. We all know that at some point we may face the same meeting, and we all dwell on our own ideas as to our choices.

Wednesday, January 28—With one week to go it is once again "media day." Today the Warden will meet with the various reporters to provide whatever information he sees fit to disclose. My friend will also have this opportunity to speak to the media—if he so chooses. His attorneys will want to address the media in an attempt to decry the inhumanity of the execution, to state my friend's innocence, and to call for clemency by the Governor. Beyond the vultures—the media—nothing pertaining to the execution or my friend will happen today.

Thursday, January 29—I was called out to collect my weekly commissary order. My friend was also out, collecting his. As I greeted him, he asked me if I'd like to go out and play cards that afternoon.

At 1:00 p.m. my friend shows up with two bags. He passes out cokes, Chex-mix, Nacho chips, and Snickers bars. We all know what this is. We all know that it is "Goodbye." So we play. We laugh and tell old jokes. We talk about Obama. We talk about everything and anything, as long as it's not what we are all thinking about.

Way too quickly it is 4:00 p.m. and the guards call an end to our rec period. This is my last visit with my friend. As he slowly stands up, his jaw is firmly set and he slowly steps away from the table. He looks at me for a long moment. He nods his head and puts his hand on my shoulder, and quietly walks away. My friend, my brother, has said "Goodbye," not only to me, but to years of friendship—years of shared visits, of spades games, pinochle, dominos, and dirty hearts. I will miss him.

Friday, January 30—The United States Federal Court for the Sixth Circuit in Cincinnati, Ohio, has ruled against my friend. This ruling provides the perfect introduction for the local media to the upcoming execution. This day's coverage consisted of the county's District Attorney, local police commentary, and parts of the propaganda video provided by "the angry people." What I did not see was any mention of my friend's side of things. He sat for hours with the various television reporters, yet there is no mention at all that he had anything to say. What I did see was a local police chief trying to explain why the very fabric of our society depends on executing my friend. Oddly enough, this officer, his department, even his county, have nothing whatsoever to do with my friend or his case. The original offense occurred several counties away. Nevertheless, with today's report, the circus has come to town. The train has pulled into the station, and soon the elephants will be marching down the street.

Saturday, January 31—This will be my friend's last day in the unit, and it will, no doubt, be a very difficult day for him. He has been given several special visits over an eight-hour period. I will mention only two moments during those eight hours. The first visit was from 8:00–10:00 a.m. with his daughter, son, grandson, and his six year-old granddaughter.

At 10:00 a.m. a terrible scream echoed through the unit, and I saw guards running towards the visiting area. Soon our assigned guard returned to the pod, visibly shaken. In his words, at the end of their visit my friend picked up his granddaughter to hold her this one last time. She refused to let go. The scream heard throughout the unit was only a small part of the drama. This little girl was begging "them" not to hurt her grandpa. She was begging for someone—anyone—to save her grandpa.

It is a credit to the unit's officers that they did not interfere, allowing this terrible scene to play out. As it was, it took all three family members to separate the hysterical little girl from her grandfather. I watched out my window as my friend's son carried a crying child down the sidewalk.

My friend's parents had the 2:00–4:00 p.m. visit. This would be the final visit of the day. At 4:00 p.m. I watched my friend's parents as they walked slowly away from the unit and their only son. His mother was barely walking as she leaned against her husband; her body was bent and visibly shaking as she cried her heart out. My friend's father tried to give comfort and support to his wife, but you could see the tears on his face also.

In my opinion, it is this picture that the media should be showing to the world. They should show a little girl clutching her grandfather and begging for mercy. "The angry people" should see this elderly woman, her heart broken in grief, being half carried from the prison. That should make the evening news. I do not say this in anger. I say this simply because I cannot believe that anyone—no matter how angry, callous, or spiteful—could truly want this.

At 10:00 p.m. tonight I will begin my vigil. It will be during the next eight hours that they will come for him, and I cannot allow my friend to pass this time alone.

I walk slowly
One last mile
Bound in chains
Wrapped in shame
One last time
To see the stars
The warm night breeze
Dries my tears
I can see the lights
Beyond the wire
I smell the grass . . . And whisper goodbye
I walk slowly
One last mile
To pay a debt
That I do not owe

Sunday, February 1—It is 2:00 a.m., and I am quietly waiting for the sound of keys and chains. I am rather surprised by the number of men still awake. As I look out my cell door I can see the flickering lights of the televisions on the smooth waxed floor, but no bright lights, no loud music, and no mindless chatter. Many want to keep this watch with me, and no one will disturb the solemnity of these last hours.

3:00 a.m.—Standing on my bunk looking out of my rear window, I can see the back wall of Building 8. I can see the four tall, thin windows of the deathwatch cells. I stand at my window watching the night sky, searching for stars, and watching the mist rolling over the riverbank. It is at times like this that I truly regret that from this cell I cannot see the moon. However, I can see that the lights are now on in Building 8. It won't be long now until they come for my friend.

4:30 a.m.—Four officers enter the pod. The nighttime security lights are on and the four men walk to my friend's cell. I know that he is awake, and the soft voice of the Lieutenant in charge is polite and respectful. The sound of chains and handcuffs and leg-shackles is oddly loud and clear. As my friend steps out of his cell and into the common area, many quiet words of support and good luck pass through the pod.

And as quickly as that, my friend is gone.

5:00 a.m.—My friend is slowly walking past my cell window. After so many years, my friend is finally walking in the grass. I had planned to knock on my window to wave a last goodbye, but I can't interfere with his last wish for himself. So, with a "slightly" lighter heart, I watch as my friend slowly walks towards his last moment under the sky. No one is trying to make this ordeal any more difficult for him, and as my friend slowly walks by he is talking with the officers. Four times I've watched as a friend took this last walk, and all four times I've been grateful for the compassion and professionalism of these officers.

When my friend reaches the sidewalk leading to the side door of Building 8, he steps out of the grass. These final difficult steps will be made on the concrete he hated.

As my friend got to that brown door, as he reached that final step that would forever separate him from the earth, he turned slightly towards our unit and spoke to the officers with a small shrug. Then my friend looks up to the clear night sky, he took a deep breath and slowly let it out. The guard detail steps up, and my friend is gone. I stare at a solitary door.

6:30 a.m.—The unit guards come into the pod with our breakfast. Everything is done in the quietest way. For the next three days, in fact, this will be a very quiet place. The only satisfaction I have is from the local news, who seem very upset that the prison moved my friend before dawn. Apparently, they had hoped for some film footage to air with the morning report.

The clock continues its countdown until my friend dies, and the uncertainty is like some awful and perverse funeral that just doesn't seem to end. As I sit with my visitor, quietly holding her hand, my mind is with my friend. His daughter is visiting him in Building 8. He is bound hand and foot, and behind thick glass. His daughter had to run a gauntlet of film crews and stupid questions just to have this last time with her father. There are fourteen news vans and trucks out in the visitor's parking area, so "the vultures" that had been circling in the sky have now landed in the branches. Their evil eyes and sharp talons are just waiting for death.

I will end this first day of deathwatch as I started it, standing at my window looking out over the prison. Looking at the lights in the cell windows of Building 8, I can't begin to imagine what he must be feeling right now.

The Grass

I walked upon the grass last night
The first time in many years
A few moments of personal happiness . . . Before the time of tears
Above my head a bright full moon
It's glow to light my way
My heart expands to touch the night . . . I won't see another day
Around me walk four silent men
Not a word to speak their mind

I've seen this show played out before . . . They are trying to be kind
I walked upon the grass last night . . . I heard an owl's cry
I stopped a moment at the door . . . And whispered a last goodbye

Monday, February 2—At 6:30 a.m. I turn on my television to see the local news as I eat breakfast. Over grits, I watch quite a bit of coverage concerning the execution. Most of it is prosecutors calling for "justice," activists demanding revenge, and a local police chief declaring that this execution will send a strong message to criminals everywhere. On and on they talk. What I find so interesting—and it is always this way—is that after hours of interviews, the only air time my friend gets is reduced to a sound bite: "I'm an innocent man." In other words, he gets four words in as many seconds. So far, the media hasn't seen fit to show the attorneys for my friend. Evidently, that side of this story is not important, and won't bring the viewers back for more.

9:00 a.m.—A clemency hearing is held by the State Board of Pardons and Paroles, which is a big part of the news at noon. All five of the board members are present. All five look very severe and stern. What I saw on the news report, and what I can never understand, is that after they all vote "No" to mercy and grace—which is, after all, what clemency is—after a vote to deny my friend any level of forgiveness, the spokesperson for the Board will close the proceeding with the words, "May God have mercy on your soul." I don't think that I can add any commentary to such a ridiculous statement.

We are now down to less than thirty-seven hours. We no longer count months, or weeks, or even days. My friend is counting hours. Because I know my friend, as well as the good reverend, I'd bet anything that they will spend a lot of that time on their knees.

10:30 p.m.—There has been no legal news, and the cell lights in Building 8 are off. My only hope is that all the sleepless nights have finally caught up to my friend. I want him to have one last night of sleep and rest. We know what awaits him with the new day, his last day.

I stand in my window watching the snow falling out of the darkness and into the lights high above the prison. Even in such a place, at such a time, the beauty and majesty of God will always make itself known. I know in my heart that even though the people on the State Board didn't really mean it, I know that God *will* have mercy on my brother's soul.

Tuesday, February 3—It's 3:00 a.m. The snow has stopped falling and the sky is clear. Will my friend be standing in his window tonight? I can't imagine what he must be going through. I've thought about trying to sleep part of this time away, but if I don't care enough to stand-watch with my friend, how can I ask anyone else to care?

6:30 a.m.—All through the pod I can hear the questions: "Any word yet?" "Did the courts rule?" "What do you think?" All through this day the questions will pass from cell to cell. Not a single newscast will be missed. The light is on in my friend's cell in Building 8. I can see his shadow as he stands in the window watching his last sunrise. As the sun rises, the sky is shades of the deepest blues, rich and regal. Has God tried to give some measure of comfort to my friend on this terrible day? Then, all too quickly, the sky turns gray and dismal. A harsh and cold winter's day seems all too appropriate for the situation.

10:00 a.m.—All is quiet in the pod. This is all I really know, solitary confinement may be great when one wants to be left alone, but it is also very limiting for those times when we require current information. So, we do what we do best and we wait. We sit in our cells and watch as the minutes slowly pass. My friend is down to fourteen hours and I still have two hours to wait for the local news at noon. With fourteen hours to go, only the Supreme Court of the United States stands between my friend and his death.

Noon—The local news reports that my friend is set to die at 1:00 a.m. I was counting it to midnight, so my friend gains an hour. The news commentator also says that my friend's attorneys are preparing their eleventh hour appeals for the State courts. Things will begin to move very fast for all of the parties involved. However, at noon, with thirteen hours to go, nothing has changed. The media lottery has been held, choosing the reporters to witness the execution. The "winners" have been notified and will soon gather for the show.

5:00 p.m.—The local news has now begun its coverage of the execution. The only real information they have, however, is that my friend's last meal will be a seafood platter—fish and shrimp. It is also known that his son and daughter will be there to give their love and support to their father as he faces such an ordeal. His afternoon was spent saying goodbye to his family. He will spend these last seven hours with his minister and his attorneys.

6:00 p.m.—As I wait for the latest reports on the television, I am listening to the various thoughts and theories as to what the attorneys will, and should, do.

The United States Supreme Court has denied my friend his appeal. It is looking worse and worse for my friend.

7:00 p.m.—A prayer vigil is now being held at a local church. The prison has set aside an area for a midnight protest vigil, side-by-side with an area for those in support of the execution. Of course, this area is out in a large field, far from the prison, on the other side of a hill. So, even if a large crowd is willing to brave the frigid temperatures to protest the execution, no one is likely to notice. With six hours to go things look grim.

8:30 p.m.—I watch the light come on in the cell in Building 8. Whoever my friend was with, is now gone. Unless an attorney visits with some news, my friend will remain in his cell until they come for him. I can only hope that he won't face these final hours alone.

9:00 p.m.—Fox News reports no change in the situation. Shown were clips from the prayer vigil, which had a very good turn out. Also, I saw the victim's family. I can't say this enough—*no one* in this unit has said anything against this family, or their right to be angry.

We are down to four hours.

10:00 p.m.—A lot is going on. The Governor has refused to get involved and will not grant a reprieve or pardon. My friend's minister has returned to the prison from the prayer vigil to share these final hours with him, to share communion, to pray, and to try to give strength and support.

It truly is a circus out in front of the prison. With every news report there are more and more people. There is noise and laughter in the background. And right in the middle of the visitor's parking lot is a big white tent.

With three hours to go my friend is running out of options, and I am running out of hope.

11:00 p.m.—I've been watching many people in long coats coming in and going out of the prison, passing between Buildings 1 and 8. A small, gray mini-van—the hearse that will carry my friend from the prison—has now backed into the small garage at the end of Building 8. With two hours to go there will be no news on television to let me know what is happening. I must wait the next two hours for whatever news there is.

Momma I'm scared
It's raining outside
I see shadows on the wall
Something is under my bed
Momma . . . Please turn on the light
I'm so all alone
I hear voices outside
Momma . . . Please hold me tight
I'm afraid of the dark

> Chase the monsters away
> Momma . . . Please sit on my bed
> And tell me a story
> The one with the bears
> Momma . . . Where are you
> It is so dark in my room
> Someone is at the door
> Momma . . . They're here
> Momma . . . They're here
> I hear voices and chains
> Momma . . . They're here

February 4—After more than 23 years on Death Row, thirty minutes remain. A large number of people are now passing into the prison. The unit guards have conducted a visual count of all the men in Unit Two. They have checked by hand every cell door to ensure that all the cells are secure.

If something doesn't happen in the next thirty minutes I don't see any hope for my friend.

12:40 a.m.—The light has gone out in my friend's cell. My friend is now laying on a gurney, strapped down, arms and legs and chest. Someone—hopefully with medical training—will be inserting a large-bore I.V. needle into his arm.

Shortly before 1:00 a.m. my friend will be rolled into the death chamber. He will be attached to the waiting tubes, which have been pre-set by the Warden. Both the victim's family and my friend's family (along with other witnesses) will look down on my friend from raised theater seats. My friend will be allowed to make a final statement. He will be able to say a final prayer with either the prison chaplain or his own minister, and he will no doubt be looking toward his children. Because I know my friend, I know that all his pain, all his worry, and his only concern will be for his children and his family.

12:50 a.m.—I stand in my window watching and waiting for any sign of hope . . . mercy . . . or reprieve. I flip through the local T.V. channels trying to find some word, some news. My friend's life is now measured in minutes.

> Into the darkness
> Into the night
> The shadows are coming
> To steal the light
> All things are fading

You can't even pray
The voices all vanish
As life slips away
Alone on a table
You watch yourself die
Surrounded by hatred
You can't even cry
The poison enfolds you
In it's deadly embrace
Your last thought is slipping . . . of God's loving grace
Into the darkness
Into the night
A lifetime is fleeting
Another soul takes flight

At 1:00 a.m., early in the morning of February 4, the Warden did what the Warden had to do. He pushed a button, and my friend died.

As my friend's children stood, pressed against the glass, the reporters sat casually behind them in their theater seats, chatting and taking notes. This is merely another story to them. As chemicals, which are deemed by law to be too "inhumane" to euthanize an animal at the pound, as these chemicals flow through my friend's veins his daughter's tears flow down the glass partition. The curtains close. Her father is gone. My friend's son takes his sister into his arms. The great strength that she gave so freely to her family for all these months is spent. All that is left is a little girl's tears. As my friend's son helps his sobbing sister from the room, the reporters watch the show. What a wonderful story this will make for the morning news.

1:45 a.m.—A small gray mini-van slowly exits the prison. My friend is gone.

Out in the parking lot, my friend's son makes a statement for the family—forgiving those who took the life of his father. Through his tears he declares one last time his father's innocence.

In Memory of My Friend — Steve Henley

Remember me
From yesterday
When tomorrow held promise
And life was free
Remember me
When we were young
Those summer days

At the swimming hole
Why did we want to grow up
Why did we ever leave home
What was the big hurry
To let it all pass
Remember me
In better times
When we owned the day
And the future was ours
Remember me
In some small way
With love and forgiveness . . . Then let me go

3:00 a.m.—I stand on my bunk, looking out my window at a clear night sky, listening to the newscaster covering the big show. The local news is doing all it can to turn a five minute story into a six hour circus. All I can think of is the old question, "Why do we kill people who kill people to show people that killing people is wrong?"

This morning a man died and his family was shattered. For whom is the pain lessened? How is the loneliness eased? What peace was found here last night? The only thing satisfied tonight was revenge.

14

Tearing Down the Temple to Rebuild the Kingdom

JEANNIE ALEXANDER

NOVEMBER BROUGHT NASHVILLE NEW life born in the streets in defiance of indifference, new life preparing us for Advent and the waiting to come. New life in the form of a homeless child born directly onto the filthy streets of Second Avenue, *unto us a child is born*. As I write this the last few days of Advent lead us to hope in the messianic promise fulfilled, in the fullness of time the revolution in Mary's belly revealed. And my boasting and fearlessness is put to the test as I preach to a crowd that the crosses that we wear around our necks are a symbol to all that the very worst they can do to us is put us to death, and there is no power in death for we believe in the God of resurrection. And the world obliges, and puts us to death.

I look to the God of resurrection at 1:00 a.m. on December 2 as my friend and brother in Christ, Cecil Johnson, is injected with chemicals deemed too inhumane to be used in the euthanization of animals. It's so cold outside as he dies. We stand in the freezing rain in a field adjacent to Riverbend Maximum Security Institution, marking the minutes; bleeding heart abolitionists, *Jesus too had a bleeding heart*. I watch the ambulance slowly pull into the prison ten minutes before murder and I begin to shake, this madness need not continue, and he doesn't have to die. Or does he?

Days before his death *The Tennessean* reported on Cecil's impending execution and Governor Bredesen's refusal to commute his death sentence. As I scanned the reader's comments in response to the story my stomach churned. My sweet brother in Christ was called a "monkey," an "animal," a "monster," and it was suggested in good Southern fashion that this nightmare "should have ended 29 years ago at the end of a rope." Was he a murderer? It depends upon which Cecil we are speaking of. The old Cecil committed acts of murder and yet I cannot love him any less. If God is reconciled to Cecil through Christ, and God is, then who am I to reject him? If I crucify Cecil, I crucify Christ. You see, Cecil has already died. Years ago he was put to death. Through his baptism Cecil was baptized into Jesus' death. The old Cecil died to sin and was resurrected in Christ. We speak so much of being born again and neglect the truth that before we can be reborn we must die to this world. Cecil was bought at a price, yet what is good enough for God is not good enough for man. We demand every pound of flesh from the new Cecil, willfully blind to the reborn creature before us.

If we refuse Cecil's first death, as a society we must convince ourselves that Cecil is an animal, an ape, a monster in order to kill him. We must refuse to see that Cecil is made in God's image, and we must ignore the last twenty-nine years of his life. We must ignore the fact that Cecil is more like Saint Paul than the dangerous monster the state would paint him to be, but most of all we must refuse to see how he is so like us.

Cecil was raised poor in the country, a barefoot boy in overalls. He was brought up in church, a loved boy living a life in the rural South, a boyhood that sounds so like the childhood of my father and grandfather, your father and grandfather. I recall hearing the story of Cecil as a young boy playing around an old barn-like building with his brother. They noticed a young white pigeon on a rafter, too young to fly and almost sure to die, and so Cecil scaled the rickety beams and boards to capture the bird. As he grasped the pigeon the board he was standing on broke and as he fell he tossed the pigeon to his brother. He was saved from injury by a nail catching on his overalls and breaking his fall. I can see the young boy in overalls dangling in the air, face flushed with excitement, happy that he had saved the bird. Cecil tamed that pigeon and it followed him around everywhere for years. Relatives laughed and shook their head at Cecil's pigeon.

If I wanted to I could feel sorry for Cecil and blame his current state on a life so different from my own, but that would simply not be true. I could try to remove myself from the reality of the history and context of my own family and instead offer a carefully constructed fiction that shows how different I am from my poor black brother cast in chains and scheduled for death. I could hide in multiple graduate degrees from Cornell Law and the Religion Department at Georgia State University. I could feel self-satisfied about my erudite taste in fiction and sophisticated urban commitment to sustainable living. But scratch the surface and my past is not so different from Cecil's. I too grew up barefoot in the rural South in dirty overalls and cut off blue jean shorts. Our family car was an old '65 Chevy truck that my mother had to learn to fix herself because it might or might not make it back from a trip to the vegetable and fruit stand. Scratch the surface and two generations back I come from Georgia sharecroppers and Tennessee snake handlers. I suspect that my grandfather and Cecil's grandfather were only truly differentiated by skin tone.

Two weeks before Cecil's execution, Jerry Welborn, the chaplain at Riverbend, and I were walking over to Unit 2 to visit with Cecil and two other inmates on death row, Ron Cauthern and Don Johnson. As we walked we had an encounter with Cecil's past and perhaps the Holy Spirit. Jerry and I were in deep discussion concerning Cecil's faith and steadfastness and whether or not he was at peace with his impending death. As the words "Cecil's faith" left Jerry's lips a large white pigeon, the only solid white pigeon I had ever seen at Riverbend, flew directly towards us, at the last minute pulling up, its wings all but brushed our foreheads. I could smell its feathers as it looked me directly in the eye. We had no doubt that it was Cecil's pigeon, and it seemed to be an answer to a question and a harbinger of peace before the storm.

And now, numb in the cold I meditate on the voice, the smell, and the joyful presence of my beautiful brother reconciled to his God, reconciled to his death, reconciled to a world that could not be reconciled to him; a world motivated by fear, a world that continues to choose law over grace, a world that chooses the false security of power, authority, and hierarchy over relationship and vulnerability. And so my brother will die stretched out, strapped down in the shape of a cross. I begin to pray: *Father forgive them, Father forgive them, Father forgive them.* And I scream inside as the ambulance pulls up to the death chamber. *Hail Mary full of grace the Lord is with thee. Blessed are you among women and blessed is the fruit of your womb Jesus. Holy Mary Mother of God, pray for us sinners now, and at the hour of our death. Amen.* I pray not for a miracle but for mercy, mercy in death. *Our Father, who art in heaven, hallowed be thy name. Thy Kingdom come. Thy will be done, on earth as it is in heaven.* And the old black spiritual plays in my mind "Were you there when they crucified my Lord? Oh! Sometimes it causes me to tremble, tremble, tremble. Were you there when they crucified my Lord?" And I tremble because I am there. I hold tight to my faith in the Son of Man executed by the state as another son of man is executed by the empire of our day. Fists clenched, nails digging into the palms of my hands, I weep as I pray that he does not feel forsaken. Do I believe in the power of God? Yes, and also in the indifference, hardness of heart, and the fear that leads to so much sin in man. But above all I believe in grace. What are his last words? "I love you." My brother dies with the word "love" on his lips. Sweet mercy.

As the prayer echoes in my head my heart begins to rage. *On Earth as it is in heaven.* May God damn the cities where thy will is not done! May God damn the walls that hold my brother and the needles and machines that crucify him! May God damn a system that incarcerates over 30 percent of black males between the ages of eighteen and thirty-five, and millions upon millions of their poor "white trash" brothers! And may God damn the prison walls and bring them crashing down, another Jericho in our time!

And tomorrow the church choirs will sing, and their congregations will grow, and the giant American flags will hang high in the church parking lots, blocking out the cross (if there is even a cross at all). And we good Christians are entertained and laugh, and we pray to a safe domesticated Jesus through songs with a saccharin beat where Jesus becomes our boyfriend. And we good Christians line up to feed Caesar's war machine, onward Christian solders! And we take great pride in our idolatry, and great volumes of heresy spring forth from the lips of the teachers of the law as we back our political candidates because that is where our real faith lies, and we justify our standard of living on every broken back beneath our feet, and we raise our Bibles high! Oh God we do *not* tremble!

Woe to you Pharisees, Sadducees, and teachers of the law who have taught us to submit to the state, deny God, and to crucify our brother. You teach us that the Kingdom of God is our reward after this life if we do as we are told, become upright citizens in good standing with the Chamber of Commerce and the Rotary Club, vote and pay our taxes, go to church on Sunday, and believe in the righteous power of free market capitalism. Oh you deceivers. But we *are* the body of Christ, we *are* the living church in the world, and we could see the Kingdom among us if the temple were not blocking the view. And so my final prayer on that cold night is not the Our Father, or a prayer for peace. We are to pray boldly before the Lord, and so my final prayer is for the courage and faith to tear down the temple, all of the temples: the temples on Wall Street, the temple of the state capital, and the temples of Christendom, the temples of the academy, and the broken temples of our mind that make us prisoners of powers and principalities of a realm we do not apprehend. Let us tear down the institutional temples to reveal the Beloved Community. Let us tear down the temple to rebuild the Kingdom.

One week and a day later it is still so cold, so very cold. In the morning hour just before dawn another man dies, a poor white boy from Memphis, a man without a home, burning, burning so hot like a star fallen to earth, silent as a burning Buddhist monk protesting the brutal regime of the South Vietnamese government. Another dead brother sent off into the wilderness, seeking a better life in Nashville's Tent City where he heard that a poor man could find some help. Like a wise woman struck dumb following a star, I stand at Kevin's deathbed in the dirt under a bridge. Three hours after he burns I arrive at his camp, a camp marked now with the carbon etched form of a body staining the ground curled up against the stones of the fire pit: our own little Hiroshima in Tent City. His camp mates say there was not a sound, no screams from the dying man. Silent resignation perhaps or perhaps he was dead before he ever hit the ground, infused with yet more killing chemicals, as primed as the creosote-soaked timber he was burning.

We pray as a group trying to understand, and I tell the members of the dead man's camp, "This is not God's will. This is not the Kingdom among us. This is society's failure to abide by God's will. This is our sin, our refusal to live reconciliation. In the beloved community *every man shall sit under his own vine or under his own fig tree undisturbed.* Kevin's death was not the result of divine punishment, but of human indifference."

Bobby, Kevin's camp mate and friend pulls an old dirty grey blanket towards us; it is filled with what the police left behind after their investigation: burned twisted shards of glass, plastic, shoes, and charred bits of Kevin. The cold air holds the faint smell of roasted sweet meat and my stomach turns. He tells us that it was Kevin's wish to be buried at sea. Although he could not swim, Kevin said it was to be his baptism. And so we grant his request in the sea of the Cumberland as his friend proclaims "I baptize you in the name of the Father." It is finished, and we stand on holy ground, on tortured ground.

Standing in the wilderness of Tent City I apprehend the chemical induced deaths of a system designed to bear false witness to the reality of an America that praises Jesus on Sunday and kills Jesus on Monday, and I can feel Cecil burning from within and Kevin burning from without.

One black, one white, poor Southern men, Levitical scapegoats, crucified because, unlike the God we profess to follow, we will continue to hold men's misdeeds against them; indeed they will pay the ransom for our own misdeeds. Two men, their lots cast. One will die a terrible death in the wilderness, banished from the community long ago to make atonement. The other kept and well tended (death row inmates receive the best medical care the prison has to offer) prepared for the sacrifice to our true god; complete with a feast for all in attendance, the unblemished goat in the prime of his life. And so we slaughter the goat, slaughter our brother, as a sin offering, for deep down we know that the sin is our own. The very existence of the prison is proof that our way is a failure, a counterfeit rendition of truth and justice. Retribution is dearer to us than grace, more real to us than salvation.

Both men killed by a culture of death: one man directly murdered in a clinical sanitized pantomime of a medical procedure; the other man killed indirectly, but no less assuredly, by a society that will pay millions for the death penalty (hundreds of thousands more than the cost of life in prison, never mind the possibility of restorative justice over the current model of retribution), billions for war, and a brass farthing for low income housing. The poor will always be with us, why fight it?

I stand at Kevin's last sanctuary and my heart burns and my vision blurs. As I touch the still warm sand and let it run through my fingers I wonder, where were all of you so called pro-life members of the community? It's so very easy to be pro-life when the person in question is one so innocent they've not yet touched the earth, but what about the condemned man, what about the homeless man? Where are your demands for life? You hypocrites of omission, your silence kills. And I am bitter with hate for a system that I cannot be reconciled to, and I struggle to love the blind children of God trapped in the hell they created, we created, for us all.

Either we are all reconciled or none of us is reconciled. Cecil told me weeks before his execution that "God doesn't lie, we are all reconciled." Every Jew gripping a stone at Stephen's martyrdom, every angry black man with a gun, every white supremacist stockpiling weapons, every CEO making the decision to foreclose on thousands of homes while his bonus continues to grow, every frightened woman seeking an abortion, every prison guard who supports the death penalty, every child born addicted to crack, every prostitute with broken nails and AIDS, every child molesting priest, every abusive husband, every soldier in war, every raped and murdered civilian—we are all reconciled; it has been accomplished.

God would give us the best, the Kingdom of God is among us, and yet we choose the comfort of the deceiver, false promises of safety secured with bars, steel doors, concertina wire, chemical cocktails of death, and mandatory sentences. We choose the temple gilded with gold, draped with flags, decked out with bejeweled crosses (so many distractions to hide the rot), over a lowly stable.

Cecil was a letter from Christ, a new creation, no longer Greek or Jew, master or slave, murderer or saint. He was persecuted but not abandoned, struck down but not destroyed. His final words whispered, "I love you," in defiance of the final solution of the human justice system, a final testimony to reconciliation. My brother strong and full of life, a chest ripped with muscles, a mind educated beyond his earthly means, a dove tamer and an artist, departing from us as one 2,000 years before, leaving us with the only truth we will ever need, love. And so through and past anger, tears, and exhaustion I pray to the only God I know, a God Thomas Merton described as "mercy, within mercy, within mercy." I believe in reconciliation, I believe in the Beloved Community, and I believe in the executed Nazarene who takes us there.

PART 5

The Scandal of Community in This Institution

THE DEATH-DEALING NATURE OF the American prison system can quickly tempt us to despair and abandon all hope. Even if we do not give up, we nonetheless feel the weight of frustration. Will Campbell's exasperation with the system made him want to act. He tells a story about a man who came to his house to talk about the authority of Scripture. Campbell eventually asked if the man believed the Bible "literally," to which the man responded, "Yes." As Campbell tells it:

> I stood up, gave him a courtly bow and ceremoniously got my hat and cane, extended my hand and said, "I didn't know there was anyone else in the world who believed the way I do. The Bible says that the day has come to proclaim the opening of the doors of the prison and letting the captives go free. I've been looking for years to find someone who agreed with the literal interpretation of that scripture 'cause there's this prison in west Nashville and I can't tear the thing down by myself, but if there's 15 million folks out there who believe in the literal interpretation of Scripture, we can get them all together and raze that prison to the ground."[1]

1. Campbell, *Writings on Reconciliation and Resistance*, 70.

On the one hand, I suspect Campbell wanted to reveal that his visitor might not be the "literalist" he imagined, but on the other, Campbell provided a quixotic editorial on his commitment to take down prison walls. Like Campbell, the frustration we feel for our imprisoned brothers and sisters entices us to *do something*. Don't tell anyone, but as a means of "taking down the walls," I have occasionally considered driving my car through the fence of the Charles B. Bass Correctional Complex. My dear friends and confidants have convinced me, however, that such a strategy would be much too violent a way to proclaim the good news of freedom to the captives. Still, we are a people called "to proclaim release to the captives," aren't we? So, let's tear down those walls.

One creative way of tearing down walls is by *being* community together with prisoners—being *Beloved* Community. I am, for example, part of a group of men and women who meet together at Riverbend Maximum Security Institution in a Benedictine-inspired community. Although we have had our fair share of "just what the hell are we doing" moments, our Riverbend community shines as an embodied witness to the egalitarian kingdom of God. We sit around a table at which everyone has an equal share in what happens. Because life together involves meeting one another in vulnerability, we try desperately—although we sometimes fail miserably—to avoid prison-politics and power grabs. Our fundamental desire is to live the Rule of St. Benedict in our context, e.g., embracing practices of Scripture reading, prayer, hospitality, service, mutual accountability, and "being there" for each other. Like all communities, we are a motley work in progress, but even works in progress can be life affirming and value giving. Thus the characters in Will Campbell's novel, *The Glad River*, resonate with and inspire us because when it comes to owning and controlling the community, we take a vow of poverty. "We don't make community any more than we make souls. It's created."[2] And once it has been created, community practices the "will to embrace"[3] unable to recognize any walls between *us* and *them* since such "[b]oundaries act as a form of *separation* between the self and the other, often signaling the failure of love."[4] In my experience, sitting in a room—simply being present with men and women gathered—can be as wall-destroying as Will and his 15 million biblical literalists chipping away with pick-axes at the physical walls around a prison.

2. Campbell, *The Glad River*, 77.

3. Volf, *Exclusion and Embrace*, 29.

4. Beck, *Unclean*, 127.

Community is therefore scandalous because it subverts the narratives of the prison system. Perhaps the subversiveness of being community with prisoners is most evident in the case of confession: for the prison system, confession leads to punishment, but in Beloved Community, confession leads to absolution and pardon. Appealing to the "prophetic imagination," Randy Spivey begins this section by highlighting this very contrast of narratives. Indeed, throughout the essays in this section, the theme of confession is heard because confession creates space for receiving reconciliation. Confession allows us to see ourselves as we really are—broken, yet dearly loved—and it allows for both individual and communal transformation and renewal. Thus, a former prison chaplain, Marlin Elbon Kilpatrick, shows how he was transformed out of the corrections system, which coerces through violence, and into community, which witnesses the nonviolent love of Jesus. Jeannie Alexander proclaims that even though the prison system may dehumanize those entering baptismal waters by making them wear chains, community baptizes the shackled prisoners, proclaiming that freedom comes from God and cannot be taken away. And Richard Beck speaks the scary truth that even though the dogma of the prison principality announces "Blessed are the violent," the community of our Lord reminds us that "those who are persecuted for righteousness' sake" are really the blessed. These subversive narratives question the "reasonableness" and efficacy of the narratives of the powers-that-be.

Yet the only reason that these communities can subvert the prison system's narratives is because they are gatherings that anticipate the coming of the kingdom of God in its fullness—a kingdom where the least is the greatest, the last is the first, and where all are welcomed around the messianic banquet table. Call these communities "eschatological" because the death-dealing powers that claim to frame the narratives for reality are exposed as shams and imposters. They are defeated by the life giving— the life renewing—kingdom of God. We are members of the community formed by the "ridiculous" norms of the cross and resurrection of Jesus. Therein is our hope. Therein is our reconciliation. Let's go be ambassadors.

Craig D. Katzenmiller

15

Questioning Society's Criminal Justice Narratives

RANDY SPIVEY

SEVERAL YEARS AGO TWO immigrant store clerks were killed during
a robbery in Madison, Tennessee, a suburb of Nashville. The immigrant community was outraged. A priest who served the community
stated clearly that "we are hoping for this, that the death penalty will be
applied on all three of them, even the juvenile person [. . .] This will set
an example for others [. . .] If justice does not take revenge for these killings, this incident will be repeated once again . . . We need to be tough
on these kinds of criminal."[1] Shortly after this occurred, Lipscomb University began the LIFE Program, a project that provides college classes
and college credit to inmates at the Tennessee Prison for Women (TPW).
These classes consist of fifteen inmate students and fifteen traditional
Lipscomb students. The traditional Lipscomb students travel to the
prison for a weekly three-hour class.

The first class taught in the LIFE Program was Judicial Process, a
class designed by its professor, Preston Shipp, to take a critical look at the
American criminal justice system. The class centered on two questions:
What is justice? Does our current system promote justice? These questions
permeated the entire semester in the hope that the different perspectives
present in such a unique educational community would challenge traditional assumptions of justice.

1. Allen, "Tears and Anger," 3.

At the beginning of his course, Prof. Shipp had his students read a newspaper article describing the Madison killings to provoke a conversation on how American society defines justice, and why the American concept of justice is so closely tied to retribution and even revenge. During the program's first semester, the discussion of the Madison killings provoked thoughts of faith, forgiveness, revenge, hate, racism, and the responsibility for juveniles. However, when a new cohort of fifteen students began the program, the same newspaper article provoked a different reaction from the second cohort. When the new TPW students read the article, they recognized a name. The young woman, a juvenile at the time of the killings, who had been arrested and convicted for her part in the crime, was now incarcerated at the TPW. After the class, the students approached the young woman, showed her the article, and questioned her in detail. The young woman was devastated. Even in prison, she did not want her worst moment opened up for discussion. She was worried that the class discussion would affect her appeal. She was confused as to how she had become the subject of a course on judicial process. This semester the article did not provoke conversations about faith and forgiveness, but rather it provoked accusations and judgment.

When we learned that several of our students had accosted the young woman mentioned in the assigned article, I asked to speak to her. I did not know what to say, or if she would speak to me. I was taken to an empty classroom and told to wait. After several minutes, the principal of the education program at TPW came into the room with the young woman. She sat down across from me, but would not look at me. She looked so young and scared. She carried with her the same fear and pain and shame that each one of the inmate students in the LIFE Program carried as they walked in to their first college class.

In his song, "The Lonesome Death of Hattie Carroll," Bob Dylan beautifully describes how important it is to be fully aware of the pain around us before we can begin to adequately understand and lament. The song describes the death of Hattie Carroll at the hands of a wealthy, young man named William Zanzinger. In four verses, Dylan walks his audience through the victim's life of poverty and struggle, Zanzinger's life of privilege, the senseless killing, the arrest and trial, and finally the judgment. After each verse, Dylan warns:

> You who philosophize disgrace
> And criticize all fears
> Take the rag away from your face

Now ain't the time for your tears.

We are tempted to weep without knowledge and to mourn without action. As Dylan progresses deeper into the story, he will not allow unexamined tears. Here, Dylan, as artists before him and after him, serves as a spotlight—the prophet interrupting social convention and condemning political presumptions. Dylan's refrain holds the listener in place far beyond the point when the listener may feel Dylan has made his point. The artist denies society the luxury of "moving on," holding before society—with searing clarity—the things society would rather forget. As those of us who have been privileged to teach and participate in the LIFE Program have grown closer to the women at TPW, it is more difficult to accept that the wonderfully bright, creative, and kind women we know must remain in prison. Neither can we be satisfied with simply mourning that people must go to prison without questioning why people must go and who and how many are going.

Confession and Community

While concrete solutions are beyond the scope here, there must be a first step, a starting point from which a new approach to justice may begin. Those of us who have worked with the LIFE community have discovered this first step, seemingly by accident. This first step is part apology and part question. It is a step that criticizes and laments. It is a step that the prophets, who see injustice clearly, provoke us to, whether it is the interruption of John the Baptist crying for repentance or Bob Dylan holding the awful truth before our eyes. In this step, we must lament all of statistics, all of the racism and injustice and hold them up in contrast to the fourth chapter of the Gospel of Luke.

> The Spirit of the Lord is on me,
> because he has anointed me
> to preach good news to the poor.
> He has sent me to proclaim freedom for the prisoners
> and recovery of sight for the blind,
> to release the oppressed,
> to proclaim the year of the Lord's favor. (vv. 18–19)

We take this first step when we see how far short of Jesus' bold proclamation we fall and when we question how far we are willing to extend grace. This first step is confession.

In January 2007, the inaugural LIFE course met at the TPW and began a narrative of questioning and confession. The fifteen women from TPW were tested and screened from more than one hundred applicants. They were required to have a good behavior record and a high school diploma or its equivalent. They were also required to have at least two years left on their sentence. Those fifteen inmates were promised 18 credit hours over the course of two years. The fifteen inmate students were joined by fifteen traditional Lipscomb students, who, prior to this inaugural class, had undergone a forty-five minute Department of Correction orientation that included a directive to never hug an inmate and instructions on what to do in a hostage situation. The inmate students, having just been strip-searched, entered their first college class with their heads down, terrified.

I sat in the back of the classroom and watched the fifteen denim-clad women file into the room and take their seats in the circle of chairs that had been arranged, inevitably divided neatly into semi-circles of the free and the felon. The class felt like a courtroom, silent and waiting: the young Lipscomb students shaken from the security check, the razor-wire, the slamming metal doors, and the inmates facing judgment again from all of the "good" Christian kids who now sat across from them. Professor Shipp took in the circle and then simply said, "OK, now breathe."

With that Shipp began a semester long confession. The confession began with the simple acknowledgment that everyone was nervous and unsure of what they had gotten themselves into, but it continued into the substantive matter of the course. Shipp challenged the class to define justice in a new way, and confessed how far short of the biblical model of reconciliation our system of punishment via warehouse falls. Shipp confessed the racial, economic, and gender inequalities that are inherent in the American justice system. He confessed that the escalation of imprisonment has destroyed families by taking away mothers and fathers, providers, both economic and emotional, when their crimes could have been more appropriately addressed in another way. Shipp, an appellate prosecutor for the State, confessed his own frustration, in being a cog in the wheel of a system that actively rebels against the proclamation of Luke 4.

Shipp, by assigning readings and leading discussions that challenged the traditional notions of retributive justice held, not just by the traditional Lipscomb students, but by the inmate students as well, confessed to and repented of how the American system of justice had fallen short of the bold proclamations of Jesus. Shipp evoked healing, a healing that "begins with confession—with recognizing when we have participated in wrongdoing, owning up to it, and being held accountable."[2] This healing through confession continued as the class learned of preliminary hearings, appointed lawyers, and arraignments. As the semester progressed, the inmate students became more and more open with their own stories as the ongoing confession freed them from their fear of judgment. The system that imprisons them was being mourned by a college professor and the books he was assigning, and the students were finding their voice in a community of trust, confession, and honesty.

Walter Brueggemann, in his book *The Prophetic Imagination*, provides a vision of a community that laments the broken systems of its age and provides hope for the hopeless: a community that seeks to fulfill Luke 4. Brueggemann describes the task of this community as "prophetic ministry." This community, "bring[s] people to engage the promise of newness that is at work in our history with God."[3] This newness is brought about by a compassion that "announces that the hurt is to be taken seriously, that the hurt is not to be accepted as normal and natural but is an abnormal and unacceptable condition for humanness." True compassion is not simply "generous goodwill," but rather *"criticism of the system, forces, and ideology that produce the hurt."*[4]

Beginning the LIFE Program with a course that takes seriously the hurt of arrest, conviction and imprisonment, and the poverty, abuse, or sin that is at the heart of crime, not only begins a process of healing, but also creates a community where the inmate students may learn and grow. It does not change the system, after all, it is just a class, but it does "enable a new human beginning to be made." The TPW women do not have to apologize for where they are, what they have done, nor are they burdened by the fear that their cries of injustice will be heard as jailhouse complaints. Their complaints have been given voice and confessed. They are now free to move beyond those complaints into a "new human beginning."[5]

I have seen these new human beginnings. I saw one that first semester when a ten page final paper assignment became a forty page treatise simply because Natasha had so much to say. I saw one the next semester when Erika proudly drafted her own appeal brief. I saw one in the Prison Literature course when Kita's two and a half inch margins slowly crept back toward the edges of the paper as she became more and more

2. Magnani and Wray, *Beyond Prisons*, 3.
3. Brueggemann, *Prophetic Imagination*, 59.
4. Ibid., 88–89, emphasis added.
5. Ibid., 101.

confident in her ability and freedom to express herself. And I see one now in Sarah, a nervous bundle of child when we first met, who is now free on parole, counseling others as they are released in the very same halfway house from which she only recently graduated: Sarah, our poet-muse whose audacity inspired these women to create their own literary magazine, and who became a traditional Lipscomb student attending classes on the traditional campus.

The new beginnings of community are possible because confession, the acknowledgment of the wrongs and the hurts of the criminal justice system, is more than lament. Confession is lament moving to repentance, and repentance "entails specific action by those who have done harm: acknowledgement of the harm, assumption of responsibility for doing the harm, and the agreement that change must take place to ensure that further harm will not be done."[6] Confession, or "prophetic ministry," is not simply criticism that "stands against" the criminal justice system, but a confessed repentance that "stands with" those who are hurt and oppressed by the criminal justice system. As Brueggemann describes it, it is not a criticism of "triumphant indignation but one of the passion and compassion that completely and irresistibly undermine the world of competence and competition."[7]

Prophetic ministry takes seriously the injustice, prejudice, and pain, and because of that it is unable to lightly offer solutions. It will not indulge the glib demand for quick fixes and cheap change; it demands more. This confessed repentance "does not lightly offer alternatives, does not mouth assurances, and does not provide redemptive social policy. It knows that only those who mourn can be comforted, and so it first asks about how to mourn seriously and faithfully for the world passing away."[8]

To be clear, when we speak of the injustice and hurt that the inmate students have faced, or that all those incarcerated in America face, the confession of those wrongs must not be heard as the denial of guilt or culpability for the crimes they have committed. The students of the LIFE Program have committed terrible acts that have ruined or ended lives, destroyed relationships, and scarred both perpetrator and victim. To confess our own culpability in a criminal justice system that warehouses and punishes without rehabilitating while ignoring the need for repentance of the criminal is a denial of true justice that heals and reconciles broken people

6. Magnani and Wray, *Beyond Prisons*, 5.

7. Brueggemann, *Prophetic Imagination*, 95.

8. Ibid., 99.

and relationships. But to require repentance before offering the hand of grace denies the radical power of grace to bring about repentance. It is the offering of a prayer of thanks that we are not like the sinners around us as we betray the Gospel by accepting that not all are within the reach of the hand of grace, and that forgiveness and reconciliation are simply too hard. After all, "[i]t [is] one thing to eat with outcasts, but it [is] far more radical to announce that the distinctions between insiders and outsiders [are] null and void."[9]

We have learned from our students that the distinctions between us are immaterial. One "traditional" Lipscomb student, having escaped an abusive marriage, saw this vividly as she heard her classmates relate their histories of physical and sexual abuse. The professors in the program see how alike we all are each time they sit to grade papers, and the inside students believe in our sameness each time they have a conversation about television, or art, or children, or music with an outside Lipscomb student who is allowed to leave the prison when the class is over. This is the prophetic ministry that Brueggemann describes. It is not "spectacular acts of social crusading or of abrasive measures of indignation." It is, rather, the "offering an alternative perception of reality and in letting people see their own history in the light of God's freedom and his will for justice."[10] The LIFE Program is not a social crusade, nor is it a prison ministry. The Program offers only questions and a few credit hours. Within the questions and the too-few hours is the beginning of a community that is unafraid of the injustice it faces because the community has named and found freedom in spite of it.

Conclusion and Call

When we examine the American criminal justice system, we must acknowledge our own culpability in a broken system. We must lament the injustices, but we must not lament them as the acts of another. They are our own acts. Realizing this calls the Christian, not to strategies, tactics, and ministry programs, but to presence. The Christian must be present within the system in order to confess his responsibility for it and to stand with those who suffer at its hands in a confessing community.

As I sat in the room with the young woman convicted in the Madison killings who had been unwillingly made a part of the Judicial Process

9. Ibid., 109.

10. Ibid., 116–17.

class, I was reminded of the LIFE Program's first class and how the inmates filed in, heads down. I was also reminded of how, during the course of the semester, as they mourned the system that held them in place, so much of their shame was released and their confidence and worth restored. I was reminded of how the lamenting of injustice had transformed those women; how, having someone else acknowledge the power that oppressed them, freed our students to move beyond that oppression.

I looked at the woman across from me and simply said, "I'm sorry." I wondered how long it had been since someone apologized to her. Her head immediately lifted, and we began to talk, about her case and her concerns about her appeal, about her work towards a G.E.D., and about the conversations of justice that her story had provoked in the LIFE Program. I encouraged her to continue working towards her G.E.D. so in two years, she could enter the LIFE Program.

I hope she understands that her story, her narrative, is not written in the words of a newspaper article, the lecture of a professor, or the boxes of a verdict form. I hope she understands that statistics of crime and incarceration may describe her, but they do not define her. I hope that she will find a place in our community as together we confess, "that the hurt is to be taken seriously, that the hurt is not to be accepted as normal," and in that I hope she will hear the faintest echo of Jesus outlandish proclamation of freedom.[11]

11. Ibid., 88–89.

16

The Confession and Correction of a Former Correctional Chaplain

MARLIN ELBON KILPATRICK

> "*Behold, I send you forth as sheep in the midst of wolves . . . And ye shall be hated of all men for my name's sake: but he that endureth to the end shall be saved . . . Whosoever therefore shall confess me before men, him will I confess also before my Father which is in heaven. But whosoever shall deny me before men, him will I also deny before my Father which is in heaven*" (Matthew 10:16, 22, 32–33).

THIS IS MY CONFESSION and correction of an evil that I participated in from April 28, 1996, to March 9, 2001. Through my employment as a prison chaplain, I supported a system of coercion and deadly violence called the Federal Bureau of Prisons. It was by my presence as a Christian minister endorsed by my then denomination—the Christian Church (Disciples of Christ)—that other Christians could believe prison employment is morally justifiable for a Christian.

I made an "about face" in two "quarter turns." The first turn began with the experiences of listening as a youth to my father and grandfather, both Church of Christ ministers, discuss *Civil Government* by David Lipscomb, founder of Lipscomb University and the *Gospel Advocate*, a mid-nineteenth century Christian periodical circulated among the membership of the Disciples of Christ and Churches of Christ. My grandfather, Lawrence Elbon Kilpatrick, adopted Lipscomb's view that a Christian could not participate in human governments because such systems violated the teachings of Jesus found in the Sermon on the Mount.

Lipscomb, who lived in Nashville, Tennessee, witnessed Northern Christians and Southern Christians take up weapons against each other in the 1864 Battle of Nashville during the American Civil War. He saw their warring against each other as contrary to Jesus' teaching to love enemies.

My father, Lawrence Marlin Kilpatrick, adopted the view of Foy Wallace, a mid-twentieth century editor of the *Gospel Advocate*. Wallace contended Christians should participate in human governments because government was the sword of God against the wicked. With the rise of fascism and communism, my grandfather later sided with my father, who preached about hell in the pulpit and would burn my butt and the back of my legs with a belt when I broke his rules at home.

It was the experiences of physical, emotional, and spiritual abuse by my father and witnessing his violence toward my mother that led me to research the relationship between violence and religion. After a quarter century of life experiences I turned to the writings of Rene Girard, who by this time was the Andrew DuPont Chair of French Literature and Civilization at Stanford University. This completed my first "quarter turn" from the broad way that leads to destruction toward the way that leads to eternal life.

Girard developed a theory about the creation of culture, positing that human behavior is mimetic. In other words, when an object is desired by more than one person, rivalries result, and with the multiplication of rivalries a mimetic crisis is generated. To avoid chaotic violence, a community, Girard theorized, displaces its internal violence upon a victim whose murder brings an experience of peace within the community.

Girard elaborated that laws designed to prevent mimetic crises gave rise to cultures, cultures that used sacrificial rituals to achieve peace. Law and order, for instance, are sought through violence directed against victims. First the violent sacrificial rituals were directed at humans, and later animal victims. Yet the violence in mimetic cultures is justified by myths that mute the cries of their victims. The violence the victim experiences is in service to gods/goddesses and society. Girard recognized that the Old and New Testaments of the Bible reveal the scapegoat as the social mechanism of sacred societies.

Providentially, I was able to attend informal colloquium meetings at Stanford while employed as a hospital chaplain at Doctors Medical Center in Modesto, California. I listened to Girard, Robert Hamerton-Kelly, Gil

Baillie, and others apply the theory of mimesis and scapegoating to studies in anthropology, economics, history, literature, psychology, sociology, theology, and other academic fields of research.

In regard to the criminal justice system, Vern Redekop, a Mennonite, applied Girard's theory of scapegoating in "Scapegoating, the Bible, and Criminal Justice: Interacting with Rene Girard." After reading his essay I desired to minister as a chaplain to the scapegoated criminals in prisons. My opportunity came upon my selection for the position of Supervisory Chaplain at the Federal Correctional Institution, Englewood, in Littleton, Colorado.

It was during the Introduction to Correctional Techniques course—the Federal Bureau of Prisons (BOP) three week orientation of new employees at the Federal Law Enforcement Training Center in Glynco, Georgia—that I experienced the separation of chaplains from firearms training and was instructed in the BOP policy on the use of force. The BOP understands that a chaplain cannot be effective in ministry if the inmate knows the chaplain is trained to kill him or her. However, the BOP expects the chaplain to support prison staff's use of violence when the institution deems it necessary.

During my BOP chaplaincy I grew to understand the relationship of the prisoner as the *pharmakos* (ancient common Greek word for "scapegoat") of society, and his/her purpose as *pharmakon* (ancient common Greek word for "drug, remedy, poison"). Society experiences the punishment of the criminal as a remedy for the poisonous mimetic rivalries that erode community boundaries and laws. Order is established by "peace" officers, who initiate communal violence upon society's scapegoat victim, the criminal, through its sacrificial ritual called a trial that separates the wicked from the righteous community.

I witnessed this ritualizing of communal violence as the chaplain assigned to Timothy McVeigh and Terry Nichols, both men housed in the Special Housing Unit at FCI Englewood during their federal trials in Denver for the 1995 Oklahoma City bombing. In the eyes of his fellow Americans, McVeigh's military service to his country was never questionable. But when the violence he learned to perpetrate skillfully against an evil foreign enemy during the Persian Gulf War—a war that transformed the mimetic crisis of an American recession economy into an American mythic television experience of watching Iraqi "devils" get bombed while listening to TV news anchors, generals, and evangelists collude in the muting of the Iraqi screams of horror with a chorus of accusations against their enemies—was used against the American people, the scapegoating mechanism transformed this victorious veteran into a vile criminal. No one critically examined the connection of the military's brainwashing of this country's children with society's use of violence against enemies.

But even with this revelation of systemic evil, I believed I could serve God as a correctional chaplain within the violent incarceration chambers of the violent "kingdoms of this world." I was about to take another quarter turn in my about face.

After my BOP transfer and promotion as Supervisory Chaplain at the Federal Medical Center, Lexington, Kentucky, in 1998, I met Rev. Emmanuel Charles McCarthy at Boston College during the 2000 Colloquium on Violence and Religion. I noted his commitment to truth during our several conversations, and welcomed his offer to send me audiotapes of his Ireland workshops on Gospel Nonviolence.

Soon, I received "Behold the Lamb" and "The Kingdom of the Lamb." I repeatedly listened to the tapes and was enamored by the historicity and simplicity of original Christianity's faithful following of the Lamb of God. I contacted Rev. McCarthy about further readings and other resources on Gospel Nonviolence. It was the videotape "Father George Zabelka: The Reluctant Prophet" that led me to examine my complicity with systemic violence. Fr. Zabelka was the Air Force chaplain who served the squadrons that in 1945 dropped the atomic bombs on the Japanese cities of Hiroshima and Nagasaki.

Inspired by Zebelka's conversion to the nonviolent Jesus of original Christianity, I quickly became convinced that Christian clergy in military and prison chaplaincy—and their respective ecclesiastical endorsing bodies—ordain as "justifiable" the homicidal and coercive violence of military and correctional institutions. In the name of protecting society, they proclaim as "good" what Jesus rejects as "evil." I began to think about the upcoming execution of Timothy McVeigh as an ultimate punishment for the capital crime of murder in a hierarchy of punishments for crimes that are named capital. If state killing is good, what other evils is the state calling good? The justification of the lesser evil is contained within the justification of the greater evil.

I thought about the crime of kidnapping, for example. I saw the police invasion of a home, taking a family member from his home, and requiring the family to pay a bond for his release as not different from a kidnapper who takes a family member from his home and requires the payment of ransom. Both police and kidnapper use violence—an evil that

Jesus commanded disciples to overcome through the goodness of nonviolent suffering love toward all in all circumstances.

Dennis Burkett, an inmate, brought my own complicity with state violence to my attention. After I preached a sermon contrasting the kingdoms of this world and the kingdom of God, he responded: "Chaplain Kilpatrick, I really enjoy your preaching, but you still wear the keys." Recognizing he was contrasting the prison keys that hung on my side with the keys of the kingdom of God, I knew I was serving in the wrong kingdom.

My presence as chaplain was little more than an ecclesiastical blessing of Christians in a correctional institution that rejects Jesus' teaching of nonviolent love through the use of coercion and deadly force. So, I resigned my position as Supervisory Chaplain at FMC Lexington, effective March 9, 2001. After looking into the mirror of God's Word, I completed that second quarter turn in my "about face" and began my march out of fear's prison on that ninth day of March into the freedom of Christ's nonviolent love of friends and enemies: "There is no fear in love. But perfect love drives out fear, because fear has to do with punishment. The man who fears is not made perfect in love" (1 John 4:18).

Prior to my resignation, I was interviewed and called by Bethany Christian Church (Disciples of Christ) in Jackson, Tennessee, to be their pastor. Also, prior to my departure from FMC Lexington, Rev. McCarthy came in October 2000 to the prison and held a Gospel Nonviolence workshop attended by over thirty inmates. As a result of the workshop, a weekly inmate discussion group was formed that listened to the "Behold the Lamb" audiotapes. After my departure, the group received the prison warden's approval to attend group sessions in place of the prison's Anger Management Program. I was informed by a released inmate, who attended the original discussion group, that the group was replicated in fourteen other federal prisons after group members transferred to other correctional facilities.

Outside the security fence of the United States Penitentiary in Terre Haute, Indiana, on June 11, 2001, I protested the execution of Timothy McVeigh. Soon afterwards, several insecure church leaders at Bethany Christian Church complained about the local *Jackson Sun's* front page story about my protest and asked that media stories of future protests not mention the congregation's name.

Three months later, the September 11 attacks occurred. I preached about the love of enemies and wrote a letter to the editor against the Army's recruitment of seminarians and clergy for their chaplaincy. With the

War in Afghanistan beginning on October 7, 2001, I was fired at the end of October by the church for my defense of the faith in the nonviolent love of Jesus for friends and enemies.

Again, after two months of pulpit supply at First Presbyterian Church USA in Selmer, Tennessee, the congregation leadership terminated my services after I preached about Jesus' command to love enemies immediately after the U.S. invasion of Iraq in March 2003. Rather than be led by the Good Shepherd's crook, the Christians of this church in Selmer seemed to be led by the big stick of the town's legendary sheriff, Buford Pusser, who was immortalized in the movie "Walking Tall" for his beatings of the county's crooks.

With anger, hatred, and malice, Christians do the works of the Devil, "a murderer from the beginning" (John 8:44). We must not have read the Scripture that says, "Anyone who does not love remains in death. Anyone who hates his brother is a murderer, and you know that no murderer has eternal life in him" (1 John 3:14b–15).

So ends this Christian's written confession and account of my correction since former employment as a correctional chaplain. May the reader come to know the Jesus of the Gospels as the nonviolent Christ who calls us to follow Him in the nonviolent love of friends "and the criminals with Him."

17

Freedom out of Bondage
The Baptism of Walter Pride

JEANNIE ALEXANDER

WALTER PRIDE COULD NOT have a more perfect name if God himself had named him. A diminutive man in stature, but large in spirit with a mischievous streak, at times crossing over into the criminal. Walter is an inmate at Riverbend Maximum Security Institution in Nashville where I serve as a volunteer chaplain. Shortly after meeting Walter he asked me to baptize him, and it was for that purpose that Ben Grady and I waited expectantly for Walter on an early spring day. As we waited I reflected on my surroundings. The chapel at Riverbend is small and nondescript, and the baptismal is a large square box with narrow stairs leading up into the pool. Baptism at Riverbend is a full immersion affair, which sits well with my Baptist upbringing. Over the pool hang three banners which proclaim "Peace," "Love," and "Hope." Such declarations at a maximum security prison may seem incongruous to an outsider, but for some of us who live, worship, work, love, and die at Riverbend, we know the presence of the Holy Ghost permeates every corner of this institution.

My thoughts were interrupted as my brother was led into the chapel, and my heart skipped a beat. Walter was chained in the manner known as full restraints. He wore a blue jean jacket over his white t-shirt and white state issued pants inscribed with "Tennessee Department of Corrections" down the sides. His ankles were chained together, and his wrists were chained together and locked with a metal box. Connecting his ankles and wrists was a long strong chain which then wrapped around his waist. He shuffled towards us and looked small, and awkward, and just a little afraid. But then Walter saw me and smiled a big beautiful smile that I have come to love, and in his face I saw his name, Pride.

But the chains did not come off. I asked one of the officers escorting Walter to remove the wrist restraints so that we could at least take his jacket off. The officer complied but told me in no uncertain terms that the wrist restraints would be locked back into place and the rest of the full body restraint would remain locked in place as well. I felt a small tremble inside. How, oh God, do I baptize a man in chains? I took a deep breath and asked "Walter Pride, are you prepared to die? Are you prepared to die to this world and be reborn in Christ through whom all things will be reconciled?" "Yes," he replied and the tears began to fall across his sunken cheeks, tracing the lines etched by years of pain and anger. And as I proclaimed the liberating truth to Walter that we no longer live under law but since the coming of faith we live under grace, the tears flowed unchecked from Walter's eyes and my own eyes began to blur as I read from St. Paul's letter to the Galatians: "For as many of you as were baptized into Christ have put on Christ. There is neither Jew nor Greek, there is neither slave nor free, there is neither male nor female; for you are all one in Christ Jesus." And oh Walter, there is neither prisoner nor guard.

We approached the baptismal and there was barely enough give in the chains for Walter to raise his foot to the first step, and so carefully and gently I, Ben, and the two escorting officers lifted my brother into the baptismal pool. As I lifted him I felt wrenching compassion and the humiliating pain of his chains. The sacrament of baptism is the shedding of the garments of the world to accept reconciliation and to engage fully in the symbolic ultimate act of freedom and defiance. Through submission we die and are reborn as full participants in the kingdom, fully clothed in the armor of God, which is love. It is this unending, all powerful, transformative love that marks us as new creatures fully alive for the first time.

And yet this most holy of acts, this moment of liberation, was occurring while Walter was physically bound in chains. As I cradled his head in one hand and covered his nose with the other, my tears mixed with Walter's tears and the water, and I was struck by how utterly vulnerable and dependent he was on me to bring him back up into life after guiding him back and fully submerging him into the water. At that moment, I understood the role of priest to also be that of midwife. As my arms lifted Walter back up into the air of this world, *ruah*, the breath of God filled and transformed us. And there were no chains as the drops of water on Walter's face and on the end of his nose hung suspended in a moment outside of time and space; and as the Comforter descended my eyes met Walter's eyes, but I do not think he saw me, heard me, or felt me. Walter was free. At that moment, I experienced and understood the reconciling, liberating, tearing-down-the-temple power and love of God. This is how Jesus can be tortured and executed, Stephen can be martyred, Paul can be imprisoned, and Walter can be chained, and yet they remain free. That one small baptism on an early spring day was an act of insurrection against the illusion of worldly power and force, and a rebirth for both Walter and me; in that one simple baptism I witnessed freedom born out of bondage. As for Walter, he remains an ambassador in chains.

18

On Fear and Following

Reading the Beatitudes in Prison

RICHARD BECK

AFTER MONTHS OF WAITING for my paperwork to clear with the Texas Department of Criminal Justice, I'm finally attending the training class that should be the final hurdle in getting my clearance to assist in the Monday night Bible study at the prison. During a break in the session the Prison chaplain turns to me and asks why I want to come out and help with the Bible study. I smile and say, "I guess it's a Matthew 25 thing. You know, visit the prisoners." The answer seems to satisfy. And it's the truth, though not totally accurate. What I'd like to say is that I'd been reading a lot of Will Campbell lately. I'm out here looking for God. As Brother Campbell observes, "It is not we Christians on the outside—safe with our money, respectability, and connections—who tell the prisoners the Scriptures. It is the prisoners who tell us."[1]

And it's the truth. In the first weeks of the study I'm consistently struck by how strange the Bible sounds on the inside of the prison. Familiar passages, rendered banal and dull from repeated hearings, come alive, infused with new potency and energy. New interpretations rise to the surface. And time and time again the radical call of Christian community comes crashing up against the harsh and dehumanizing realities of prison life.

Perhaps there is no better example of this than the Beatitudes.

1. Campbell, *Writings on Reconciliation and Resistance*, 19–20.

For my part of the study I've been working through the gospels, and a few weeks ago we reached the Sermon on the Mount. I anticipated facing a challenge with the Beatitudes. My fear was that our discussion of the Beatitudes would be reduced to platitudes and sentimentality. But I knew, if we really confronted the Beatitudes, we'd be talking about something closer to life and death.

I started by asking a question. Before we read the Beatitudes, I said, I want you to think of the "Beatitudes" that govern the world in which you live, the life behind these concrete walls and barbed wire. Who is blessed in here? Who gets ahead? Who comes out as "number one?" Fill in the sentence, "Blessed are the . . ."

All I get is silence.

This isn't surprising. Generally speaking, prisoners have to live two lives. One life is the face the prisoners present to the guards and other prison officials. This is a nice compliant face. And for the most part this is the face the prisoners show us, the chaplaincy volunteers. The other face is the face they show on the inside, among their fellow prisoners. This is the face they show to survive day to day. And as you might expect, these two lives don't go together very well.

Week to week, as you lead a Bible study with prisoners, you can come to believe that this is the most holy, devout, and saintly bunch of Christians you've ever seen. This is, incidentally, one of the joys of prison ministry, how nice, grateful, and cooperative the men are. You'll never have a better audience.

But I know that this is a bit of an illusion. To be sure, the men are grateful. The time they have with us is, perhaps, the only non-coercive, relaxed, and egalitarian interaction they have during the week. So they are truly grateful and happy to be a part of the Bible study. And many have become committed followers of Jesus.

Still, for the most part I know that the devoutness on display during the Bible study is hiding a great deal of darkness. And we don't talk much about that darkness. I'm not sure why. Perhaps it's too scary, or demoralizing, or depressing to talk about. Still, even though unspoken, the harsh and brutal realities of prison life are always in the background. And I wanted, for this class at least, to talk a bit about those realities before reading the Beatitudes.

So I wait. Then ask again, "Inside the prison, who is blessed?"

Finally, a man answers: "The violent."

I nod. Everyone nods.

"So that is Beatitude number one. 'Blessed are the violent.' What else?" The floodgates open.

The thieves.

The liars.

The manipulators.

The hypocrites.

The wealthy. (There is an underground black market economy.)

The strong.

The brutal.

The cruel.

On and on it goes. These are the "virtues" that are "blessed" and rewarded inside the prison. These are the "virtues" that help you get ahead, survive, and thrive. And I wonder, is it any different on the outside where I live?

After creating this list we turn to Matthew 5 and read aloud:

Blessed are the poor in spirit . . . Blessed are those who mourn . . . Blessed are the meek . . . Blessed are those who hunger and thirst for righteousness . . . Blessed are the merciful . . . Blessed are the pure in heart . . . Blessed are the peacemakers . . . Blessed are those who are persecuted because of righteousness . . . As we read these words the room becomes very somber. Very quiet. In light of what we'd just been talking about the radical call of Jesus shines like a white hot light. It burns. When you read the Beatitudes on the outside of a prison it all sounds so nice and happy. But read inside a prison you suddenly see just how crazy you have to be to be a follower of Jesus. You see how the Beatitudes are a matter of life and death.

I ask the men, can you be meek, poor in spirit, or merciful in prison? I'm wanting them to say yes. Because isn't that the right answer? But things have gotten too honest in the last few minutes, so there isn't a quick response. Just more silence. They are thinking about the darkness they face everyday, about what they have to do to survive. And they are trying to determine if the Beatitudes have any place in their world.

Finally opening up, they said no, you can't. You can't be meek or merciful in prison. You'd get hurt, taken advantage of, raped, killed. Your days would be numbered if you tried to live out the Beatitudes.

And it pains them to admit this. I can see that on their faces. They feel trapped by the call of Jesus and the Darwinian fight they must endure everyday.

And suddenly, I don't know what to say. For it has become very clear to me what it would mean for me to preach the Beatitudes to these men. I'd be asking them to give their lives to Jesus. I'd be asking them to die.

So I hesitate. For one simple reason. I don't know if *I'm* ready to make this commitment. And sensing hesitancy in my own heart, my own fear of Jesus, I can't ask these men to do something that I myself lack the courage to do.

None of this is verbalized. After the men describe how it would be suicidal to live out the Beatitudes inside the prison we start to talk about how, in small moments here and there, they can let their defenses down to show a little meekness, to show a little mercy. We start to figure out ways they can fit Jesus into the gaps and margins of prison life. Where their shell of violence and toughness can be dropped for a moment.

Basically, we talk about compromise. About how to accommodate Jesus to the brutal and ruling ethic of prison life. And on this night I can't ask for anything more. Who am I to push them for more mercy and meekness when I'm walking out of the prison gates in less than an hour? I don't yet understand what I am asking them to do. Nor am I confident about what I would do if I were in their shoes.

The sun was setting as I walked through the prison gates toward my car. I stood for a moment looking at that gorgeous West Texas sky. But my heart was troubled.

What was Jesus asking of these men, and in a prison of all places? How could these men find the kingdom of Heaven in the violent world in which they lived? And where would they find the courage to follow?

And I also knew, deep down, that the choices the prisoners faced were not so dissimilar from my own. Is a life lived on the outside according to the Beatitudes any less radical, crazy and suicidal?

This is what happens to you when you read the Bible in a prison. For the first time in my life I'd read the Beatitudes . . . and was afraid.

But perfect love casts out fear. That's what I believe. So all of us, the men and I, needed to revisit this discussion. Fear couldn't—shouldn't—have the final word. We found an opportunity when we reached John 13 and the story of Jesus washing the disciples' feet.

After reading the story I returned to our prior conversation. I asked, echoing our earlier conversation, "Can you serve people like Jesus did here in the prison?"

As before, there was general skepticism. The comment "kindness in prison is mistaken for weakness" was repeated. But I pushed a little harder this time and waited a little longer.

"How can you find moments to serve in this place?"

There was a long silence.

Then one man, Norberto (not his real name), raised his hand.

I was intrigued by what Norberto would say. He is a big, intimidating man. He could snap me like a twig. You can tell he commands a lot of respect from the other men.

I called on him and, given his intimidating presence, figured he'd stay with the "you can't do that kind of stuff in here" consensus.

He began, speaking softly.

"Well," he started with his heavy Hispanic accent, "I don't know if this is what you are looking for, but I help my celly [i.e., cell mate]."

"How?" I ask.

"Well, my celly isn't too bright. Something is wrong with his head. He was in an accident so he's not too smart." Guys who know Norberto's cellmate nod in agreement and elaborate. Apparently, he's borderline mentally handicapped and needs a lot of help taking care of himself and navigating prison life.

Norberto continues. "Well, when my celly first got put in with me I noticed that he never took off his shoes. He always left them on. So one day I finally asked him, 'Why don't you ever take off your shoes?' He wouldn't tell me. Finally I got him to tell me. He was embarrassed. He didn't know how to take care of his feet. So his toenails were all overgrown, smelly, and ugly looking. So I asked him to take off his shoes and socks. And his nails were awful. But he didn't know how to cut them.

"So I sat him down and had him put his feet in water. Then I took his foot in my lap and cut his toenails for him. I don't know what people would have thought if they walked by, his foot in my lap. And I would never have thought I'd be doing something like that."

There was now a deep silence in the room. The image before us was so unexpected. Here was this huge, intimidating man taking the time, almost like a mother, to gently wash the feet and trim the nails of his mentally handicapped cell mate.

Breaking the silence Norberto looked up at me and asked, "Is that an example of what you were talking about?"

"Yes," I said. "Yes, that is an example of what I was talking about."

PART 6

Reconciliation is Our Story

LEFT TO OUR OWN devices, we seem to prefer an intellectual world that is two-dimensional. We pit, for example, "good" against "evil." We fight, or we take flight. We calculate victories according to our ability to defeat enemies. We live, in other words, in a zero-sum game of our own creation. This 2-D vision is certainly evident in our practice of justice. "What could possibly be wrong with restoring a person in the name of justice?" Wendy Murphy rhetorically asks. "It's evil," she answers. Restorative justice is actually a "strange" and "criminal-loving" injustice, and a "truly warped philosophy that allows the most dangerous criminals to be set free early—or never locked up at all." If restorative justice "weren't so cruel to victims and dangerous to society, you'd have to laugh out loud," she concludes.[1] Here's that 2-D world again. Our support of victims is measured by the vengeance we exact on criminals. To demand anything less than maximum punishment of the offender is simply to violate the victim again.

Will Campbell's life and work, of course, has always been out of focus in a 2-D matrix. His frequent response to an "either-or" question, for example, has been a stoic "possibly" or lamentable "maybe." Recall his 1962 *Christian Century* essay on the Albany Movement, "Perhaps and Maybe,"

---

1. Murphy, *And Justice for Some*, 145–6.

which infuriated progressive Civil Rights activists who wanted buffoon-ish villains to lampoon and vanquish. Campbell held out hope for, and community with, even a racist police chief like Laurie Pritchett. Perhaps. Maybe.[2] Also recall his 1977 *Christianity and Crisis* essay on the last of the Scottsboro trials, "The Last Act of a Tragedy."[3] Here Will explained his inability and unwillingness to choose sides in the courtroom. In fact, with any tragedy "you really don't take sides with any satisfaction," Will confesses. Instead, once you appreciate the tragedy before you, "you quit blaming one side or the other. You quit choosing up sides, and you start to minister wherever the hurt is, as best you can."[4]

So, when there's violence in our world and one neighbor has harmed another, why do we presume only two options (i.e., privilege either the victim or the offender)? There *is* a third way. Instead of choosing sides, be an alternative to division-as-usual. Rather than another facile resolu-tion where one side wins by defeating the other, be betwixt and between. "Stand in the tragic gap." "Hold the tension between the *reality* of the mo-ment and the *possibility* that something better might emerge," to employ the counsel of Parker Palmer.[5]

Here's an authentic nonviolent justice that restores. Not by "good" defeating "evil," but by holding the ground between all the alienated, pre-cisely at the most difficult, contested, divisive moment. In other words, refuse to label, categorize, and scapegoat. Reject the zero-sum game. Live the reconciliation that social convention refuses to acknowledge, but we know has already occurred. The Black Nationalists and the Klan may live as enemies, for example, but our place is with both—and for the tri-umph of neither. As Will has illustrated, our place is in that tragic gap. Stand forgivingly in that gap—come what may—as an incarnation of our reconciliation.

Harmon Wray found his life's vocation in that tragic gap.[6] Cyntoia Brown and Preston Shipp highlight the difficulty and promise of stand-ing together in that gap. Risk-averse institutions will shun that space, but communities who see the value of every sister and brother can locate themselves nowhere else.

2. Campbell, "Perhaps and Maybe," 1133.
3. Ibid., "Last Act in a Tragedy," 189–91.
4. Campbell and Goode, *Crashing the Idols*, 30.
5. Palmer, *A Hidden Wholeness*, 174–7.
6. Dark, *The Sacredness of Questioning Everything*, 245–47.

What does the reader need to know? Community must be incarnated, because an "imagined community," as Lee Griffith counsels, "is no community at all."[7] We must find the wherewithal simply to see, hear, and be with the exiled, which will look differently for discrete collections of differently gifted individuals.

In his 1972 *Katallagete* piece, "Vocation as Grace," Will tells of an unnamed friend who described Campbell's professional career as "acrobatics." "At first I was amused by his choice of words to describe my ecclesiastical meanderings. At least I thought I was amused, tried to act amused," he confessed. "But I kept going back to read that letter over and over. It was a long letter and I began to notice that I always paused when I reached that sentence about my acrobatics." Eventually Will's reaction evolved from amusement to offense. "Acrobatics" stuck in his craw as a demeaning affront, a term questioning his integrity and probity. Nevertheless, as Will surveyed his resume of short-term employment (e.g., from a steeple, to a university, and parachurch organizations), he came to the conclusion that his friend's assessment may be right. "I am an acrobat. Praise the Lord!"

In his life Will has discovered how institutions (e.g., the University of Mississippi and the National Council of Churches), by their nature, have clear mission statements with precise job descriptions for employees. By contrast, communities are irregular, ad hoc, and unscripted. Instead of institutional controls, communities are full of risk and grace. "If you want to find yourself, then lose yourself and quit all the navel gazing," Will concedes. "All I know to do [is to] just jump and hop and summersault around, hoping occasionally to be in the right place at the right time." Thus Will concludes:

> Well, thank you, brother, for calling me an acrobat. It was not such an insult after all. For I have seen them high on that wire, standing on tiptoes, jumping, flipping, turning, leaning this way and that, never trusting their own skills and strength alone to catch them for there is always the team around. And as soon as that evening's performance is over they are always ready to move on to the next town. It is an elusive thing for them too, an elusive dream and scheme, always somewhere else, always beckoning them on, only to find that it isn't at the next performance either, never becoming a reality, always a driving, pushing, haunting upper that keeps them jumping, walking on tippytoes,

7. Griffith, *God is Subversive*, 97.

swinging and summersaulting high over the crowd at Municipal Auditorium—God's world.[8]

We conclude this collection, therefore, neither with an impassioned, rousing call to action, nor some proscribed legislative blueprint for remedying the problem of prisons once and for all. Instead of outlining what to do, we offer a call to be. Be the reconciled community. Be a community of confession rather than control, of presence rather than policies. Be a community that cares to see our sisters—like Felicia—who are exiled by the principalities and powers, and a community that listens to what she has to teach us. As Janet Wolf counsels, such Campbell-inspired communities will run afoul of conventional norms and often flout institutional protocol, but they may just be the most beautiful, Beloved Community we'll experience.

Richard C. Goode

8. Campbell, "Vocation as Grace," 80–86.

19

Punitive Justice vs. Restorative Justice

A Meditation on the Spirit of Punishment and the Spirit of Healing[1]

HARMON WRAY

I WOULD LIKE TO ask you to consider with me two images. The first image is that of The Executioner, or The Incarcerator. Surely, as the last Western democracy still using the death penalty, and as the nation with seven percent of the world's population and twenty-five percent of the world's prisoners, we should be able with no trouble to envision this image. It is our own nation, our own people, our own criminal justice system. This image is what we should see when we look into the mirror.

The second image is that of the Healer. In invoking this image, I'm not talking about an image of a physician. Is it "corrections" I am talking about? Whenever I hear this term, especially as it relates to the dominant, incarceration part of the field, I always wonder, precisely what—or who—it is that we, those who say we work in corrections, are actually correcting. So no, that's not it, either.

Perhaps the image of the Healer brings to some minds the idea of rehabilitation. But that's not what I have in mind, either. I do not believe that the dichotomy of retribution—represented by the Executioner/

---

1. This essay is a revised version of an address that Harmon Wray delivered on August 15, 2001, to the Interfaith Prayer Breakfast organized by the American Correctional Chaplains Association at the American Correctional Association's conference in Philadelphia. It was published in the November/December 2001 issue of the *Offender Programs Report*, and is used here by permission.

Incarcerator image—and rehabilitation really exhausts the possibilities. These concepts don't even get at what I think the real issues are. So I want to hold off for a little while identifying what I mean by the Healer image.

The Real Issues I Have in Mind

The Issue of Prevention

Under the general principle that an ounce of prevention is worth a pound of cure, what we do or don't do to prevent crime from occurring in the first place is more important than what we do or don't do to react to it after it has taken place. This principle is also the measure by which we should judge our after-the-fact efforts. This is, basically, a call for a public health approach to crime. But our blind, retributive reaction to crime, based on the questionable theory that the way you get people to change is to scare the hell out of them—whether by what you do to them or by what you do to others (the logic of "deterrence")—is having a counter-deterrent effect. It's making criminals worse more than it is making them better.

Meanwhile, we are skinning so many of our limited public resources into this reaction that we are depriving truly crime-preventative measures—education, low-cost housing, job training, drug and alcohol treatment, early childhood family intervention, etc.—of the funding they need to be effective for large numbers. And the way we think about and practice rehabilitation—as programs for prisoners—exhibits a failure to understand that the retributive prison context and its overwhelming focus on security and punishment limit the effectiveness and the reach of such programs so much that they have little chance of success within such an oppressive environment.

Issue of the Victims

Both retribution and rehabilitation are focused on the offender, not on the victim. We often say that we are punishing perpetrators "for the victims," but the primary effect on most victims is to raise their taxes in order to build and operate more prisons. They still don't get their lost property back, or their damaged property fixed, or their insurance deductable returned, or their medical and therapy bills paid, nor do they get their peace of mind returned to them, much less enjoy the "closure" that we promise them.

We say we are giving them what they want when we severely punish their victimizers, but what we are often doing is merely exploiting their vulnerability and anger to serve many prosecutors' and judges' political agendas. And we do it in a way that ensures that there will be many future victims of the damaged and embittered men, women, and children that we will release back into the community after taking a few pounds of flesh out of their hides. And on those rare occasions when we do attempt "rehabilitation" with the offenders, we seldom include a primary, restorative focus on helping them to understand what they actually did to their victims and what they should do to make it right.

Value of Incapacitation

The third issue that the retribution/rehabilitation polarity fails to illuminate is the very real value of incapacitation as a function of intelligent sentencing. Retribution is so eager to make the offender's life miserable, and rehabilitation is so focused on making him/her better, that each—taken alone—fails to address the very real question from the serious offender.

This is where the value of the fourth function of penal sanctions (along with retribution, deterrence, and rehabilitation)—rendering him/her incapable of continuing predatory activity—becomes clear. Sometimes this can only be done by short- or long-term (for the truly dangerous) incarceration, during which we should not forgo rehabilitative and restorative efforts. But often it can be done less expensively, and with far less long-term damage, through the use of such methods as electronic monitoring and intensive probation/parole.

Ah, if only this whole realm of criminal justice policy were so rational that common sense arguments and cost-effectiveness analysis could carry the day. But we all know that both policy and practice in this field are so eaten up with passion, politics, money, and theology that to really understand it and to have a chance at changing it, we must sometimes operate on a whole different level from that of reason, of utilitarian and fiscal analysis, and of policy critique.

Helpful Metaphors

To lead us into this perhaps deeper level of analysis, I ask you to consider with me five or six metaphors to help us understand what's really going on in this whole arena of crime and our criminal justice system.

Toxic Waste Dump

First, I have found it helpful to look at our prison system as the human equivalent of a toxic waste dump. Many of our corporations seek to put their dangerous wastes out of sight and out of mind by dumping them in somewhat isolated spots where no one, except perhaps small groups of poor people, live. Similarly, our criminal justice system and private, for-profit prison corporations often seek to isolate what many think of as human waste in prisons usually built in rural communities having economic difficulties, promoting these prisons as economic development. In both cases, there seems to be the assumption that if it's over there, it won't bother us over here.

But it's not so easy to get rid of the problems we create. In both cases, the toxicity seeps into our environment and—like bad karma—comes back to us. In the case of prisons, it can be seen locally, where the prisons are, in a higher incidence of job stress, domestic violence, divorce, alcoholism, drug abuse, and other problems in the lives of "correctional" officers. But it also seeps into the larger community, since most of those we incarcerate are eventually released to come back into our communities, often more damaged, bitter, hopeless, and sophisticated in their criminal skills than when they entered. As a society, we usually get what we deserve, and there is another example. We can run, but we can't hide. Unfortunately, there is no EPA to clean up our human toxic waste dumps.

Medieval Morality Play

A second metaphor that I believe illumines at least most visible manifestations of our criminal justice system is that of a medieval morality play. When we look at most of the big "show trials"—Rodney King, O. J. Simpson, the Menendez brothers, Tonya Harding/Nancy Kerrigan, William Kennedy Smith, Mike Tyson, the Bobbitts, the Unabomber, and Timothy McVeigh—there is a strong flavor of the theatrical, the dramatic, in which the key players are larger than life, symbolically representing whole classes of people and social forces beyond their own persons.

Most of these trials seem to represent our collective effort to somehow dramatize and process major social conflicts between groups within our society—the races, social classes, the sexes, religious groups, and groups holding conflicting political ideologies. It's as if our society is looking to our criminal justice system to resolve once and for all these ongoing battles that make our lives so difficult, and that the primary institutions of our society—family, faith community, workplace, health care, school system—have failed to address effectively. But the criminal justice system only replicates and heightens these conflicts, so they are never really resolved. And what is writ large in these high profile cases is played out on the micro level every day in courtrooms throughout our nation, in which lawyers, judges, and occasionally juries re-enact these same social conflicts and struggles, supposedly on behalf of mostly anonymous victims, defendants, and families, in plea bargains and courtroom battles that often change forever the lives of defendants and victims and both their families.

Prison Industrial Complex

The third metaphor has several twists. One is the concept of the Prison Industrial Complex that is analogous to the Military Industrial Complex, a notion that surfaced during the Cold War and was identified by President Dwight Eisenhower in his 1961 farewell address. Basically, the idea is there are now so many politically powerful, corporate economic interests, which profit from incarceration, that they drive and often determine criminal justice practice. In other words, they use their political clout to pursue their expansionist economic goals by promoting pro-incarceration policies. Another part of this concept is the revolving door between government criminal justice executive jobs and corporate prison industry jobs, much like that between the Pentagon jobs and jobs with military contractors.

Another facet of this military/incarceration analogy is the degree to which both our Cold War and post-Cold War military policy and our retributive justice system rely on an assumption of the logic of deterrence to exercise control over others. We seem to think that might makes right, and that the threat and exercise of violent power will intimidate others, whether globally or domestically, into playing the game according to our rules and interests ("we" being the dominant forces in the economy and the government). Our continuing commitment to executions and to the greatest use of incarceration the world has ever known suggests we may be replicating our Cold War policy of violence and arms buildup even to the point of mutually assured destruction.

Yet a third twist on this military/prison metaphor is more psychological in nature. Most social groups seem to have a need for an enemy or enemies. It seems to me that during the Cold War we had that enemy embodied in what President Ronald Reagan called "the evil empire." Clearly, the Soviet Union and "Red" China, primarily, constituted that enemy for a half-century. Now that we don't have the Communists to kick around any more, except for a few marginal countries like Cuba and North Korea, we have had to find some new enemies.

Globally, our primary enemies have been categorized as "terrorists," and personified primarily as Middle Eastern. Domestically, we seem to have identified several categories of persons who, at different times and in different ways, serve us quite well as enemies—the poor, people of color, children, immigrants, and criminals. When we can identify persons who exemplify several of these characteristics, as many do, all the better. Since, in our view, they are totally responsible for their poverty, their political powerlessness, and all their negative behavior, we feel totally justified in punishing them and otherwise pushing them around.

The mixture of fear, hatred, guilt, and self-righteousness the dominant groups in our society feel toward these groups means the latter always get the short end of the stick. If we doubt the truth of this, especially in the case of children, we should simply look at the low wages we pay child care workers, the extent to which we are eviscerating our juvenile justice system by transferring more and more cases over to adult court and adult prisons, and the fact that children are the age group in our society with the highest percentage living in poverty—through absolutely no fault of their own—a reality that our vaunted "welfare reform" is probably making worse.

The Scapegoats

I am not saying that criminals, for instance, do not often play very well into this collective psychological need that we have for an enemy by doing some very bad things. But as a society we are highly selective in how we punish criminals. This is where the fourth metaphor, that of the Scapegoat, comes in. Contrary to popular assumption, scapegoats are typically not innocent victims. Usually they have transgressed social boundaries and mores. But so do most of us, in one way or another.

In the realm of crime, the numbers of lives taken, injuries and illness suffered, and property lost or damaged due to crime in the suites committed by corporate criminals—who are seldom prosecuted and almost never incarcerated—are staggering, much higher than the corresponding numbers due to crimes in the streets. People commit the sorts of crimes for which they have access to the tools, but we choose to punish only those committed by the poor with the tools available to the poor.

Similarly, the percentages of illegal drug users and sellers who are people of color correlate roughly with their percentage of the population, yet at every stage—arrest, conviction, and incarceration—our criminal justice system punishes those who are not white at ever-increasingly disproportionate levels. At the height of apartheid, when South Africa was considered the most racist society on earth, a black man in his twenties was eight times as likely to be locked up in the USA than he was in South Africa.

What underlies this highly selective punitiveness? I believe that we all have a dark and mean side, which most of us do not want to face, so we engage in various forms of denial and rationalization about it. Scapegoating involves displacing and projecting this dark side onto others; conveniently, there is always an Other handy for assuming this function. So, if we project our own fantasies of revenge, seduction, rape, mayhem, and violence onto Ted Bundy or Timothy McVeigh, the ritual act of sacrifice of their lives becomes cathartic for us as a collective, relieving us by conveniently taking from us our deep-down suspicion that we, too, given certain circumstances, are capable of similarly horrifying acts.

Addictions to Crime and Punishment

Finally, I want to turn to a fifth and sixth metaphor that I hope can shed some light, not only upon our compulsion to punish, but also upon crime itself. You see, I do not follow the conventional wisdom of society in believing that crime is the problem and punishment is the solution. I see crime and punishment more as two sides of the same coin, and both as symptoms of deeper, more profound problems. It was a revelation to me when I realized that the root word for "punishment," and for other words like "penitentiary," "penance," and "penal," is "pain," and so punishment is, basically, the intentional infliction of pain upon human beings by human beings. But what is crime? At least for those crimes that have victims, isn't it pretty much the same thing, and isn't that why we don't like it and try to discourage it?

So these two sets of metaphors—numbers five and six—are intended to help us get at the roots of both crime and punishment. Number five is crime and punishment as an addiction, whether individually or socially. If the language of addiction expresses certain psychological dynamics of both crime and punishment, then, similarly, the biblical language of idolatry expresses in theological terms the mixture of compulsion and willfulness, which seems to characterize both crime and punishment in our world.

I believe there are basically three addictions/idolatries that lay at the root of both crime and punishment in our society, and this goes for crimes committed by both the rich and the poor, and for punitive policies promulgated by the rich and powerful, and carried and supported by the poor. First, there is the addiction to money and "stuff." Rich or poor, outraged middle-class burglary victim or criminal, individual or private prison corporation—we want to keep what we have and we want to get more. No matter how much or how little we have, there is never enough for us, and no matter how big or how small we are on the scale of things, we want to grow larger. Biblically speaking, we worship the god Mammon (Property). Many of us will do whatever is necessary to keep what we have and to get more, even take human life, legally or illegally.

A second addiction is the addiction to violence, or to magical, "quick fix," thinking and coercive action. Theologically, it is often expressed in the Old Testament, or Hebrew Scriptures, as the reliance upon, trust in, chariots and other war making equipment. Or we might speak of the idolatry of worshipping Mars, the Roman god of violence. Again, it goes both ways, with punishment as well as with crime. Just as armed robbery, assault, rape, kidnapping, and murder are violent crimes, locking someone in a cage, as well as executing someone, is a violent and coercive punishment. In a similar vein, restorative justice practitioner Howard Zehr makes the argument that both crime and punishment are profoundly disrespectful of their targets.

The junkie/robber with an itchy trigger finger, the cold hit man, the domineering spouse- and child-abuser, the knowing but uncaring manufacturer of dangerous consumer products—all are violent criminals. Likewise, the brutal and racist cop, the politically ambitious pro-death penalty prosecutor, the politically cowardly governor refusing clemency or legislator voting for still more prisons, the private prison company executive with beds to fill—all are violent punishers. And in this democratic republic, to the extent that we let it happen, so are we all.

The last addiction, akin to the first two, is what we might call the addiction to power, or control over others. The biblical expression of this is the idolatry of Caesar, as read in Jesus' response to a question intended to trip him up, "Render unto God that which is God's, and unto Caesar that which is Caesar's." In our uniquely incarcerative society and our distinctively death-dealing society, power is not only an aphrodisiac, but also, like money, something of which there is never enough. Our addiction to it is also at the root of street crime, committed by those who have too little power, and corporate crime, committed by those who have too much of it.

On the crime side, the need for control over others, our victims or competitors, and for control over perceived or feared threats to us (the addiction to "security") underlies much criminal activity. On the punishment side, the excessive exercise of ultimate (capital punishment) and penultimate (lifetime imprisonment) power by the state over its citizens raises—at least for Christians—the question that if absolute power over human life, death, and liberty are placed in the hands of Caesar (the state), with so little effective opportunity for redress, precisely what is it that is left to God?

If we believe in the twelve-step recovery folks and those who participate in communities of faith following various religious traditions, both addiction and idolatry are spiritual issues. If I am right, crime and punishment are issues in which the language of addiction and idolatry is appropriate and illuminating. This means that, at least for some folks, crime and punishment are spiritual issues as well as issues of law, psychology, sociology, criminology, economics, and penology. So it may not be too outlandish to talk in terms of the spirit of criminal and penal greed, the spirit of criminal and punitive violence, and the spirit of exercising power over others present in crime and punishment.

Spirit of Revenge

I want to turn now to a closely related issue: the spirit of revenge. In practice and in effect, I see no fundamental difference between punishment, retribution, retaliation, and revenge. There may be some fine distinctions concerning how and by whom it is carried out, but in reality, in our society, it is beside the point whether the aggrieved party or the state, acting on behalf of the aggrieved party, carries it out. As is whether the act of revenge is performed with the aid of a rope, a gun, gas, electricity, a guillotine, a cross, poison, or a lifetime sentence to a prison cell. It is the spirit that I am interested in, and the spirit of revenge is the same, whatever the precise manner in which, and the chosen implements by which, that spirit is expressed.

It also makes little difference whether revenge is executed by an individual or a government, whether it is done in the heat of passion or in cold blood, and whether it is done legally, constitutionally, and with "due process," or against the law and without the pretense of due process. We are at such a basic, primitive level here, that what makes the most sense is to say, simply, "Revenge is revenge, period." It is the spirit of it that is important, for our purposes.

Proponents of state killing often argue that the death penalty is not about revenge, but is rather a matter of providing "closure" to the families of murder victims. And murder victims' families sometimes argue something along the lines of: "As a Christian, I forgive the person who murdered my loved one, but the law calls for the death penalty, and the law must be carried out." While such views are natural and understandable, both of these responses are efforts to have it both ways, to disguise revenge as something else. Sometimes, the person is disguising it to herself or himself. Sometimes, it's just an effort to short-circuit the dialogue by playing the victim card or the law card, each of which begs fundamental questions.

There are other problems with the death penalty as well; for instance, we sometimes execute the wrong people. And then there is the matter of racism in determining who gets the death penalty, and what color does the person you killed need to be if you want a better chance of not getting it, and so on. And what is true of the race of the victim and the perpetrator is also true of social class. Truly, those without the capital get the punishment. In terms of the "do it for the victims' families" argument, there are at least two problems. First, a number of victims' family members do not want it. Second, it tends to distort and drag out the natural grief and healing process through which victims' family members need to go.

But perhaps the worst thing about the spirit of revenge, as it is embodied in our retributive criminal justice system and personified in our image of the Executioner and the Incarcerator, is that it appeals to the worst part of our human nature—the bitter, vindictive part of us all that wants others to suffer, because they have made us suffer. If the logic of deterrence makes the mistake of assuming a truncated view of human nature whereby the way one gets people to change their behavior is to terrorize them, the spirit of revenge doesn't even care about changing people. It just wants a pound of flesh, or more.

It has often been said that Timothy McVeigh is the "poster boy for the death penalty." In truth, there is no better case for letting us see the moral bankruptcy of the spirit of revenge that is behind the death penalty. As has been pointed out by Bud Welch, father of a young woman killed in the Oklahoma City bombing, what the execution of Timothy McVeigh was about is revenge. And the reason his daughter and the other 167 people died in the bombing is the same: revenge. McVeigh expressed his revenge against the U.S. government for Ruby Ridge and Waco. We expressed ours against him in Terre Haute. Might it not be time to question the basic validity of the spirit of revenge? It is a never-ending descending spiral, digging us all deeper and deeper into the hole. As Gandhi put it, an eye for an eye and a tooth for a tooth will eventually just leave the whole world blind and toothless.

The Work of Healers

It is time to turn away from the image of the Executioner and the Incarcerator. It is time to return to the image of the Healer. This image is one that insists that the primary goal of our social response to crime should be neither retribution, deterrence, incapacitation, nor rehabilitation, but restoration and healing. Incapacitation and rehabilitation have their place, but healing should be foremost. The Healer focuses not on what laws were broken, but on what harm was done. Healing justice asks not so much whom we can blame for the lawbreaking, but what do the victims need for healing. And instead of asking how we can best punish the blameworthy one, the Healer asks who is accountable for meeting the needs of the ones who have been harmed.

The image of the Healer stands for the perspective and the movement that is variously known as community justice, transformative justice, and—most often—restorative justice. For those who walk in the Judeo-Christian tradition, restorative justice is rooted in the biblical witness of Jubilee justice (Leviticus 25), which theologian Walter Brueggemann has summarized like this: "Justice is to sort out what belongs to whom, and to return it to them." It is also biblically rooted in the work of the Hebrew prophets, the Hebrew concept of shalom (peace with justice, and right relationships), and—for Christians—Jesus' Sermon on the Mount (Matthew 5–7). Restorative justice is also based on communal processes used by a variety of aboriginal groups in New Zealand, Africa, and North America for addressing conflicts and disputes within their villages.

Restorative justice takes victims' needs and rights seriously, yet insists victims' rights not be reduced to a right to have the state take revenge on behalf of victims. Instead, it empowers victims, offenders, and the local community—the primary stakeholders in any crime or other conflict—to engage in face-to-face dialogue and make decisions about what must be done to "make it right." It redefines crime from breaking a law to actually harming human beings, redefines the victims of a crime from the state to the actual person harmed, and redefines accountability from passively taking one's punishment to actively taking responsibility for what one has done and for doing what one can to make amends. It replaces the notion of externally imposed punishment with the concept of agreed upon restitution and internalized self-discipline.

So, which image will it be that represents our criminal justice system in this country? Will it continue to be the Executioner/Incarcerator? Or will we follow the lead of most of the rest of the world, and of our own scriptures, and explore what we might learn from the values, practices, and policies symbolized by the image of the Healer and embodied in the restorative justice perspective?

On July 28, 2007, friends of Harmon Wray gathered to celebrate his life's work on behalf of the "least ones." To conclude the service, Rev. Janet Wolf offered a powerful benediction. It is fitting here to include some of her petition.

> And now, O God, I pray that you would not only comfort us, but that you would also disturb us and anoint us with your Spirit. Send us back into the world to live with the same kind of vision and holy boldness that we celebrate in Harmon. Allow his life and witness to challenge and change us so that we, too, might invest everything in out-loud loving, so that we too might agitate and advocate, organize and strategize, reconcile and redeem, companion and comfort, trouble and transform until all the chains are broken, all the prison doors opened and your justice flows down like a mighty river.

20

"Misjudging"

Part One
CYNTOIA BROWN

WHEN I LEARNED WHO my first professor in the LIFE Program would be, I thought I knew exactly who I would be dealing with. I'd done my research on the man by speaking with the group of women who studied under him several semesters before. He used to be a prosecutor, taught Judicial Process, and was named "Preston Shipp." I expected a disconnected, pompous, set-in-his-ways, old guy who was only teaching to push his agenda on "irreparable criminals." I was nervous. I thought I knew who he was before he even strolled into the classroom that first evening. But the wrong person began addressing the class.

While I was waiting for Uncle Sam to arrive, some young guy had taken over. His teacher's aide maybe? He started talking to us about the course, witty remarks emerging here and there. I was so taken by the way he addressed us—as friends, as peers, as members of his community—that it didn't register that he'd referred to himself as "Preston." Talk about misjudging someone.

Mistake in judgment was a recurring theme that semester. Preston was such an amazing professor—whatever parallel universe he came from truly gifted him. Each Wednesday night I went to class it seemed like he shrunk by a thousand times and crawled around inside our minds. There he would pick up pieces of us and examine them: testing thoroughly every belief, idea, and prejudice—leaving them strengthened, dissolved, or replaced.

I never knew a prosecutor like him. Perhaps he was not meant to be one. After all, he'd had a change of heart and a change of employment after he began teaching out here. Whatever the case, I was never able to see him in that light. When I envisioned a prosecutor I always went back to my personal experience with the one involved in my case.

At sixteen years old, I had boarded a speeding train headed to the pit of death and destruction. By some turn of fate, I exited the train at the Juvenile Justice Center. Charged with a major crime, I faced life in prison. I was supposed to have an open road to endless possibilities, but now I was left standing on a road where the bridge had given out, cut off from a meaningful future.

My situation drew the support of a few people, and I was most grateful for it. I was at the lowest point in my life and the people who believed in me were the people who enabled me to believe in myself. But there was one person who claimed I was beyond redemption, that my young, still developing, and very impressionable mind was unable to be rehabilitated—although he himself was a father of children. That prosecutor crusaded to have my life ended abruptly because of the mistake I made.

I'd thought many days and nights about the duty of a prosecutor— albeit with a scornful bias. Ideally, (as I like to think) I believed a juvenile court prosecutor should seek to reposition misguided youth onto a more promising path—to issue tickets of transfer from the train of perdition to the train of promise. The sad reality I witnessed was that the prosecutor was out for blood and intent on sealing off the path to the "land of second chance."

The prosecutor spoke of me at hearings as if he searched every chasm of my heart and mind, and found no good, or seed of good whatsoever, therein. In truth, he couldn't even tell you whether my oral hygiene was up to par, because he never even sat down to speak to me outside of the adversarial proceedings. The prosecutor did not know me, but still set his heart on labeling me a vile and unconscionable creature. And I did the same to him, and all other prosecutors. A classic case of how preconceived notions are formed. Behind our enmity for each other was a sea of ignorance.

I couldn't fit Preston into that box. As a matter of fact, his mental excavations did their best work on my demonization of prosecutors. Preston knew me. He was a brother, an ally, a zealous believer in the salvation of lost souls. He was my friend.

As the class progressed, my heart opened to viewing the prosecutor as a man instead of a demon. I came to see a man concerned with righting wrongs and keeping society safe. A man of intentions so grand they at times worked to their own detriment. In the course of zealously protecting one party, he over time created a demon of the other. His religion urging him to conquer the other on the battlefield of Moral Highground—not swayed by "tricks" of the demon to seem human: *For the devil is a liar.* He removes from the defendant any trace of civility, of humanity—and he proceeds with his case in such a manner. But can he be faulted? However erroneous in his convictions, with an original intent so noble, how could I harbor anger for his tunnel vision?

I couldn't. Because if I failed to forgive the inadequacies of the man who chose to be a prosecutor, then how could I, without hypocrisy, expect him to see my own faults as attributable to my humanness? My loathing for him was without merit, and as the semester went on it crumbled.

As is commonly known, one can relapse back into bad habits. It is the same with prejudice, even after ignorance has dissipated. For a second, I fell weak to it. Not towards the prosecutor in my case though—toward the man who helped me do a 180 degree turn on my heart and mind.

It was a Wednesday night, after class ended. Preston was standing in the prison hallway among everyone else saying their goodbyes, see you next weeks, and other exchanges. I was smiling when I came out of the classroom—another great night of college for a girl in prison for life. So, I didn't understand Preston's concerned expression at seeing me, or why he would ask whether I was okay. I paused to look at him curiously and assure him that I was fine, and then resumed my smiles and exchanges as I floated down the hallway waving goodbye to everyone.

I fell to earth with a hard thud the next day as I realized the reason for his concern. I was called to the prison's visitation gallery where legal mail was always picked up. I had been awaiting the court's decision on my appeal from the conviction in the trial court. I had it all planned out, I would get a good plea bargain, continue going to college while I was in here, and finish when I got out. I would go to law school. I would be the advocate for youth who so deserved a second chance. I'd help reform the justice system. I'd change lives the way mine had been changed. I'd have my second chance because the God above who sees my heart and the transformation therein would will it so.

All these thoughts pumped me up so high into the clouds as I signed to receive my mail. I'd rehearsed this moment a thousand times in my head while lying on my cell bunk. I'd scream and jump for joy—the mail lady would share my happiness and praise God with me. Everyone on the sidewalk would know as I passed them in route back to my unit—they too would praise God with me. They'd be inspired; faith renewed that one day their day would come too.

The world stopped around me as my eyes took in the second line. All I could hear was the blood rushing heavily in my ears. I could barely see through the cloud of tears that suddenly sprang up.

> *"I am sorry to say that we did not prevail*
> *with the Court on any of our appeal issues."*

My lawyer said. Certainly I must have continued to breathe, lest my heart have stopped—but I gave no conscious effort. Were I not breathing today, I wouldn't hesitate to tell you that I died in that moment.

It was only my dreams that suffered, though.

I was too distraught to carefully read the decision that day—fortyfour pages of reasons why I should be denied a second chance. All I could think of was the Lipscomb function scheduled that night, a reading of *Chiaroscuro*, the LIFE Program's literary magazine. I was anxious to see Preston. I knew he could help me—he'd become to me a superman of sorts. He wasn't God, though. God is ever present, and that night Preston wasn't there.

The next day, a Friday, I sat down to read the opinion. Everything became clear: the concern of Preston on Wednesday night, my question of how he knew the decision before I did. On the second page of the decision, where the parties of the case were named: *Preston Shipp, Assistant Attorney General*. His name was right in line with the other prosecutor he helped me to forgive. He was on their team. He was against me. If I ever knew confusion, it overcame me then.

Betrayal was the instant feeling. Then disbelief. And guilt. I felt guilty for feeling this way toward the man who'd become my friend. I wrestled with the common sense that it made no sense to feel betrayed by him—the date he prosecuted my appeal was before I had ever met him. It must have been one of the last cases he worked while still a prosecutor. Still, I had difficulty reconciling Preston my friend, and Preston my adversary. I couldn't understand how this man who would no doubt love to see me excel outside of prison, who saw for himself how I was not beyond salvation, who I *trusted*, could ever stand against me while I fought for a second chance. His level of articulation, of intelligence, his excellent reasoning when arguing his position, I always saw him as a stellar debater. To know those skills were put to use to sway the court to deny my appeal, crushed my soul.

I didn't know whether I would go back to class that Wednesday or not. I wondered if I would be my usual outspoken self and turn my weekly rant of injustice towards him and show the entire class the fraud he was. My anger sought to draw a line—"us," the class, crusaders against injustice, advocates for second chances and forgiveness, vs. "him," the one who crushes dreams, snuffs hope from our life, the oppressor of us all. I relapsed into demonizing the prosecutor; I turned my back on a friend. I wrestled with myself the whole weekend.

Wednesday came and I was dead set on what I was going to do. I marched into the classroom and took my seat, as I had every Wednesday before that. Everyone else filed in and class began. Whatever was discussed that night, I can hardly remember. I was too distracted on what I'd been planning to say. I followed the discussion as best I could until it was time for me to confront him.

When he announced that it was time for a ten-minute break, I approached him. I asked if we could go outside the classroom, into the hallway, to talk. He obliged. I told him I was not angry at him. I had worked through that over the weekend. I let him know that I didn't want him to feel bad—I understood. He was only doing his job. I think he was relieved.

I went through several feelings after that night. Even though I had dropped my anger towards Preston and was determined to continue on as his friend, I was insecure concerning how he felt toward me. The case files the prosecutor worked from painted a monstrous caricature of what was a troubled sixteen-year-old. I was less secure in the classroom with him—I felt like there was a mind in the room who judged me the way the media, detectives, prosecution, and some of the public had through the stages of my trial. I felt like the girl I used to be, regardless of how much I knew I'd changed. My participation in class suffered some—I lacked the confidence I had before when I thought the sixteen-year-old me was dead and buried. The resurrection of my awful past was the demise of my newborn self. I'd relapsed.

On the last night of class, Preston gave me the greatest gift someone in my situation could have ever hoped to receive. We talked openly about my case. He revealed to me that he had trouble putting the me as he presently knew me, with the me as I was portrayed at sixteen. In the moment, seeing that a former prosecutor in my case acknowledged a transformation in me, I was filled with hope once again. I was once again convinced that I was worthy of forgiveness, of acceptance, of friendship, of love. I was shown by a man that I was never beyond salvation, that there was always hope for me. I was renewed with faith for a second chance; for if God opened the heart of a former adversary and changed his mind about my humanity—then I knew it was possible God could do it again. My soul tells me He will.

I think it is safe to say that in the justice system, the prosecutor and the defendant rarely become friends. Most times, they never even seek to look beyond what is presented inside the adversarial proceedings. The result is all too often a dangerous demonization of each other, and if my situation is anything to go by, a missed opportunity to receive a gift from God Himself. I believe it is when we venture beyond the ordinary, beyond the accustomed, that we best see the work of God. In a prison classroom, between a prosecutor and a defendant, God created friendship, acceptance, and redemption. To this day, Preston and I keep in touch; he was formerly my prosecutor, but forever my friend.

Part Two

PRESTON SHIPP

I FIRST BECAME ACQUAINTED with Cyntoia Denise Brown from a safe and sterile distance. I did not know what she looked like, what her hobbies were, or where she grew up. At the time, I was acting in my role as an appellate prosecutor, a cog in the wheel of the criminal justice system, and Cyntoia's case was assigned to me. By the time I received the case, Cyntoia had already been tried and convicted of first degree murder and sentenced at sixteen years old to life in prison. The transcript of her trial, which I carefully reviewed, filled a banker's box, and she had raised numerous challenges to her conviction on appeal. My job as an assistant attorney general was to argue to the appellate court that the issues Cyntoia presented were without merit and that her conviction and sentence should be affirmed. At this point, Cyntoia Denise Brown was not a *person* to me. We had never met. Instead, she was just another *case*. She was a brief that I had to write. As in so many of my prior cases, Cyntoia was a name without a face, and all I knew about her was the worst thing she had ever done.

This is how the fallen powers tend to operate. Systems, institutions, and authorities thrive when people are dehumanized, stripped of their humanity. It is easier to marginalize, oppress, and discard a person when that person has been labeled based on worldly categories such as race, religion, economic status, and education. The principalities, such as the media and political parties, encourage society to think in terms of "us" and "them." Nowhere is this dichotomy more pronounced than in the criminal justice system, the arena in which I worked for about six years. I wore the label of "prosecutor," and the people on whose cases I worked were generally labeled "criminals," or more specifically "murderers," "robbers," "rapists," and "thieves." I tended to think that as a prosecutor, a representative of the state, I was "good" and "right," waging a professional war of words against people who were "bad." I was encouraged to think this way, and it certainly made my job of arguing for the punishment of law-breakers a lot easier. I served as counsel in over 250 cases, and never did I have to meet any of the defendants in my cases. I remained insulated and secure, protected by the illusion of an us/them dichotomy, and able to argue day after day that the convictions should stand and the sentences should not be disturbed. I was helping to put the bad people away so the good people would be safe. I slept well at night. But then I met Cyntoia Brown.

In the spring of 2009, I was scheduled to teach Judicial Process for Lipscomb University. The class would meet at the Tennessee Prison for Women and would include an equal mix of traditional Lipscomb students and inmates who were earning college credit. One would think that when I received my class roster and saw Cyntoia Brown's name that I would immediately recognize her as a defendant in a case that I worked on. But, as noted above, she was not a person to me. The thought that I might cross paths one day with a defendant from one of my cases was an abstract possibility, but not something that would ever actually occur. So the fact that the Cyntoia who was present in class each week was, in fact, Cyntoia Denise Brown escaped my notice. I ignorantly went forward and began to teach the course. In class, we critiqued the criminal justice system, called the legitimacy of the adversarial system into question, and noted how little room is left for victims to express their anguish or for offenders to express their remorse. Reconciliation, far from being a goal of the system, is replaced by mere retribution. We discussed an alternative approach to criminal justice that seeks to restore, to transform, and to heal both parties, not simply to ask what law was broken and what the punishment should be.

Cyntoia was an excellent student. If any of the students really grasped the glaring inadequacies of the current system, which tends to demonize the offender and offers little support for the victim, it was Cyntoia. She also perceived the benefits of a different kind of judicial process, one in which justice is measured not by adherence to procedural rules but by the healing that is achieved in and between the parties. Cyntoia was fiery and outspoken, quick to voice her opinion. She was enthusiastic about learning and most grateful for the opportunity to attend college while in prison. She and I had productive exchanges in class, and we got to know each other a bit outside of class. We became friends during the first few weeks of the semester. I always looked forward to seeing her.

On April 20, 2009, the Tennessee Court of Criminal Appeals released its decision in Cyntoia's case, in which it affirmed the judgment of the trial court convicting her of first degree murder and imposing a life sentence. As counsel in the case, I immediately received a copy of the opinion. Finally, I realized that the Cyntoia in my class, my outspoken friend and student, was the Cyntoia Denise Brown in the case that I had just won on behalf of the state. My heart sank. I felt like I had betrayed a friend who had placed her trust in me. I had argued that the most appropriate outcome was for Cyntoia to spend the rest of her life in prison. Had I known Cyntoia before I worked on her case, I would not have been able to make that argument.

I began to wonder how many arguments I had made while standing behind the veil that separates prosecutors from defendants, "good" from "bad," which, had the veil been lifted, I would not have felt comfortable making. Had I been afforded the opportunity to know the person, to meet him or her, to listen to the person's story, would I have persisted in my argument that the person needed to be imprisoned for five, ten, twenty years, or life? If the illegitimate dichotomy had crumbled and the imaginary chasm that separated me from the person been bridged, would I instead have been an advocate for the person? Why was I ever content to read a transcript and author a brief against an individual whom I had never met, whose story I had never heard, whose context I had never learned? How could I seek to persuade a court to take action against a person I did not know?

I did not know how I would face Cyntoia in class the following Wednesday night. I assumed she would hate me. I feared she would drop out of the class. Despite all our academic talk of reconciliation, I did not see a way past the fact that the powers had pitted me against Cyntoia, I had gone unquestioningly along with it, and she was paying the price. I felt I had no credibility left and that she would think that all my sophisticated talk of a different kind of justice was just a hypocritical sham. After all, in her case and many others, I was an agent of a system that seeks only to condemn and punish, never to forgive.

Cyntoia and I had a brief conversation in the hallway during a break in class. I remember little of the conversation. I apologized, and she told me it was okay. She recognized that I was only doing a job and that I did not know her at the time. She understood that I had left my job as a prosecutor due to the tension the work caused me. She knew that I had been unwilling to continue laboring in a system that demonizes and incarcerates people at a rate higher than any other country in the world. Her words offered little comfort, however, because she was clearly hurt and disappointed. Not only that, but she was intensely vulnerable. Now she was confronted with the awful truth that I was familiar with the details of her crime. Without her consent, her worst moment had been laid bare, like a wound reopened. I could tell that she was afraid that armed with this information, I could no longer think of her as Cyntoia the outspoken, bright student with the quick smile. Her past had followed her into the haven of the Lipscomb classroom. Our friendship was tainted by an enormous power imbalance. I was still the prosecutor, and she the criminal.

These worldly labels do not easily pass away. I happen to have a law degree, and that degree enabled me to teach the Judicial Process class in the first place. I am not a convicted felon, so I can vote, if I am so inclined. Others do not enjoy these privileges and opportunities. The labels that are placed on us dictate how society views us and the value it places on us. I was unsure whether Cyntoia and I would ever be able to move beyond our labels, especially now that they were so out in the open and intimately connected. But what is not possible with people is possible with God. Not only possible, but accomplished! The work of reconciliation is done. Our task is simply to live it.

So Cyntoia and I returned to class and to our discussion of how the system is broken and what could be done differently. The semester concluded, and we had a party on the evening of the last class meeting. During the party, Cyntoia and I found time to talk. I expressed to her the difficulty I had in reconciling what I had read about her in that court record with the person I knew her to be now. She explained to me more of her story, her context, and her upbringing. She filled me in on the details of the life she was caught up in and the terrible circumstances she had endured since she was a child. These details were not contained in the trial transcript, and were never presented to the jury that found her guilty. I came to see that had I been in Cyntoia's position, I may have made the same choices and might be dressed in prison garb. But Cyntoia has refused to allow the label that society placed on her when she was sixteen years old to define her, and she has likewise refused to define me by the role I used to play in the criminal justice system and in her case.

Cyntoia and I are not very different. We are both passionate about justice, real *shalom*-based justice, we both value education, love to read, have strong opinions, and are suspicious of institutions. Through continued correspondence and dialogue, we have learned more about each other and have become good friends. Cyntoia is not bad; she never was. And I was never good or right. We are both simply children of God, loved and forgiven by Him, and reconciled in Christ.

21

Reframing Academy and Community

The Prison and the Power of Art

LAURA LAKE SMITH

> It is often said that the goal of incarceration is rehabilitation,
> but what does that mean? Isn't rehabilitation simply changing
> the way one thinks? For some, landing behind bars is enough
> to prompt change, but for most, major obstacles, such as anger,
> resentment, fear, or lack of self worth and education keep not
> only the body, but the mind imprisoned.

THIS STATEMENT WAS WRITTEN by Shayne, one of my students at the
Tennessee Prison for Women, and while reading this perspective on
incarceration, I could not help but think of the vivid yet haunting images
of Giovanni Battista Piranesi's *Le Carceri d'Invenzione* (*The Imaginary
Prisons*). Piranesi created the now infamous series of etchings during
the eighteenth century. It was a century that boasted the Age of Reason and the Enlightenment; it was also a period in which structures of
restraint such as asylums like Bedlam to configurations of prisons like
Jeremy Bentham's panoptikon were proliferated. But Piranesi's etchings, by comparison to other rational pursuits of the time, reveal a more
emotional and expressive response to the reexamination of confinement.
Piranesi's is a nightmarish view into the world of prisons. The dungeon-
like spaces are overwhelming and their staircases and ladders seem to
lead to nowhere. The feeling of suffocation, despite the enormity of the
space, is palpable. It is well known that these images were borne out of

a fever-induced sleep and that the visions of what Piranesi places before us are the same visions that haunted him during this brief illness. Yet, it was common for eighteenth century artists, writers, and radicals to compare their social order to a prison.[1] But while Piranesi's incarceration was symbolic and analogous to society and its issues, Shayne's incarceration is more than emblematic; she is physically restrained and thus she inhabits a place of corporeal domination that Piranesi does not. But Shayne's comments are more about the mind, rather than the body, and are similar, metaphorically, to Piranesi's phantasms of prisons.

As evident too in Piranesi's etchings, Shayne's words convey the mental oppression and the psychological anxiety of the incarcerated experience. However, her statement also speaks to the inadequacies and deficiencies in attaining significant rehabilitation in the current prison system. Yet, both Shayne and Piranesi successfully criticize and defy positions which we might consider as conventional notions and beliefs—Shayne, the status quo of the prison system and Piranesi, his oppressing artistic and social reality. In many ways, Shayne and Piranesi are like artists before them and after them in that they confront, with resilience, institutionalized standards and forces. For Piranesi, art is more than an aesthetic interlude—his work asks uncomfortable questions and jars the viewer, making it a visual which is not easily digested or quickly experienced. Correspondingly, Shayne questions the notion that prison is simply incarceration—a perceived effortless rehabilitation, a mere interlude in between life events. In fact, each of their responses to their individual circumstances implores us to begin with them a moral adventure of sorts.

The LIFE program (Lipscomb Initiative for Education) embodies such an adventure as it provides higher education, individual empowerment, and restorative change to inmates at the Tennessee Prison for Women by way of unique academic engagement in the liberal arts and in the reframing of the university community. LIFE educates traditional Lipscomb students alongside those incarcerated in the Tennessee Prison for Women, and in the process, both groups, the "inside" students from the TPW and the "outside" students from Lipscomb, earn college credit for their various graduation requirements. My responsibility in the program has been to teach the art history courses and to do so in an unconventional manner.

At 5:15pm, every Wednesday, our limited allowed belongings were x-rayed, our bodies patted down in an intrusive manner, and our left hand

1. Jones, "No Way Out."

stamped with a special ink that indicated approval for entry and exit. Escorted by a corrections officer, we walked through high security gates and across the prison courtyard to the education wing. Once inside, one might be surprised to know that the surroundings were reasonably normal and resembled learning environments that we might have known during our own "outside" studies. This, however, did not deter the initial fear in some of our traditional students. In their reflective writings, they revealed how nervous and frightened they were on the first night while waiting for the inmates to join us; they second guessed their choice in taking this course. But, a few weeks later, it was normal, and the scenario was as comfortable for the outside students as Facebook.

In building this course, I confess that I was uncertain how the class would come together and what exactly would be required for assignments. I soon learned during a pre-class meeting with the first cohort of inside students in 2008 that they were concerned about studying art. They had no background, knew none of the "expert terms" for art and did not know the rubric by which work was assessed. The women noted that they felt powerless with this rather elitist subject and were vulnerable for the first time in the series of courses offered in the LIFE program. I assured them that art was much more accessible than they thought. Though the meeting exposed many pre-conceived notions about art and its worth in the inmates' eyes, their comments gave me insight into organizing the course in a dynamic and exploratory manner. My art history course was entitled "The Power of Art," and considered specific and complex issues related to art and its power dynamic within the art world and beyond.[2] Through this thematic template, we examined art as a way of investigating issues of race, gender, rights, economics, cultural perspectives, and political ideologies, issues that have long plagued those on the inside of the prison system and issues that our traditional students might not otherwise encounter, at least not at this point in their lives. Ideally, the course would break down the seemingly constricting barriers in learning and understanding art and in the process, hopefully, destroy the barriers between the outside and inside students as well as challenge, perhaps, some of our outside students' perceptions about incarceration. In other words, our experience with art would be more than an aesthetic interlude.

2. The course was initially (and rather loosely) based on Simon Schama's *Power of Art* series, mainly as a pedagogical methodology, but the course soon became an investigation of important voices in art (scholars, critics, and artists) and its profound affects throughout the history of culture.

The Power of Art: Encountering Moral Adventures

Throughout the semester, we covered the tenets of a general art history course, but did so through different frames of reference. We considered, for example, depictions of African Americans during the Civil War and Reconstruction periods and focused on the artist, Henry Ossawa Tanner. In their discussions, the students felt that he was the only artist that treated African Americans with dignity and respect. While viewing other artists' treatments of the subject matter of African Americans, the students were quick to point out that their images resembled grotesque drawings or caricatures rather than renderings of human beings. We examined some of the racially insensitive beliefs held about slaves—that they were "gator bait" or "animals." The students noted that African Americans were depicted as just another form of entertainment for the whites, rather than another equally important human being. In many of the works, they discussed how slaves were performing or entertaining with various antics and dances. Several of the inside students mentioned that these particular depictions were stereotypical and unfair to the sense of music and song that was so important to the slaves. Their observation that stereotypes dominated the field of African American images was correct. Tanner himself even said that "many of the artists who have represented Negro life have seen only the comic, the ludicrous side of it, and have lacked sympathy with and appreciation for the warm big heart that dwells within such a rough exterior."[3] However, through his painting, Tanner reconstructs the African-American identity. In *The Banjo Lesson*,[4] he pays tribute to the lineage of music in this culture as the banjo was developed from a type of stringed instrument brought to the states from Africa by slaves. Here Tanner focuses on the act of teaching and passing on knowledge, an honored exchange of music between generations. Tanner's depictions do not desecrate but venerate the character and selfhood of African Americans. The discussion of Tanner led to other African-American artists such as Jacob Lawrence, Bettye Saar, Kara Walker, and Renee Cox who also investigate their ethnicity, its stereotypes and historical injustices, and react visually to the marginalization of their race. These artists, like Tanner, engage the audience in critical discourse and in the perception and apperception of racial matters.

We also analyzed gender politics of the late nineteenth century and particularly examined the diverse reception of the works of Berthe Morisot

3. Eisenman, *Nineteenth Century Art*, 203.

4. Henry Osswa Tanner, *The Banjo Lesson*, 1893, Collection of Hampton University Museum, Hampton, Virginia, museum.hamptonu.edu

and Mary Cassatt. Because Mary Cassatt was an unmarried and child-less woman living in Paris, an advocate for women's rights, and possessed a distinctly strong and bold brushstroke, she was dubbed as masculine. Her work was constantly criticized because she did not paint "as a woman should." In Cassatt's images, she empowers women, even in those well-known images of the mother and children. Conversely, Morisot painted as a woman should, at least, according to critics, and was praised for her depictions of suitable females performing suitable domestic activities like laundry and caring for children as in *The Cradle*.[5] That she was married and also had children especially satisfied the critics and the greater public. Her artistic style was womanly and sanctioned; her painting was frenetic and messy, but this is how women were perceived, mentally speaking. Our discussion on this topic centered on an essay by Tamar Garb which explained how women were documented by cultural historians and scientists in the late nineteenth century as being uncontrollable and irrational, particularly because they menstruated. Women, it was believed, stopped developing intellectually at the onset of puberty so that their bodies could better develop for procreation. Therefore, women lacked the abilities to hone certain skills needed for solid, detailed painting because their basic make up simply would not allow it; this type of skill was reserved for men only.[6] Such erroneous notions and misogynist conventions regarding women and art propelled us into examinations of female artists of the twentieth and twenty-first centuries as we investigated issues of gender politics, body image, artistic protest, and feminist artistic responses.

These examples by no means encompass the entire semester but serve to highlight a selection of the course content. Throughout our class, we analyzed art in order to find power dynamics within the art world and the world that it touches just outside, to recognize the goodness of humanity as well as its less humane moments, to discern the justices and injustices found in race, gender, and economics, to discover the power of artistic individualism and the power of authoritative groups, and to learn from those who creatively use art to solve problems in society as well as

5. Berthe Morisot, The Cradle, 1872, Collection of the Musée d'Orsay, Paris, France, www.musee-orsay.fr

6. Garb, "Berthe Morisot and the Feminizing of Impressionism," 230–45. Garb's research, art historically, culturally, and scientifically, sheds great insight on gender politics for female painters as well as male painters. She focuses on the style of Impressionism and artists related to that movement. Her work was instrumental in our reading assignments for this time period and her findings help to shape the viewpoint of the students as they analyzed the work of Morisot and Cassatt.

those who use art as abusive or divisive. A primary goal in teaching this type of art history course was to introduce students to the salient material which can be learned from art history, no matter the time separation or the density of the "metanarratives." Additionally, this pedagogical approach encouraged each student to create their own narrative of art, preferably one which would be an ever-evolving but integral part of how they see themselves in the world. For the sake of art history, and for any prevailing narrative for that matter, it is crucial to question, reflect, and create our own story for our time and our place. The art historian James Elkins, in his *Stories of Art,* said that thinking about the shape of art history and what it means to us and how it moves our imagination is a necessity. "Otherwise," he wrote, "art history is just a parade, designed by other people, endlessly passing you by."[7] More importantly, the types of art discussed in this class exposed pretenses and shatter engrained customs and beliefs. The exploration of these artworks illuminated the issues inherent with mere "aesthetic interludes" and championed the worthiness of the "moral adventure" in art. Evident, too, in this juxtaposition were the larger contentious power relationships between institutions like governments, academies (even the ruling art elite), and the loosely grouped, organic communities of artists—individualistic, unique, and sometimes, idiosyncratic.

Reframing Academy and Community: Reconciling a Paradox

After lectures and discussions each week, the class continued inquiry and analysis in their weekly response papers and topical and service-learning reflective essays. The papers were powerful, from both the inside and outside students. I observed perspectives shifting and minds opening from week to week and read some of the most insightful work that I have ever encountered as a professor. Certainly, art became something that was more approachable for both the inside and outside students. They also saw the interconnection of information between various disciplines and enjoyed the ability to be interdisciplinary in reading and understanding art history. Moreover, they realized that art history taught lessons for life—in cultural, ethical, and political situations—and that through art, the individual had a voice and could be empowered. Some of the students, particularly the inside students, saw themselves much like the artists who we discussed and/or simply felt a kinship to the situations in the struggles,

7. James Elkins, *Stories of Art,* 11.

the injustice, and the need for personal expression. Students also noted that they learned to be more critical of information—particularly of stereotypes—in the history of art and in their relationships with each other. The artist and teacher Joseph Beuys noted that "[T]ransformations of the self must first take place in the potential of the thought and mind . . ." Furthermore, Beuys stated that "[I]f one of my students should one day rear her children in a better way, then for me, that is more important than just having taught a great artist . . . art and the perceptions gained through art can create an element of backflow into life."[8] And this experience did just that—the interaction and collaboration through this initiative brought about meaningful impact to all participants, transforming and permeating the lives of the students on the inside and the outside.

The outside students became advocates for the program at large. This was particularly visible in the open community forum at the end of the class, their service learning culmination for the course. All outside students spoke about their experiences, the change that took place once "they got it," and perceptions they initially held and ultimately relinquished. On behalf of their inside colleagues, they read personal reflections and were the inside students' voices to the outside world. Friendships were forged and the traditional students realized that these women were not all that different from themselves.

In the last reflective writing assignment for this course, I asked the inside students to comment on the LIFE program thus far and to discuss their experiences, both personally and intellectually. The following are excerpts from these writings:

> We were all students in a class there to learn what we could— about art and about each other. . . . Coming from the situation that I do, it is easy to have who you are overshadowed by the uniform you wear, and what the media says you are (more often than not, you are painted as a monster or heartless beast in need of a cage). Being involved in this learning experience in this [art history] course has helped me to understand why people pay millions of dollars for art and why you can't put a price on the educational experience that [these] classes offer. ~Cyntoia

> The concept of punitive—of the beating down, of degrading the women that reside here—is complicating an existing problem within each inmate. I feel it is a tragedy of this country that instead of helping to fix broken individuals in humanitarian

8. Fineberg, *Art Since 1940*, 233.

manner, [the system] has further degenerated and actually destroyed those lives and others involved. On the contrary, this program is lifting up individuals, giving each offender the chance to successfully challenge the "criminal stigma" by transforming themselves, to contribute again to society. ~Beth

Many people don't understand what all prison can take away from a person . . . I realized how far from society I was during my first Lipscomb course. . . . I had been stripped of a majority of my self-confidence, and with that, the ability to make eye contact. That was a startling realization I was not ready to accept; nevertheless, [it is] one I have worked very hard on in the past year to overcome. Now, when I speak, I hear a new voice. Gone is the girl who allowed her surroundings to dictate her attitude and decisions. Say hello to a woman who is determined to succeed in an institution deliberately designed to break. ~Billie Jo

For all of us involved in this experience, it was certainly more than an intermission from the average week for analysis and discussion of art; it was a time of reflection and revelation. Here were two, quite unlikely groups of students coming together to study and learn in a unique environment, one not usually encountered between the academy and the community. One might even view the LIFE program much in the spirit of the community of artists discussed in "The Power of Art" course—challenging the oppressive "aesthetic interludes" of institutions of art as well as the prison-like infrastructures that both Shayne and Piranesi bring to light, and affirming the vitality and liberation of the moral adventures, in art and in life.

22

The Transformation of X, Y, and We

FELICIA YBANEZ

FACED WITH PRISON TIME, I have found it necessary to peel away my former nature and clothe myself in a better version of my previous life. While I don't want to completely cover up or remove who I used to be or the experiences that have led me to where I am today, I enjoy being the person I have developed into.

Once incarcerated, the options were to "do the time" or "let the time do me," as is often the counsel in this environment. I can "do the time" by taking advantage of the opportunities this institution has to offer, not rebelling against the policies and in-house rules set before me, and possibly pursuing higher education during my many hours of free time. This could lead to a peaceful and productive life inside prison by staying out of segregation and not engaging in hostile situations between other inmates. It could also have positive effects once released, such as better job opportunities and improved social skills.

By "letting the time do me" I would be sitting idly, misbehaving, and staying in trouble, which could lead to a poor institutional record and hinder my early release from prison. Also, without the positive influences, I would remain apprehended by my past and would not progress. There would be no room for closure. Once released from prison, I would continue to be emotionally and educationally dormant. How I spend my time in prison will produce drastically different results in important areas of my life once I am released. Employment prospects, social situations, and even my religious and political views will be altered.

While adversities do bring out the true nature and state of mind of individuals, let us not forget that people can be locked up in a variety of "prisons." Some prisons may be institutions, while others are physical disabilities or states of mind. Everyone faces prisons of adversity. Any prison can be the perfect breeding place for either education or idleness. The decision is up to the individual and his/her own convictions. The time and opportunity for conversion of thought and belief are certainly present for each offender incarcerated for any amount of time. I am not advocating for longer sentences, or for offenders to be immediately sent to prison without pursuing other avenues of reconciliation. In fact, I wish to propose just the opposite. With the right amount of support and resources, we, as a community of healers, volunteers, and leaders, can shine a light for any distressed person.

The Transformation of Malcolm X

Since I've been locked up, I've read the *Autobiography of Malcolm X*, a story that shows the possibilities for religious and political conversions during periods of incarceration. Like me, Malcolm X knew he could "do the time" or "let the time do him." Malcolm X's story isn't mine to tell, but I have experienced a lot of the same moral dilemmas he often found himself in.

Before he became Malcolm X, he was known by his given name, Malcolm Little, and then in prison, the men in the cellblock called him "Satan" because of his reputation. In chapter 9 of his autobiography, Malcolm X recalls the limited values, and limited vocabulary of Malcolm Little. For example, he believed a woman to be simply "another commodity"; he didn't place much value on any human life, his own included. He smoked a lot of marijuana and his non-standard English was laced with profanity and slang. He was a hustler, making money by illegitimate means, just to get by.

Although I have learned a lot from Malcolm X's experiences, as well as my own, this part of his story is not what I relate to best. I relate to his being lost, and his drive to be delivered from his own personal bondages. When Malcolm Little got locked up, his initial commitment to "going straight" was motivated by a desire for early release. But while under the watchful eye and complete control of someone else, he was forced to be still. Being still allowed him to hear his own voice and to recognize his true potential, and what he heard shaped the person he eventually became.

From the beginning of his incarceration, Malcolm Little was consistently observing his surroundings as he had trained himself to do on the streets. While taking notice of his atmosphere, he became aware of and intrigued by an inmate called "Bimbi." "Bimbi was the library's best customer," he recalled. "What fascinated me with him most of all was that he was the first man I had ever seen command total respect . . . with his words."[1] Bimbi held a quality that Malcolm Little had always desired, but seldom rightfully deserved—*respect*. To have the respect of others in this manner was similar to the kind of prestige that Malcolm had been trying to obtain on the streets with his lifestyle and hustles, but he learned from Bimbi that respect is earned by individual attributes rather than coerced through fear and intimidation.

Over time, as Malcolm developed an earnest interest in language, his curiosities and priorities changed. Prison became a pool of opportunities, and he chose to modify his lifestyle. Malcolm's brother drove this point further by stating, "You don't even know who you are. You don't even know your true family name."[2] Such statements prompted Malcolm's search for "truth." He became interested in history, not just his history, but America's history. What he discovered—stories of human trafficking that tore down a race of people and erased their identities—angered him. He recounts how the truth was similar to that of a "blinding light." Often he would find himself in a catatonic-like trance, ingesting and absorbing the world around him and the account of how a nation kidnapped and oppressed its people. Ultimately, these moments clarified who Malcolm was as an individual. They helped to shape Malcolm Little into El-Hajj Malik El-Shabazz, more famously known as Malcolm X.

Once released from prison, Malcolm X maintained the beliefs he gained while incarcerated. He prayed each day earnestly and even began preaching at The Nation of Islam's Temple Number One. The love and devotion he held for his Muslim beliefs transported him into a life advocating for the Nation of Islam, "fishing" for others to join, and recounting the truth of America and the teachings of Elijah Mohammad. The years of hustling and ill-gotten gains were forgiven. During Malcolm's visit to Mecca, after twelve years of following Elijah Mohammad, Malcolm declared:

> I've had enough of someone else's propaganda, I'm for truth; no matter who tells it. I'm for justice, no matter who it is for or

1. Malcolm X and Alex Haley, *The Autobiography of Malcolm X*, 157.
2. Ibid., 164.

against. I'm a human being first and foremost, and as such I'm for whoever and whatever benefits humanity *as a whole*.[3]

The Transformation of Felicia Y

I went through something similar when I first came to this prison. I watched everyone and took small mental notes concerning the type of personality traits I would like for myself. I begrudgingly refer to this stage as my "adjustment phase" because, while I was learning from others, I was still a slave to my useless attitude problem. It seemed like every time I turned around, I was disrespectful to an authority figure (namely the prison staff). I was the bitter recipient of several disciplinary infractions, many of which landed me in segregation. I didn't realize at the time that my self-destructive behavior, which landed me in prison in the first place, had followed me into the prison. Family members had repeatedly told me that I was at the wrong place at the wrong time, but I always knew it was my choice to make, and I have always owned up to my responsibility for the crime. The problem was that I didn't understand how to change the way I would react in certain situations.

In awkward emotional situations, every feeling translated into anger. I soon began to believe that I wasn't truly *happy* unless I was in the middle of an anger surge. I misunderstood all emotions, even genuine happiness. What I thought was happiness was actually convenience and familiarity. Being angry all the time was easy; if I was sad, it was easier to be angry; disappointed . . . angry; embarrassed . . . angry. The cycle was comfortable—until it became an obstacle to what I wanted out of my life. I didn't get the response I desired from other people because of my *attitude*. I didn't know how to convey my thoughts and feelings in a coherent, effective manner. Likewise, I couldn't politely articulate what I wanted. If anger didn't achieve for me what I desired, my version of being civil was to be emotionally unavailable—a blank slate, if you will.

I also responded to unpleasant situations with daydreaming. I have always been a daydreamer. In school, I would cook up scenarios in my head that seemed much more pleasant than my real life. Daydreaming always beat concentrating on what the teacher had to say, and it was certainly better than doing homework when I went home—or so I thought at the time. While living in Kentucky I would skip school and go to the

---

3. Ibid., 373. Emphasis in original.

creeks. Sometimes I would lie out on the banks, look up at the sky and create an alternate life for myself. Occasionally, I would walk the creeks exploring, creating, and dreaming. My dreams were always so vivid and clear to me. I always knew what I wanted but never figured I could accomplish my visions. I thought they would always just be dreams, and I was content to just dream.

I stopped dreaming for a while when I got locked up, because of all of the time and energy it takes to go through our criminal justice system. After I received my sentence and settled in to "doing time" I began to dream again, only this time I wanted my dreams to become reality. I slowly discovered the story of my life: experiences, guilt, pain, shame, and accomplishments. This inventory of feelings and thoughts allowed me to undergo a slight transformation and see my past and my present in a new light. I had to begin to distinguish between reality and the inaccurate feelings that clouded my judgment. I never got very far before I noticed another minor adjustment needed to be made. The several small steps I took in investing in my future proved to be the glue that gave me the staying power I needed to continue. If I had tried to change overnight it could have been disastrous; I would have failed. I decided that excuses were not acceptable, failure was not an option, and excellence was my goal. So I paced myself.

With each change or adjustment I made, I gave myself more opportunities for a positive change in my life. In essence, I decided to empower my future self so that I might become successful when I got released from prison. I developed a higher sense of self-worth and the realization that no other person determined my value. As an inmate, these adjustments test what boundaries I am capable of setting for myself. In doing so, I have found I created my own limitations within the institution and all of its rules. I simply decided that the prison confined my physical body, but it must not possess my mind. The institutional policies and rules may limit me, but there are some things that this institution offers, such as confusion, mischief and negativity, that I will not tolerate in my life.

I made every effort to separate myself from the oppressive attitudes that stifled my personal growth. First, I separated myself from my own bondage to ignorance, recognizing that if I lingered too long in the state I was in, I would be limited, I would regress and self-destruct. My oppression would be of my own doing—not that of the institution. Always changing, adjusting, adapting, or even peaceably non-conforming to inmate stereotypes has allowed me to accept exploration of other cultures, thus gaining an open mind. Refusing to wallow in the past for too long has made me teachable. Instead of stagnant, I am always moving toward a destiny I create.

These are my declarations to maintain my own distinctiveness, and to defy the stereotype of the ignorant prisoner. The inmate we see depicted on television is very rarely in the state of bettering themselves. I've watched countless programs depicting inmates who refuse to move forward, and upon their release they are always looking for another scheme, a way to get over on an unsuspecting victim. One example is the mini-series "Scoundrels." In the first season, the father of the West family is arrested and the rest of the family is under constant surveillance for life-long criminal activity. The mother is left to fend for her family of four children and one father-in-law, and despite the family's efforts to "straighten up," they all continue in their unlawful and immoral activities. The father, while doing time, steadily tries to con his way out of prison in the most unrealistic situations, and he continues illegal activities to keep his family afloat financially.

While stereotypical inmates are always scheming or manipulating a person or situation to benefit themselves, my experiences with inmates are slightly different. After being locked up for fifteen years I can attest to the fact that not every inmate is a bad person: people can make mistakes of the worse kind, yet be fundamentally good people. Bad decisions can be made based on a number of factors: poor upbringing, emotional distresses, psychological issues, abusive circumstances (physical as well as emotional), sexual abuse, and the list goes on. The fact that some states don't have a self-defense law means that there are more spouses being locked up for defending themselves against domestic violence. I don't attempt to justify the bad decisions of offenders. I'm simply saying that all is not as it appears on the surface. True, not every convict becomes a Malcolm X, craving more, looking to further his education, and expand intellectual limits. But at the same time, not every inmate has the desire to wreak havoc on American communities, creating chaos, and only living for such moments.

My own transformation includes always trying to evaluate if my feelings about situations are valid or if they need reassessment, making me a more compassionate and understanding individual. I now have a canvas of emotions that I can choose from, instead of just a "blank slate." Therefore, I very rarely get truly angry, but have found myself frustrated *without* fear of pushing the anger boundary. Yes, even my feelings have boundaries. I learned to create the limits by determining what was truly important and a priority in my life.

Just recently, I was standing at the property room window, waiting for the contents of my personal property order I had purchased. The officer in the property room asked if I had a brown paper sack in which to carry my items back to the dorm. When I replied that I did, he asked me if it was open, he wanted to see if he could toss the items in the bag from where he was standing in the middle of the office, with one Corporal between us. This was the perfect opportunity for me to either comply and file a grievance on the officer for unprofessional conduct or start running my mouth about just how childish he was being. I opted for another avenue. While I continued to sign my property list, without looking up at him, I stated, "Sir, I would rather you didn't throw my property at me." There were no underlying tones in my voice, nor did the officer feel belittled or embarrassed by what I had just said. It made sense, and the minor hiccup of the officer's attempted misconduct was barely noticed. He placed my property in the sack for me and I left the property room with an exchange of a slight grin between the jokester and myself. I have allowed myself to rise above my circumstances and flourish where I have been planted.

The Transformation of We

Transformation can occur when a person is truly made to be still—even by unappealing circumstances. Everyday life and its responsibilities need not interfere with the overflow of personal inner growth. It's often during traumatic events and distressing circumstances that people who want to prevail often do. Traumatic events could include a young single parent on her/his own, trying to provide for his/her family. It's traumatic because it's a distressing situation that disturbs the normative standards of morale in everyday American living.

I further propose that once an individual in prison has a taste of the kind of freedom that only true inner searching can provide, enlightenment is desired and often sought after. I've seen it countless times. A good support system, however, is often missing. Without it, the struggle for validity is ever more tiring.

I have been fortunate enough to recognize the opportunities here at this institution, and I am a very good example of the personal and spiritual changes that an offender can experience. I am a firm believer that with a little encouragement, most prisoners are completely capable of making positive changes in their lives. Only the self-righteous and the bitter would simply shrug my suggestion off, but not those who have learned and experienced what it is liked to be truly transformed. Malcolm X wrote, "I don't think anybody ever got more out of going to prison than I did. In fact, prison enabled me to study far more intensively than I would have if my life had gone differently and I had attended college."[4] Malcolm acknowledged that he learned a significant amount he most likely would not have had the opportunity to learn, had he never been locked up. More importantly, he would not have recognized his ability to learn on the educational level that he did.

Community support groups provide a starting point; for example, my mother, Charlotte Neville, of Cordova, Tennessee, has recently become involved with the Equal Justice Coalition Support Group, a group of individuals and families whose lives are devastated by court injustices. These court injustices include wrongful convictions or cruel and unusual punishments. The support group provides a place of compassion and understanding for those who need comfort. They are there for one another, as well as the loved ones incarcerated, to provide hope and encouragement to an otherwise hopeless situation. In such an environment where knowledge of how the system operates meets compassion and support, this country has hope.

Malcolm X had his family to support him at first, and then the Nation of Islam. I have my family to support me, and now I also have Lipscomb University's finest faculty and students. I am part of a growing community where once a week, 30 selected inmates (non-traditional students) meet up with traditional Lipscomb students to take a class within the prison walls. This community has given me even more inspiration to move forward in my never-ending journey of investing in both my future, and the future of the community I will someday return to.

But it is not just those of us serving time who must undergo transformation. If society continues to turn its back on the ever growing population of offenders and refuses to become informed of the moral discrepancies that plague this country, then the blind will continue to lead the blind. We should all care about this issue because these are our children, our fathers, our mothers, aunts and uncles, brothers and sisters. These people are our community members, including occasionally, our political leaders. They are our neighbors and our ministers; they come from all walks of life. Sometimes they are our grandparents. These

4. Ibid., 183.

offenders, our loved ones, will be back in society again after being in-carcerated. Their prison sentence can result in either higher education or continued bad decision making. The resources are there, but without encouragement from our community, the decision to make the most of the opportunity may not be realized.

It takes one person to speak out, but it takes a community to surge towards what is right in order to get the attention of the masses. This is how transformation occurs; it is what people feel conviction for, for we are all connected.

23

To See and To Be Seen[1]

JANET WOLF

Learning to See

IN SOUTH AFRICA, a common Zulu greeting is "*sawabona.*" And the response is "*sikona.*" *Sawabona* means "I see you." *Sikona* means "I am here." In a world where those inside prisons and jails are most often invisible, what might it mean for those of us on the outside to see—*really* see—the faces, stories, scars and dreams, hurts and hopes of those who are locked up? To come close enough, to listen long enough, to be able to declare: "I see you!" And to invite those inside to respond: "I am here, fully present, being me—not a number, not identified by my charge or my sentence, not an object for your charity or proselytizing, but a human being, willing to be seen, being me, really me." What might it mean to *see* the more than 2 million human beings locked away behind razor wire and prison walls?

Closing the distance, beginning to see, started for me on Christmas Eve 1976. Edgehill United Methodist Church, a small, intentionally interracial, reconciling, urban church I had joined, held Christmas Eve service at the old state prison, "The Walls." The pastor, Bill, urged us to attend, emphasizing that the story of the Incarnation, the Word becoming flesh among us—this baby born to an unwed teenage mother among an

1. This chapter is adapted from *I Was in Prison: United Methodist Perspectives on Prison Ministry*, ed. James Shopshire Sr., Richmond Stoglin, and Mark Hicks.

oppressed, colonized, impoverished people—required a different setting than the inside of our church building. "It belongs in the streets," he said— the body of Christ in, for, and with the world.

Arriving at the prison that night, we were told we couldn't go inside. Something had happened, and we would have to hold our service outside. And even though this was Nashville, it was snowing. We were a sad, little handful of people, huddled outside the immense prison, snow and sleet swirling around us. This was not my idea of Christmas Eve. For me, Christmas Eve had included brilliant poinsettias and candles lighting up the rafters in the sanctuary. Christmas Eve was trumpets and pageantry, majestic music and bright colors, the choir spilling down the aisle, little kids dressed up like angels and shepherds.

We huddled together, trying to get the Christ-candle lit. The fierce wind extinguished the match every time. Pastor Bill was trying to help shield the flame and handed me the Bible, saying: "Read this." And I did, from Isaiah 9:2: "The people who walked in darkness have seen great light; . . . on them light has shined." Just about that time, the Christ-candle took flame; and I leaned in, trying to help my kids light their small candles. But in my heart, I was grumbling, still sure that this moment could not possibly matter to anyone. Then one of my boys tugged on my coat. "Mama, look!" I turned to look where he was pointing and saw, in cell after cell, the glow of matches and lighters being held up to the windows, spilling through the bars. As we began singing "Silent Night, Holy Night," I imagined I heard voices, inside and out, singing with the joy and awe of those who have turned to see what God is doing in the world.

Breaking through the Barriers

In Matt 25:44, those who are confronted by the king cry out: "Lord, when was it that we saw you . . . ?" Most of us do not see because we are not present inside the prisons and jails; we are not in relationship with those who are thirsty and hungry, impoverished and marginalized. As Pamela Couture argues, referring to John Wesley, we "keep out of the way of knowing." We distance ourselves, focusing our efforts on charity, which makes us feel good about ourselves while masking our cooperation with the very systems that perpetuate poverty and injustice.[2] Presence is a beginning— but only a beginning. Unless we allow the proximity to be translated into partnership, in ways that challenge and unmask our assumptions, biases,

2. Couture, *Seeing Children, Seeing God*, 56.

stereotypes and misconceptions, we will not be able to see people on the inside.

For those of us on the outside, barriers include our physical separation from people who are incarcerated and from the prisons and jails, our fear of those who are behind bars, and our assumptions about who is incarcerated and why. Barriers are also offered by the criminal-justice system itself, which is preoccupied with security and does not make it easy to actually get inside a prison. The barriers can be intimidating.

It might have been the beginning of any seminary/college class, except that we had passed through five checkpoints inside Riverbend to get here. We were required to show photo IDs at the front desk, removing shoes and jackets and laying them, along with books and pens, on the conveyer belt for the screening machine. As we passed through the metal detector, our left hands were stamped with a mark that could only be seen under a special light. One by one we were called into small rooms to be searched and patted down by correctional officers. Then into the metal "cage," a space surrounded by wire, with a gate closing firmly behind the group. And then, after what sometimes seemed a very long moment, the gate in front of us opened and we moved toward the next door. We lifted our hands under a black light to reveal a special stamp before the correctional officers behind a darkened window would unlock the next door. We walked down a long hall, past another checkpoint, waiting for the "click" that meant the next door had been unlocked. Now in the open space between buildings, we walked across the "yard," past the "high side," which houses death row, and on to the "low side." The correctional officers wanted us to keep going—no stopping, no waving, moving past lines of men in blue. We passed the mental-health lockdown ward and then the chapel, a handful of folks listening to vehement preaching. A correctional officer was waiting at the entrance to the building where the class was to be held and he escorted us, unlocking the classroom door. Insiders, scattered along the sidewalk and in the hallway, greeted us with huge grins, outstretched hands of welcome.

Since 2003, longtime prison advocate and restorative justice author Harmon Wray, Richard Goode, and I have been inviting students from seminaries, colleges, congregations, and the community to come with us inside prisons to learn with and from those who are incarcerated. It started with Harmon Wray's course on "The Theology and Politics of Crime and Justice in America." While Harmon had taught the course for a number of years at Vanderbilt Divinity School, it was not until January 2003 that he moved the course into Riverbend Maximum Security Institution, the state prison that houses death row. Ever since then, students from Vanderbilt Divinity School and the community have been coming to the prison to join students from Riverbend.

We had studied the Sing Sing model developed by New York Theological Seminary—theological education happening inside prison walls[3]—but wanted to add another component, namely, to bring students with us from the outside as partners in learning, in doing theology from the inside out. To prepare and plan for the course, we met with potential Riverbend students for several months before the first class began. It was important, before we started classes, to incorporate insiders as leaders with power to set priorities and boundaries.

From the beginning, the classes startled us. We had not predicted the raw honesty, prophetic truth telling, wide mercy, and healing power that were let loose. We were surprised how quickly strangers, with so many reasons to remain divided, became community. We often noted that the class had become church for us, and we saw that happen for so many others as well. We could not argue that this holy time was something we were orchestrating, although we thought we had some clues about what called such a community into being. Mutuality is the key—believing that everyone brings a gift. Each semester we design a class covenant that reminds us that we are all learners and all teachers; that every single voice is welcomed and valued. This is ministry *with*—not *to* or *for*—the incarcerated. It is an authentic partnership shaped by our desire for justice, not charity, and our certainty that some of the most profound, prophetic, world-transforming theology is happening behind prison walls.

In the course of many classes, we heard some of the same things over and over. From insiders: "This class is the only place I feel really human." "I never knew who I was until I came to this class. I had so much anger in me, but these classes allowed me to see a side of myself I never even knew existed." "We are always human beings in this class." "I never knew people outside cared." "I never thought I would really matter to anyone." "The classes give us all permission to shine, to believe we've been born to shine."

From outsiders: "I never knew. I thought everyone inside prison was so different from me . . . but it's not true." "I was scared to death to walk in here and then that first day I met people who became family." "This

---

3. Since 1981 New York Theological Seminary has offered an intensive 36-credit Master of Professional Studies designed for long-term prisoners in New York state correctional facilities.

course has changed my life. I will never be the same." "I have been a pastor for more than twenty years, but I never understood what prison ministry really means until now."

The experience of working with correctional administrators and prison officials varies widely. The correctional system is designed to keep people separated, and it is not easy to connect with folks on the inside. It is even more difficult to create safe space for a community of mutuality in an environment of "them or us," an institution in which officers identify themselves as "custodians of prison policy" with largely unchecked power to harass and coerce prisoners. Their job requires a focus on security; and it is all too easy to become rigid in applying the policies. As one correctional officer put it: "I'm disturbed by this whole system. Been working inside for more than twenty years. This place is a warehouse. Reminds me of rounding up cattle off a ranch and putting them in pens. Total chaos. People scared; no one answering questions; no rhyme or reason to lots of stuff here. Lots of correctional officers, even at the top, have a deaf ear— they don't see and don't care. Just wanting to make sure no one escapes. I tell them, you smack a dog on a leash so long; and when he gets off, he's gonna bite you."

The security business tends to attract people who want to enforce the law, who want to have the authority to keep order and be able to require others to follow rules. The work inside a prison is not easy and the pay is not much. It is not uncommon for correctional officers to have to work a double shift with little or no notice. There is a high turnover among staff and ongoing tension. While there are correctional officers who do care and try their best to work effectively and compassionately, they often seem to be in the minority. It hurts to allow oneself to experience the hardness of the prison. As one correctional officer commented: "I try to ease pain and give a little hope. I know these guys, and I know it's never too late. I'm no miracle worker but I can listen, care, look deeper into situations and try to get some answers. . . . It's a heartbreaking moment to see children and daddies during visitation. When it's time to leave, everyone's crying. You could slip on all the tears on that floor."

Nevertheless, the system tends to attract people who disconnect from the inside population. Some seem to be quick to exercise their power over and against those on the inside. Oftentimes the exercise of power seems arbitrary, capricious, and unnecessarily harsh. We have seen this pressure intensify as people get closer to their release time. We have struggled to build relationships with correctional officers, chaplains, wardens, and high-level administrators—to work for reconciliation even while confronting people in power in order to break through the barriers.

Orientation is provided for both inside and outside students before classes begin. It is the only time the students meet separately. The orientation is designed to make sure people understand the rules and regulations of the prison and the program. It is also an opportunity to express concerns, ask questions, and discuss both fears and hopes. The prison chaplain sometimes asks to participate in the orientation session for outsiders. This has not always been helpful. The following example helps explain why.

In one orientation session, after introductions, during which several people explained their longing to learn from and listen to people who are incarcerated, the particular chaplain began. "You need to be concerned about everyone in the prison. It's not just prisoners who are incarcerated. You have staff and officers who are incarcerated, locked up with those inmates, under the influence of criminal felons for eight hours at a time. . . . We do IQ tests, and you're going to be dealing with some people with an IQ of 75."

After going over dress codes and basic rules in the institution, the chaplain added: "You can be charged with a crime if you violate the rules and policies, so you be very careful. . . . Sometimes I wonder if I shouldn't quit my job and go on one of these work-release jobs. Some of these prisoners make more than I do. I know my clerk makes fifty cents an hour; but when I look at some of the accounts for prerelease inmates, I think I should ask for a loan."[4] And then the chaplain finished: "I believe in rehabilitation but it takes more to change minds. I tell prisoners there's just a four to six inch difference between you and me: that space between your ears—the choices you've made. I'm sure I can safely say this as a Baptist preacher in a Baptist school, it takes Jesus, getting down on your knees and accepting Jesus as your personal Lord and Savior. That is the only answer."

It was quiet in the room of Christians, Jews, Buddhists, and Muslims. Those who had never been inside a prison and those who had served time and would be going back in for the first time since release were troubled by the chaplain's comments. I offered an alternative approach, with the chaplain still sitting in the room; but it was clear that they had been shaken.

Dan, a white, middle-aged businessman, told everyone, including the chaplain, he had served two years in federal prison and that he was

---

4. Most inmates in Tennessee prisons earn 17 cents per hour. Work-release inmates must pay $485 per month in rent for staying in the bunk-bed dorm of the prerelease prison.

released more than fifteen years ago. He had completed parole almost twelve years ago. After orientation, we received a memo from the chaplain saying that Dan's application had been denied: "Not approved . . . Recent and serious Federal charges." The conviction was not recent, and he had not only completed his sentence but also met all other requirements. He has been "off paper"—no requirements for supervision or reporting—for more than eleven years. Dan writes: "If there is anyone qualified to speak to the issues facing current and former offenders, with all due respect, it is me. I not only know of the criminal-justice system, but I have been through it, come out on the other side, and have never returned. I have been the recipient of forgiveness, grace, and restoration from my Creator. . . . No one knows better than me what it takes and what I went through to get to where I am—a place where every offender can be, if he or she can receive the support necessary to help achieve restoration, to once again believe in themselves, to have the courage and willingness to be the person they really are. No one should ever be defined by their felony conviction."

When is the sentence completed? For most people, serving time inside a prison is a life sentence. The collateral damage continues for years. Dan noted that the chaplain's words during orientation put him back sixteen years—a prisoner defined by his crime, a number inside a dehumanizing system. Dan was eventually allowed to be a partner in the course, but it was not without incurring new wounds and experiencing a resurfacing of the old wounds. And it took going to high-level administrators to make it happen.

Breaking through barriers includes reckoning with the damage done by the system itself to those who serve time. As Harmon Wray and Laura Magnani write, the prison system creates mental and physical illness but offers minimal access to medical and mental-health services.[5] Anthony[6] has had severe headaches for two years, but the only response has been to send him to the clinic to try a new medicine—no tests and no examination by a physician. Lenny has been incarcerated thirteen years for possession of drugs, but has never had access to a substance-abuse treatment program. Antonio was diagnosed with mental illness as a teenager and required medication during high school. Incarcerated for more than eleven years now, he has never seen a psychiatrist or been given access to medications that might treat his illness.

5. Magnani and Wray, *Beyond Prisons*, 100, 122–26.

6. Out of respect, names have often been changed for sisters and brothers on both the inside and outside.

Don Beisswenger, ordained clergy, retired seminary professor, and social-justice activist committed to nonviolence, served six months in federal prison for his witness against the School of the Americas. This is a man who carefully prepared and planned for his time in prison, a man who practices spiritual disciplines and is part of a supportive community. He received many letters and frequent visits while he was in prison and was able to afford the absurdly expensive collect phone calls home. And yet, he speaks often of the damage he experienced in the prison system—the confusion, vulnerability, disorientation, and depression that came as a result of relentless harassment and dehumanization, the demands for conformity and obedience to an endless list of rules that are enforced arbitrarily.[7]

Terry often begins the semester by telling people how much time he has served: "Hi, my name is Terry and this is my 12,164th day behind prison walls." More than thirty-two years in prison for a rape he committed when he was twenty-two. It was a crime of force, fear, violation, and brutality of sexual violence. He was the first in his family to go to college. Except he came home—and raped a woman. He believes that his crime killed his mother. She died about two years after he was convicted and sent to prison, knowing that he would be gone a long time. He could not go home when she became ill, or be there for the funeral. He loved his mother fiercely and talks about her often. He dreams of being home with his father, who is almost ninety and has several serious health problems. His father is determined to get Terry home before he dies.

Terry was one of the five original inside students for our Riverbend class. He loves to learn and write; engage in critical, creative thinking; and figure out how to apply what we learn. He is passionate and funny, witty and prophetic. He also struggles with depression. Although he takes antidepressants, maintaining a balance inside the walls after so many years is not easy. In his thirtieth year of continuous prison, he was placed on suicide watch. They moved him from his guild to a tiny isolation cell in the lockdown mental-health unit. He was given a bare mattress, paper gown, and paper slippers. No other clothes, no blanket, no books, no shower. When Harmon and I finally got to see him, we were shocked. We stood outside in the hall, trying to look through the pie-flap opening in the metal door of his cell. The opening is just big enough for our fingers to reach through so we could touch Terry's hand on the other side. Peeking

7. Beisswenger, *Locked Up*.

through the opening, we wondered how healing is possible in such a barren place.

Prisons are the largest mental-health institutions in our country and mental-health care, like healthcare in general, is inadequate, sporadic, and often dangerously inaccessible. Terry has no regular contact with either a psychological counselor or a psychiatrist. On one visit, the chaplain lets us borrow a folding chair he uses so that we could actually sit outside the locked metal door and peer into the pie flap, instead of squatting down or sitting on the floor.

"Please," Terry urged us, "Would you ask them to give me back my glasses and my Bible? They've taken them both away." Tears, prayers, and deep, shattering sobs. On another occasion, he pled: "Take my ring and give it to my father." We refused, knowing that this is the only thing he has left that reminds him of a life that used to be. "Please," he said, "I want to die. Just let me go." But we kept coming, knowing that we don't have the right words or much in the way of solutions; but we love Terry, and presence matters.

Not long after that visit, however, the mental-health staff in the lockdown unit decided to isolate Terry even more by preventing him from having any visitors—no pastors, family, or friends. "Isolation for mental-health reasons," we were told by the nurse. We tried to argue that cutting someone off from pastoral care, from family and friends is a cruel and unusual punishment, but no one seemed to listen. We called the state department of mental health, correctional staff, and other psychiatrists; but no one intervened.

Terry survived and was eventually moved back into the population. He has been a part of the prison classes every semester. When it is time for his parole hearing, lots of people are supportive. Terry is nervous, as are most people in that situation. Parole hearings are hard. They require a big commitment of time from folks on the outside. Outsiders have to be there to check in before things start, but one never knows when the case will be called or how long the hearing will take, or if a hearing officer will actually show up for the hearing. It is not uncommon to arrive at 7:45 a.m. and still be waiting at 2:00 p.m.

People on the inside both hope for and dread parole hearings. Sometimes there are people in the community who come to protest parole for a particular person. Sometimes no one is willing or able to be there to provide support or to testify on a prisoner's behalf and so he or she faces the situation alone. One never knows which hearing officer one will get, and there is often a huge difference in attitude between one hearing officer and the next. For some family members or loved ones who do come, this will be the first time to hear details of the crime; since so many insiders were convicted through plea bargaining, not trials. Most inmates want so much to be a new person, to leave that old person behind. Many want to reckon with the harm they have done, make amends where possible, and trust that there is life waiting on the other side. Parole hearings drag prisoners into their past.

Terry's parole hearing was astonishing from the start. Two correctional officers took time off work in order to testify for Terry. They have known him for most of his time inside; and they talked about his friendship, his genuine goodness, his gentleness, his advocacy for others inside the prison, and his willingness to work with almost anyone. Seminary students and professors, pastors and church friends, his father and his counselor all showed up. Never have I seen more supportive people at a parole hearing. No one was there to protest his release. But the hearing was over quickly. The hearing officer declared: "Due to the seriousness of your crime, I cannot recommend parole." Terry's father began to cry.

They took Terry back to his cell. The rest of us moved back to the visiting gallery, the hearing officer's decision clear to anyone who saw us. At this point, several others were crying. How much punishment is enough? What good comes from locking someone up for more than thirty years? The seriousness of his crime will never change. What are we waiting for?

Apocalyptic Acts: Unveiling Hidden Gifts, Creating Alternatives

The shift in social location, from center to margins, from power over to partnership with, from distance to proximity, is central to the biblical story. Consciously changing location is an apocalyptic act—it unveils, reveals new truths, startling us so that we might recognize the ways in which we have "settled in as kept chaplains of an unjust order."[8] We discover anew the ways in which we have been seduced by "empire"—the prevailing society's ideology and theology; how we have been seduced with such power that we are no longer able to see or think beyond these narrow definitions of reality.[9]

8. The phrase belongs to Walter Wink.
9. Brueggemann, *Prophetic Imagination*, 126–30.

One of the hardest barriers to overcome is the common definition of prison ministry as good people from churches coming inside to minister to, evangelize, and "save" the lost people behind prison bars. This approach often silences the voices and hides the faces and stories of those on the inside and "forces others to inhabit your version of their reality."[10] In addition, it focuses the pastoral-care lens on the individual who is incarcerated, instead of on the systems and structures that have relentlessly pushed a larger and larger percentage of people from impoverished communities, especially communities of color, into the criminal-justice system. The Bible reminds us that sin is structural and collective, not simply individual. The tendency among mainline denominations to remove the gospel from the margins distorts our understanding of Jesus, sin, salvation, and who the church is called to be. As Virgilio Elizondo writes:

> There is something in the colonized identity of the Galilean that people who have never been colonized do not suspect. There is something which the poor and exploited, the broken and the humiliated, the ridiculed and separated of the world have perceived that the powerful of this world have missed.[11]

Brazilian educator Paulo Freire defines the conscientization process as a communal dialogue that awakens people to rename the world through their own experience; he recognizes the powers that oppress, control, limit, destroy, but also the powers of life and liberation, the possibilities for communal movement toward freedom.[12] This approach comes from a conviction that the people with problems are the people with solutions; that the most undereducated, impoverished, and struggling human being brings gifts for analyzing the world in which they live in order to identify how they might move toward the world for which they yearn. And most often, they can name the powers and principalities at work in their world with more accuracy and prophetic honesty than can the parish clergy, bishops, folks in seminaries, or congregational leaders.

Inevitably, the classes and this long-term, mutual, open, and honest community inside the prison pull the veil off the myths and stereotypes perpetuated by the criminal-justice system and our culture. It is not long into the conversation before it becomes very clear that the system is marked by race and class bias. While it is usually a surprise for outsiders, insiders know that who you are and where you come from make all

10. Gourevitch, *We Wish to Inform You*, 181.

11. Elizondo, *A God of Incredible Surprises*, 5.

12. Freire, *Pedagogy of the Oppressed*.

the difference as to how you will fare in the system. They also see more clearly who benefits and who is harmed by the way crime is defined in this country.

Building community takes time; although it always startles me to see how quickly the walls come down most of the time. A recent semester at the Annex was harder. There was significant tension around race. We were pleased to have larger group of white insiders than we had had before, but we soon discovered that several came with bad attitudes. We were not sure why they applied to participate or why they were approved, but there they were. During our first class, they refused to mingle, sticking instead to their White group. Even after being instructed to create diverse small groups, five White insiders refused to move. The next week they complained about the readings—"Incarceration has nothing to do with race. That's just hype; folks whining and complaining, and we're tired of it."

After class, the leadership team talked about the struggle. Do we ask them to leave, for the sake of the larger community? What does it mean to tolerate their racist behavior? What does it mean to challenge it? Jahi, a large Black man and a Muslim, who has been inside for more than twenty-nine years and who is part of our leadership team, responds: "This stuff is taught. It can be untaught. I got it. Just give me some time. We can do this."

And they did. The leadership team members on the inside kept on talking with, listening to, sharing with the White inmates who seemed so closed. They worked on loving those sharp edges into community. About halfway through the semester, one of the White insiders spoke up: "I want to apologize for all that stuff I've been writing and saying. I'm not really like that. I'm better than that. I can be. I will be. Thanks for giving me another chance." After two more weeks, he and Jahi were standing together laughing. "I see you." "I am here."

Shift to Riverbend, the maximum-security prison. We start the semester as usual—going around the circle, offering up first names and reasons for joining the class. We remind participants that we are not asking anyone to disclose why he is in prison, any more than we would ask outsiders to share the worst thing they've done. Folks smile, and we begin.

I suspect that it was because Phil's case had been on the news that day: another priest arrested for sexual abuse. So reporters dragged up Phil's case all over again—a Roman Catholic priest convicted of molesting several teenaged boys. In introducing himself Phil often remarks that he is the only one in the class who really belongs behind bars. But this time he spoke about the classes he had attended before, prompted, I am sure, by his sense that, because of the news coverage, everyone now knows why he was there and what he had done.

About two-thirds of the way through the semester Phil mentioned something about his crimes, clearly thinking that everyone knew. But Laura hadn't known, and she was shocked. Laura and Phil had become friends over the past weeks. They often shared similar responses to the readings and sat next to each other, joking, telling stories, and sharing insights. Laura, a local pastor in her forties and a divorced mother of two teenaged boys, was going through the ordination process and finishing seminary.

Laura asked to talk with me after class. We sat in my parked car, watching rain stream down the windows. She started the conversation with a question about the assignment but then began to cry, sharing her story of abuse experienced as a child and the struggles she has gone through to find healing. She had sworn that she would never be in the same room with someone who had sexually abused children. But there she was in the classroom, suddenly comprehending this truth about her friend Phil. She looked up after hearing his words, expecting to see a monster; but it was only Phil. And she wondered whether this might be a sign of God's healing, a sign that she had moved through some wall and found new possibilities for her life. She told me about the years of therapy she had gone through to try to reckon with the many broken pieces of her heart and body. In the middle of her tears, she began to laugh: Wouldn't it be something if after all she had tried, she found healing in the prison?

I suggested that she go back to her therapist to talk through this experience. Did it make sense for her to continue the class? Would she feel safe? What might be danger signals she should watch for if she decided to continue coming? She did. She came back wanting to talk with Phil. She thought that he could help her move through some of the pain and deep scars; and she had worked with her therapist to make sure that it was a safe conversation. I suggested that she begin by writing to Phil so that he would have time to think and respond.

Phil was unnerved and edgy and not sure that this was a good idea. But the possibility that he might contribute to healing pushed him through his reservations. He was open and honest and responded to Laura's questions and ideas.

After some time, she requested to meet with Phil in person outside of class. In fact, she wanted to design some kind of healing liturgy for herself and ask Phil to participate. I said that I would explore the possibilities and asked her to go back to her therapist to concretely define both a plan and a safety net. I talked with Phil. He bordered on the edge of panic; but he said that he would do whatever was asked of him, grateful for an opportunity to contribute to good.

I made the arrangements for the three of us to meet in the chaplain's office. Laura had asked that she be allowed to bring water, one large bowl, and two smaller bowls. She had heard a story about pouring pain into the heart of God, the only heart large enough to hold so much hurt. She wanted to pour her pain into that large bowl and invite Phil to do the same. But the officials refused Laura's request. We were lucky to get fifteen minutes.

As we began, all of us were a bit nervous, including the chaplain. He kept interrupting the conversation to talk about irrelevant issues such as surveys and new forms. And then the storm came.

In a maximum-security prison, electrical storms mean lockdown. You stay where you are until the lightning stops. In case of a power outage, no doors, gates, or cells are to be left open. So everyone stays put until the storm passes. This particular storm lasted a while, with plenty of lightning and thunder. As the three of us sat there, locked in, we discovered that each of us had brought something with us. Phil had found two plastic lids and a larger bottle cap. On his way to the chaplain's office, he had asked for a cup of water; so now we had two small containers with water and a larger something to catch it when poured. Laura brought three tiny porcelain fish from her time in Japan. I brought three small wooden stars to remind us of God's light and God's invitation to us to be sources of light and life.

Laura and Phil waded in—talking, reading Scripture and litanies, sharing, singing, praying. The priest who would never be a priest again led us through a liturgy of healing and was invited to lay hands on one who had sworn she would never be in the same room with, let alone ever be touched by, someone who had molested children. It was an extraordinary moment, a holy time. What happened in that room could not be locked up. It could not be imprisoned or contained. God broke through all the barriers.

At the end, Phil started laughing. He told us about the priestly ritual of dipping an evergreen branch into water then sprinkling the water into the congregation. He used to delight in making sure that he flung water onto those who were trying to avoid getting wet. "God is making sure everyone is splashed with grace this night!" The rain stopped and the door opened. Phil went back to his guild, and Laura and I returned to our car.

But the moment changed forever how we see one another and how we understand healing and grace.

Communal Pastoral Care: Resistance to Oppression

There is an African proverb that declares: "Because we are, I am. I am because we are." This proverb places the roots of individual identity in community and underlines the difficulty of finding our place in the world if we are isolated, disconnected, segregated, and separated. Pastoral care becomes a communal event, the creation and nurturing of "belongingness."[13] As Edward Wimberly notes in his writing on pastoral care in the Black church tradition, the dominant culture's tendency to focus on one-to-one therapy is a luxury in oppressed communities:

> To learn the methods and skills of the one-to-one healing model requires economic resources and extensive clinical and educational opportunities to which many black pastors did not have access until recently. . . . The black church had to rely upon a tradition of sustaining and guiding fashioned in response to oppression . . . finding corporate and communal means to meet the needs of persons when theoretical models were inadequate.[14]

Communal pastoral care requires uncovering the gifts and resources of the entire community in order to address hurts and struggles of individuals and to engage the systems and structures that cause the harm. This communal care embodies *ubuntu*—connectedness, a web of interrelatedness.[15] It stands in contrast to the more common and traditional approach that "isolates the individual from family, social, and economic contexts, thus ignoring the importance of relationships and systems in both forming individuals and enabling them to change."[16]

Healing happens for both insiders and outsiders as community grows. It is a miracle in and of itself: the very idea of a safe space in the middle of the prison; and, within that safe space, an invitation for people to really be themselves. People are often "listened into life."[17] So many good gifts are hidden behind prison walls. If it were not for the clothes,

13. J. Deotis Roberts, quoted in Eugene and Poling, *Balm in Gilead*, 25.
14. Edward P. Wimberly quoted in Eugene and Poling, *Balm in Gilead*, 155.
15. Eugene and Poling, *Balm in Gilead*, 186–89.
16. Magnani and Wray, *Beyond Prisons*, 159.
17. Boyd, "WomanistCare," 200.

it might be hard to tell insiders from outsiders. Here are snapshots of this communal healing-from-the-inside-out from a recent semester:

White, middle-aged woman locked up for a short time on a charge of drunk driving: She was not involved in an accident and wasn't speeding. She was stopped for a broken taillight, during which she was tested for alcohol. She knows the shame, the humiliation, the dehumanization, the fear. She remembers the women inside the jail and the way several of them took care of her, comforting her, knowing that she was new to it all. She told no one at work, scared that she might lose her job. Nor did she tell her family or her church, worried that they would think less of her, judge her, even exclude her. There, in that class, she will share this story out loud for the first time. "*Sawabona*. I see you." "*Sikona*. I am here."

Young African-American male honorably discharged from the military after service in the Gulf War: He remained haunted by images of that war, troubled by his role in the killing and by his country's actions. He had almost made it through college when he was picked up on a first-time drug offense. He had no previous arrest record; and no weapons or violence were involved in the offense. Home is almost 400 miles away; so he has had no visitors. He comes to class, quiet and shy but excited for the opportunity to study, read, and engage others in critical thinking and dialogue. He is hungry for community, for a second chance, to be seen for something more than his crime. *Sawabona. Sikona.*

Young Latino male: He laughed when he discovered that someone in the class spoke Spanish, since he hadn't heard his mother tongue in many months. He struggled with English, telling us that he could not find words in English to describe what has happened to him and the complete the isolation he felt. During those two hours in class, he said, he can come home to himself. *Usted veo. Soy aqui.* "I see you." "I am here."

An African-American male, entered the criminal justice system at age fifteen, now celebrating his fifty-second birthday: He has no family waiting—didn't have one when he came in at fifteen. Inside the prison walls he found a family and a community; and he learned something of the meaning of love. He is scared to go back out, having a hard time even imagining what that waiting world is like. Will people in this community really be family for him when he gets out? Can you see me? I am here.

An African-American female, late thirties, single mom working at a grocery store and going to school full time: She remembers being locked up, the shame and humiliation, the guards' harassment, and the strip searches. "Hurts to even think about it, but that's why I had to come back inside. I know what it's like. . . . I had to tell my kids to keep it to themselves—so scared that teachers would write them off if they knew their mom was in jail; scared they'd be taken away. As Jahi said, you don't do time alone. Your family serves that time with you. And for what? Locked up for not paying parking tickets and then driving on a license that had been revoked because I couldn't pay the parking tickets. Still don't have the money to pay. Still have to get in that car in order to get to work in order to earn the money so I can try to pay these fines that keep adding up, getting bigger. Sometimes it feels like there's no way out. It's a crime to be poor in this country, and you know that I'm right about that."

An African-American male, high-level administrator: "I don't see myself as all that dissimilar from people on the inside. . . . One time I heard that we were having problems with one of our treatment facilities, so I had myself referred there as a client. They had no idea who I was. In the intake interview, they kept asking: 'Why are you here? What were you doing?' I responded: 'I was just standing on the corner.' 'Well,' they were quick to reply, 'you shouldn't have been standing on that corner, should you?' And it reminded me of the history of jump and grabs in West Tennessee. At harvest time, they'd jump out and grab folks, dragging them in and forcing them to work the fields at harvest time. I was just struck by the fact that it's the same now—jump and grab—in urban settings. . . . We've managed to criminalize so many things in America."

> If I really see you,
> I laugh out loud at the humor of it.
> If I really see you,
> I fall silent in awe.
> If I really see you,
> I burst into a thousand pieces from inspiration.
> And if I fail to really see you,
> I am sealed in the cement and stone of my own prison.[18]

"As Beautiful as a Yes in a Room Full of No's"

This essay has attempted to close the distance between inside and outside, to identify a path through the barriers, to uncover the power of community defined by partnership and mutuality, and the resulting collective movement to engage systems and structures in ways that promote healing

18. Rumi, thirteenth-century mystic.

and wholeness, justice and transformation. One high-level administrator uses the word *habilitation* instead of *rehabilitation*, noting that one cannot restore what never was. He argues that the societal safety net has failed those who are incarcerated—Black and White, male and female, young and old:

> The net failed—whether it is education or jobs, treatment for the mentally ill or for people caught up in alcohol and drugs. The net failed. In some cases, people have been let down by churches. I want to create the opportunities for people to hear the voices inside, to acknowledge the humanity in everyone.
>
> Ninety-five percent of those on the inside are eventually returned to communities on the outside. While recidivism rates are high, most of the charges are technical violations, not new crimes. Transformation and Reconciliation from the Inside Out (TRIO), a think tank and action team that grew out of our Inside Out classes, works with congregations to design reentry support teams. Insiders who have graduated from the class and been released become leaders in this work. The affirmation of their gifts and somebodiness continues, as they give back to the community. This is communal pastoral care: we hold one another and we hold one another accountable.[19]

Kahuna, serving a long sentence at Riverbend, was taken by our focus on restorative justice. He received permission from the warden to write letters to his victim. For two years he wrote letters attempting to make amends, to apologize, praying for good for the person he had harmed. For two years there was no response. Then one day the letter came. Not too many months after that, the victim came to visit him at Riverbend—and to forgive him. "I stood tall that day, and I've been living ever since."

Mustafa, quiet, steady, gentle, and consistently responsible, has been a part of the leadership team. Recently he was put on work release and now is going home. On his last night in prison, he stands in the middle of our circle and says thanks: "This class helped me believe I could make it. It helped me see I am somebody and not to be so ashamed. But it's scary out there. I'd get to thinking everyone knew I was a criminal. I'd try to make myself small. Be real quiet. Not look at people. Then this man comes up to me the other day and shakes my hand. Not like you do when you feel sorry for someone, but like you do when you're meeting a real person, like we do in here. And he tells me I'm doing a good job and would I like to work

---

19. Bishop Kenneth Carder, retired United Methodist bishop, used in a sermon several years ago.

with him. And I felt something in myself. Something good. I remembered my family here. I gotta tell you, if I can make it, anyone can."

Zahir was released from the Annex and soon enrolled as a student at American Baptist College, where I teach. When the semester started, he came back inside the prison as an outsider who was working full time and going to school full time. He was a walking sign of hope. Every week, his presence reminded people that they too could make it on the outside. In the prison compound, a line drawn on the concrete walkway near the exit marks off prisoners from outsiders. All goodbyes must be made on the inside of the line. On the first night of reentering the prison as an outsider, completing class and getting ready to leave, Zahir came to the line: "Wait. Remember all those times I had to stop here? I told you, one day I'd walk out of here with you, one day I'd cross that line. Watch!" And he walked across the line. Insiders and outsiders celebrated as grace was made visible and hope grew larger.

Dorothee Soelle quotes a poem written by Joao Cabral: "He is as beautiful as a Yes in a room full of No's . . . Beautiful because he is a door that turns into many exits." And then she goes on: "To love life . . . where it has been condemned to death, even from its very beginning, is an old human ability to go beyond what is. That ability is called transcendence or faith or hope—or listening to the silent cry. It is the most important movement that human beings can learn in their lives."[20]

Pastoral care *with*—not *to* or *for*—people caught up inside the prison systems requires focusing on a healing process through community, observes one high-level administrator in the correctional system:

> Congregations have got to facilitate healing, a process of making the victim and victimizer whole. Go in with eyes wide open, knowing healing happens one day at a time—not just that one time they come forward in a church service. . . . Build realistic partnerships with the criminal justice system. . . . Offer up opportunities based on the possibility of making a change.

Pastoral care requires mobilizing the resources of the entire community to address the harm and create possibilities for reconciliation and transformative justice. It begins with this authentic partnership over time that redefines our understanding of the criminal-justice system, opens our eyes, ears, and hearts, and empowers us to see and be seen. This ongoing encounter in community mobilizes us to confront the systems and structures that diminish life, to work collectively for concrete changes to

20. Soelle, *The Silent Cry*, 282.

policies, and to "decriminalize behavior that involves homelessness, mental illness, drug addiction, or consensual sex between adults."[21] It empowers us to challenge zero-tolerance policies for children; educational systems that dump more than half of our high-school students into the streets, without any certificate or degree; a social-service system that abandons people to poverty; and a criminal justice system that is locking up children at a younger and younger age. "*Sawabona.* I see you." "*Sikona.* I am here."

21 Magnani and Wray, *Beyond Prisons*, 163.

Contributors

Jeannie Alexander serves as a pastor and chaplain to the amazing children of God at Riverbend Maximum Security Institution in Nashville, TN. She is also a co-founder of Amos House Catholic Worker Community, a writer for and on the board of directors of *The Contributor* street newspaper, and a flawed follower of the whore-loving, fig-tree-killing, Temple-clearing Nazarene.

Richard Beck is Associate Professor and Chair of the Department of Psychology at Abilene Christian University. His list of publications includes *Unclean: Meditations on Purity, Hospitality and Morality* (Cascade, 2011), and his award-winning blog is experimentaltheology.blogspot.com.

Shelly A. Breeden is currently incarcerated at the Tennessee Prison for Women. She is an animal lover and great supporter of Nature and conservation programs. She is a dedicated mother to three children. Shelly aspires to be a great artist and writer and seeks out every opportunity to learn and grow.

Cyntoia Brown is an aspiring writer with a passion for learning, activism, and educating others through her plight. The 2011 documentary *Me Facing Life: Cyntoia's Story*, produced by Dan Birman, highlights some of her journey. She is currently incarcerated in the Tennessee Department of Corrections where she is preparing her full memoir.

Will D. Campbell has been a Southern Baptist preacher in Taylor, LA, the Director of Religious Life at the University of Mississippi, and a race relations specialist for the National Council of Churches. He also served as the publisher for the Committee of Southern Churchmen's *Katallagete: A Journal of Reconciliation*. His *Brother to a Dragonfly* earned the Lillian Smith Prize, the Christopher Award, and a National Book Award nomination. *The*

Glad River won a first-place award from the Friends of American Writers. He has also won a Lyndhurst Prize and Alex Haley Award.

Alex Friedmann is the associate editor of *Prison Legal News* (www.prisonlegalnews.org), a monthly publication that reports on criminal justice issues. He also serves as president of the Private Corrections Institute (www.privateci.org), a non-profit watchdog organization that opposes prison privatization. While incarcerated in the 1990s he served six years at a CCA-operated prison in Tennessee.

Richard Goode is Professor of History at Lipscomb University, where he also coordinates the Lipscomb Initiative for Education (LIFE) programs.

Lee Griffith is a teacher, author, and longtime social activist currently working in Elmira, New York. His published works include *The Fall of the Prison: Biblical Perspectives on Prison Abolition* (one of *Christianity Today*'s Best Books of 1993); *The War on Terrorism and the Terror of God* (2004); and *God is Subversive: Talking Peace in a Time of Empire* (2011).

Craig D. Katzenmiller has been visiting Riverbend Maximum Security Institution since 2007. In 2009, he became part of a Benedictine-inspired community that meets inside the walls once a week. This egalitarian community focuses on prayer, presence, and service. Craig holds an MTS from Lipscomb University.

Marlin Elbon Kilpatrick was employed for nearly five years as Federal Bureau of Prisons Supervisory Chaplain at the Federal Correctional Institution, Englewood in Littleton, Colorado, and Federal Medical Center, Lexington, Kentucky. He is a Mennonite Church USA minister planting a church of prisoners and their families and friends in Jackson, Tennessee.

Andrew Krinks is the editor of *The Contributor*, Nashville's street newspaper covering issues of homelessness, poverty, and marginalization. He has led poetry workshops at the Tennessee Prison for Women and has studied theology at Riverbend Maximum Security Institution. He is currently pursuing a Masters of Theological Studies degree from Vanderbilt Divinity School.

Donna McCoy is inmate #301924. She is serving a life sentence, effective August 17, 1997, with the possibility of parole after serving fifty-one calendar years, making her earliest release date May 2054. And yet, she is a river endlessly flowing, hoping to water the earth along her journey, forever following the path God has etched out for her.

Nathan Miller resides at Riverbend Maximum Security Institution, a small gated community in Nashville. He belongs to God's Church of Weeds, and is currently working toward a bachelor's degree in Religious Studies. He meets with two Benedictine-influenced communities each week.

Reverend Stacy Rector is a Presbyterian minister and Executive Director of Tennesseans for Alternatives to the Death Penalty (TADP). She serves on the national board of People of Faith Against the Death Penalty and was the spiritual advisor for Tennessee death row inmate Steve Henley, who was executed on February 4, 2009.

Preston Shipp serves as Disciplinary Counsel for the Tennessee Board of Professional Responsibility. Prior to working for the BPR, he was an Assistant Attorney General for the State of Tennessee. Since 2002, he has been involved in his church's prison ministry, and since 2007, he has taught classes for Lipscomb University at the Tennessee Prison for Women.

Laura Lake Smith is an art historian specializing in the narratology of modern and contemporary art. She is the author of publications on the artist Richard Tuttle and on service learning inside correctional facilities. She also serves on the advisory board for the LIFE program at Lipscomb University and has taught art history courses at the Tennessee Prison for Women.

Randy Spivey is the Academic Director of the Institute of Law, Justice, and Society at Lipscomb University. His commitment is to see generations of students and community partners pursue the Beloved Community by acting justly, loving mercy, and walking humbly with their God and their neighbors.

William R. Stevens is the death row staff writer for the *Maximum Times* (the prison paper at the Riverbend Maximum Security Institution in Nashville). His poetry, articles, stories, and booklets have circulated internationally, and have reportedly brought a Queen to tears and a Governor's wife to the heights of fury.

Crystal Sturgill is from Pikeville, KY. She maintains a 4.0 grade point average, and is in her third year of Lipscomb University's LIFE program.

Despite serving a sentence of life without parole, she believes in rehabilitation, education, and the power of God to change lives.

Janet Wolf is Professor of Church and Society at American Baptist College in Nashville. She serves as a community organizer around poverty rights, and as a United Methodist pastor with urban and rural congregations. Janet also partners with leaders/teachers who are imprisoned, including SALT: Schools for Alternative Learning and Transformation, working toward restorative justice.

Harmon Wray was a lifelong advocate for the incarcerated. The Executive Director of Restorative Justice Ministries for the United Methodist Board of Global Ministries from 1999 through 2001, he authored *Restorative Justice: Moving Beyond Punishment* (2002) and *Beyond Prisons: A New Interfaith Paradigm for Our Failed Prison System* (2006, with Laura Magnani). At the time of his death in 2007, he was the Director of the Vanderbilt Program in Faith and Criminal Justice.

Felicia Ybanez was born in Murray, KY, and has strong military ties on both sides of her family. Her inspiration of hope consists of grandparents, Frank and Rita Varble, parents, James and Charlotte Neville, siblings, Frankie Ybanez and Rita Neville, and companion, Atlanta Hardy. Her life's passion is to be in the service of others.

Acknowledgments

W<small>E WOULD LIKE TO</small> thank the following friends and colleagues for their assistance throughout this collection: Andrew Krinks, Robbie Spivey, and Cliff Tierney. A special expression of gratitude to Craig "Dusty" Katzenmiller for his unflagging commitment to this work in tasks including, but certainly not limited to, editing, proofing, indexing, and research. For the support of Lipscomb University, and in particular Provost W. Craig Bledsoe, we are grateful. Thanks to Christian Amondson, Jim Tedrick, Chris Spinks, and the staff of Wipf and Stock Publishers.

We are grateful to all those who entrusted us with their stories. Hopefully we have proven good stewards of their trust.

Bibliography

Abramsky, Sasha. *American Furies: Crime, Punishment, and Vengeance in the Age of Mass Imprisonment.* Boston: Beacon, 2007.

Agamben, Giorgio. *Homo Sacer: Sovereign Power and Bare Life.* Translated by Daniel Heller-Roazen. Stanford: Stanford University Press, 1995.

Alexander, Michelle. "Think Outside the Bars: Why Real Justice Means Fewer Prisons." *Yes!* (Summer 2011) 18–22.

Allen, Jared. "Tears and Anger: Still in Mourning, Close Community Demands Justice." *The City Paper.* December 20, 2006.

Barth, Christoph. *Introduction to the Psalms.* Translated by R. A. Wilson. New York: Scribner, 1966.

Barth, Karl. *Deliverance to the Captives.* London: SCM, 1961.

Beck, Richard. *Unclean: Meditations on Purity, Hospitality, and Mortality.* Eugene, OR: Cascade, 2011.

Becker, Ernest. *The Denial of Death.* New York: Free Press, 1973.

Beisswenger, Don. *Locked Up: Letters and Papers of a Prisoner of Conscience.* Nashville: Upper Room, 2008.

Bellesiles, Michael A. *Arming America: The Origins of a National Gun Culture.* Berkeley: Soft Skull, 2003.

Benavie, Arthur. *Drugs: America's Holy War.* New York: Routledge, 2009.

Birch, Bruce. *Let Justice Roll Down: The Old Testament, Ethics, and Christian Life.* Louisville: Westminster John Knox, 1991.

Bosworth, Mary. *Explaining U.S. Imprisonment.* Los Angeles: Sage, 2010.

Brown, Michelle. *The Culture of Punishment: Prison, Society, and Spectacle.* New York: New York University Press, 2009.

Brueggemann, Walter. *The Prophetic Imagination.* 2nd ed. Minneapolis: Fortress, 2001.

Burton-Rose, Daniel, editor. *The Celling of America: An Inside Look at the U.S. Prison Industry.* Monroe, ME: Common Courage, 1998.

Campbell, Will D. *And Also With You: Duncan Gray and the American Dilemma.* Franklin, TN: Providence House, 1997.

———. *Brother to a Dragonfly.* New York: Continuum, 1977.

———. *The Glad River.* New York: Holt, Rinehart, Winston, 1982.

———. "Perhaps and Maybe." *The Christian Century* 79 (September 19, 1962).

Contributors

———. *Providence*. Atlanta: Longstreet, 1992.

———. *Soul Among Lions: Musings of a Bootleg Preacher*. Louisville: Westminster John Knox, 1999.

———. "Vocation as Grace." *Katallagete* 4 (Fall–Winter 1972) 80–86.

———. "Where to Sit in Scottsboro: Last Act in a Tragedy." *Christianity and Crisis* 37:13 (August 15, 1977) 189–91.

———. *Writings on Reconciliation and Resistance*. Edited by Richard C. Goode. Eugene, OR: Cascade, 2010.

Campbell, Will D., and Richard C. Goode. *Crashing the Idols: The Vocation of Will D. Campbell (and any other Christian for that matter)*. Eugene, OR: Cascade, 2010.

Cavanaugh, William T. *Being Consumed: Economics and Christian Desire*. Grand Rapids: Eerdmans, 2008.

Couture, Pamela. *Seeing Children, Seeing God: A Practical Theology of Children and Poverty*. Nashville: Abingdon, 2000.

Crow, Thomas. *Painters and Public Life in Eighteenth Century Paris*. New Haven: Yale University Press, 1985.

Danto, Arthur. "Hegel, Biedermeier, and the Intractably Avant-Garde." In *Art on the Edge and Over*. Edited by Linda Weintraub. New York: Distributed Art, 1996.

Dark, David. *The Sacredness of Questioning Everything*. Grand Rapids: Zondervan, 2009.

Davis, Angela Y. *The Angela Y. Davis Reader*. Edited by Joy James. Malden and Oxford: Blackwell, 1998.

———. *Are Prisons Obsolete?* New York: Seven Stories, 2003.

———. "Race, Gender, and Prison History: From the Convict Lease System to the Supermax Prison." In *Prison Masculinities*, edited by Don Sabo, Terry Kupers, and Willie London, 35–45. Philadelphia: Temple University Press, 2001.

DeWolf, L. Harold. *Crime and Justice in America: A Paradox of Conscience*. New York: Harper & Row, 1975.

Dostoevsky, Fyodor. *The Brothers Karamazov*. Translated by Richard Pevear and Larissa Volokhonsky. New York: Farrar, Straus, and Giroux, 1990.

Durnbaugh, Donald F., editor. *Every Need Supplied: Mutual Aid and Christian Community in the Free Churches*. Philadelphia: Temple University Press, 1974.

Dylan, Bob. "The Lonesome Death of Hattie Carroll." *The Times They Are A-Changin'.* Columbia Records, 1964.

Eisenman, Steven. *Nineteenth Century Art: A Critical History*. London: Thames and Hudson, 2002.

Elizondo, Virgilio. *A God of Incredible Surprises: Jesus of Galilee*. Lanham: Rowman and Littlefield, 2003.

Elkins, James. *Stories of Art*. New York: Routledge, 2002.

Ellul, Jacques. *The Theological Foundation of Law*. Translated by Marguerite Wieser. New York: Seabury, 1969.

Enns, Elaine, and Ched Myers. *Ambassadors of Reconciliation: Diverse Christian Practices of Restorative Justice and Peacemaking*. Maryknoll: Orbis, 2009.

Estes, Carol. "School of Second Chances," *Yes!* (Summer 2011) 32–35.

Eugene, Toinette, and James Newton Poling. *Balm in Gilead: Pastoral Care for African American Families Experiencing Abuse*. Nashville: Abingdon, 1998.

Farley, Wendy. "Evil, Violence, and the Practice of Theodicy." In *Telling the Truth: Preaching about Sexual and Domestic Violence*, edited by John S. McClure and Nancy J. Ramsay, 11–20. Cleveland: United Church Press, 1998.

Fineberg, Jonathan. *Art Since 1940: Strategies of Being*. 2nd ed. Engelwood Cliffs, NJ: Prentice Hall, 2000.

Foster Boyd, Marsha. "WomanistCare: Some Reflections on the Pastoral Care and the Transformation of African American Women." In *Embracing the Spirit: Womanist Perspectives on Hope, Salvation, and Transformation*, edited by Emilie Maureen Townes, 197–202. Bishop Henry McNeal Turner/Sojourner Truth Series in Black Religion 13. Maryknoll, NY: Orbis, 1997.

Foucault, Michel. *Discipline and Punish: The Birth of the Prison*. Translated by Alan Sheridan. New York: Vintage, 1979.

———. *Power/Knowledge: Selected Interviews and Other Writings, 1972–1977*. Edited by Colin Gordon. New York: Pantheon, 1980.

———. *Foucault Reader*. Edited by Paul Rabinow. New York: Pantheon, 1984.

Freire, Paulo. *Pedagogy of the Oppressed*. New York: Continuum, 2000.

Friedman, Lawrence M. *Crime and Punishment in American History*. New York: Basic, 1993.

Frye, Northrop. *The Great Code: The Bible and Literature*. New York: Harcourt Brace Jovanovich, 1982.

Gaines, Patrice. "Restoring Lives: Now That's Justice." *Yes!* (Summer 2011) 45–48.

Garb, Tamar. "Berthe Morisot and the Feminizing of Impressionism." In *Readings in Nineteenth Century Art*, edited by Janis Tomlinson, 230–45. Upper Saddle River, NJ: Prentice-Hall, 1996.

Garland, David. *The Culture of Control: Crime and Social Order in Contemporary Society*. Chicago: University of Chicago Press, 2001.

Gourevitch, Philip. *We Wish to Inform You that Tomorrow We Will Be Killed with Our Families: Stories from Rwanda*. New York: Picador, 1999.

Griffith, Lee. *The Fall of the Prison: Biblical Perspectives on Prison Abolition*. Grand Rapids: Eerdmans, 1993.

———. *God is Subversive: Talking Peace in a Time of Empire*. Grand Rapids: Eerdmans, 2011.

Gross, Bertram. *Friendly Fascism: The New Face of Power in America*. Boston: South End, 1980.

Heidegger, Martin. *Basic Writings*. Edited by David Farrell Krell. New York: HarperCollins, 1977.

Hibbert, Christopher. *The Roots of Evil: A Social History of Crime and Punishment.* Boston: Little, Brown, 1963.

Ingle, Joseph B. *Last Rights: Thirteen Fatal Encounters with the State's Justice.* Nashville: Abingdon, 1990.

Jones, Jonathan. "No Way Out." *The Guardian* (November 6, 2002).

Jones, L. Gregory. *Embodying Forgiveness: A Theological Analysis.* Grand Rapids: Eerdmans, 1995.

Kantorowicz, Ernst H. *The King's Two Bodies: A Study in Medieval Political Theology.* Princeton: Princeton University Press, 1957.

Karpowitz, Daniel, and Max Kenner. "Education as Crime Prevention: The Case for Reinstating Pell Grant Eligibility for the Incarcerated." Bard Prison Initiative. 30 May 2009. bard.edu/bpi.

Keel, Othmar. *The Symbolism of the Biblical World: Ancient Near Eastern Iconography and the Book of Psalms.* New York: Seabury, 1978.

Knopp, Fay H., et al. *Instead of Prisons: A Handbook for Abolitionists.* Oakland: AK, 2005.

Kopczynski, Ken. *Private Capitol Punishment: The Florida Model.* Bloomington: AuthorHouse, 2004.

Lampman, Lisa Barnes, editor. *God and the Victim: Theological Reflections on Evil, Victimization, and Forgiveness.* Grand Rapids: Eerdmans, 1999.

Lazare, Daniel. "Stars and Bars," *The Nation.* (August 27, 2007). No pages. Online: http://www.thenation.com/article/stars-and-bars.

Linebaugh, Peter. *The London Hanged: Crime and Civil Society in the Eighteenth Century.* 2nd ed. New York: Verso, 2003.

Logan, James Samuel. *Good Punishment?: Christian Moral Practice and U.S. Imprisonment.* Grand Rapids: Eerdmans, 2008.

Lohfink, Gerhard. *Jesus and Community: The Social Dimension of Christian Faith.* Minneapolis: Fortress, 1984.

McHugh, Gerald Austin. *Christian Faith and Criminal Punishment: Toward a Christian Response to Crime and Punishment.* New York: Paulist, 1978.

Magnani, Laura, and Harmon Wray. *Beyond Prisons: A New Interfaith Paradigm for Our Failed Prison System.* Minneapolis: Fortress, 2006.

Malcolm X and Alex Haley. *The Autobiography of Malcolm X.* New York: Ballantine, 1973.

Marion, Jean Luc. *God Without Being: Hors-Texte.* Translated by Thomas A. Carlson. Religion and Postmodernism. Chicago: University of Chicago Press, 1991.

Marshall, Christopher D. *Beyond Retribution: A New Testament Vision for Justice, Crime, and Punishment.* Grand Rapids: Eerdmans, 2001.

Maté, Gabor. "Why Punish Pain? A Hit of Compassion Could Keep Drugs from Becoming a Crime Problem," *Yes!* (Summer 2011) 24–26.

Maur, Marc. *Race to Incarcerate.* New York: New Press, 2006.

Maur, Marc, and Meda Chesney-Lind. *Invisible Punishment: The Collateral Consequences of Mass Imprisonment.* New York: New Press, 2003.

Mays, James L. "Justice: Perspectives from the Prophetic Tradition." *Issues in Religion and Theology* 10 (1987) 144–58.

Menninger, Karl A. *The Crime of Punishment*. New York: Viking, 1969.

Merton, Thomas. *New Seeds of Contemplation*. New York: New Directions, 1961.

———. *The Springs of Contemplation: A Retreat at the Abbey of Gethsemani*. Edited Jane Marie Richardson. New York: Farrar, Straus, Giroux, 1992.

Mitford, Jessica. *Kind and Usual Punishment: The Prison Business*. New York: Alfred A. Knopf, 1973.

Moore, Solomon. "Prison Spending Outpaces All But Medicaid." *NYTimes.com* (3 Mar 2009). No pages. Online: www.nytimes.com/2009/03/03/us/03prison. html.

———. "Study Shows Sharp Rise in Latino Federal Convicts." *NYTimes.com* (2 Feb 2009). No pages. Online: www.nytimes.com/2009/02/19/us/19immig. html.

Murphy, Wendy. *And Justice For Some: An Expose of the Lawyers and Judges Who Let Dangerous Criminals Go Free*. New York: Sentinel, 2007.

Orr, William F., and James A. Walther. *1 Corinthians*. The Anchor Bible. Vol. 32. New York: Doubleday, 1976.

Pager, Devah. *Marked: Race, Crime, and Finding Work in an Era of Mass Incarceration*. Chicago: University of Chicago Press, 2007.

Palmer, Parker. *A Hidden Wholeness: The Journey Toward an Undivided Life*. San Francisco: Jossey-Bass, 2004.

Parenti, Christian. *Lockdown America: Police and Prisons in the Age of Crisis*. New York: Verso, 2008.

Prejean, Helen. *Dead Man Walking: An Eyewitness Account of the Death Penalty in the United States*. New York: Vintage, 1993.

———. *The Death of Innocents: An Eyewitness Account of Wrongful Executions*. New York: Random House, 2005.

Provine, Dorris M. *Unequal Under Law: Race in the War on Drugs*. Chicago: The University of Chicago Press, 2007.

Rapske, Brian. *The Book of Acts and Paul in Roman Custody*. Grand Rapids: Eerdmans, 2004.

Redekop, Paul. *Changing Paradigms: Punishment and Restorative Discipline*. Scottdale, PA: Herald, 2008.

Redekop, Vern Neufeld. *Scapegoats, the Bible, and Criminal Justice: Interacting with Rene Girard*. New Perspectives on Crime and Justice 13. MCC U.S. Office of Criminal Justice, 1993.

Reiman, Jeffrey H., and Paul Leighton. *The Rich Get Richer and the Poor Get Prison: Ideology, Class, and Criminal Justice*. 9th ed. Boston: Allyn & Bacon, 2009.

Rosenblatt, Elihu, editor. *Criminal Injustice: Confronting the Prison Crisis*. Boston: South End, 1996.

Rothman, David J. *Conscience and Convenience: The Asylum and its Alternatives in Progressive America*. New York: Little, Brown, 1980.

————. *The Discovery of the Asylum: Social Order and Disorder in the New Republic.* New York: Little, Brown, 1971.

Shopshire, James, Sr., Richmond Stoglin, and Mark Hicks. *I Was in Prison: United Methodist Perspectives on Prison Ministry.* Nashville: United Methodist General Board of Higher Education and Ministry, 2008.

Slater, Philip. *The Pursuit of Loneliness: American Culture at the Breaking Point.* Boston: Beacon, 1970.

Sloan, Robert B., Jr. *The Favorable Year of the Lord: A Study of Jubilary Theology in the Gospel of Luke.* Austin: Schola, 1977.

Soering, Jens. *The Church of the Second Chance: A Faith-Based Approach to Prison Reform.* New York: Lantern, 2008.

————. *The Convict Christ: What the Gospel Says about Criminal Justice.* Maryknoll: Orbis Books, 2006.

————. *An Expensive Way to Make Bad People Worse: An Essay on Prison Reform from an Insider's Perspective.* New York: Lantern, 2004.

Soelle, Dorothee. *The Silent Cry: Mysticism and Resistance.* Minneapolis: Fortress, 2001.

Solzhenitsyn, Aleksandr. *The Gulag Archipelago.* Volume 1: An Experiment in Literary Investigation. New York: HarperCollins, 1973.

Spivak, Andrew. "Inmate Recidivism as a Measure of Private Prison Performance." *Crime & Delinquency* 54 (July 2008) 482–508.

Snyder, T. Richard. *The Protestant Ethic and the Spirit of Punishment.* Grand Rapids: Eerdmans, 2000.

Stringfellow, William. *An Ethic for Christians and Other Aliens in a Strange Land.* Waco: Word, 1973.

————. *Politics of Spirituality.* Eugene, OR: Wipf and Stock, 2006.

Stringfellow, William, and Anthony Towne. *Suspect Tenderness: The Ethics of the Berrigan Witness.* New York: Holt, Rinehart, and Winston, 1971.

Sullivan, Laura. "Prison Economics Help Drive Arizona Immigration Law." National Public Radio (October 28, 2010). http://www.npr.org/templates/story/story.php?storyId=130833741.

Sussman, Peter. "Media on Prisons: Censorship and Stereotypes." In *Invisible Punishment: The Collateral Consequences of Mass Imprisonment,* edited by Marc Mauer and Meda Chesney-Lind, 258–78. New York: New Press, 2002.

Tannenbaum, Frank. "The Dramatization of Evil." In *Deviance: The Interactionist Perspective,* 2nd ed., edited by Earl Rubington and Martin S. Weinberg. New York: Macmillan, 1973.

Taylor, Astra, editor. *Examined Life: Excursions with Contemporary Thinkers.* New York: New Press, 2009.

Taylor, Mark Lewis. *The Executed God: The Way of the Cross in Lockdown America.* Minneapolis: Fortress, 2001.

Vanier, Jean. *Community and Growth.* New York: Paulist, 1989.

Virgo, Sabina. "The Criminalization of Poverty," in *Criminal Injustice: Confronting the Prison Crisis.* Edited by Elihu Rosenblatt. Boston: South End, 1999.

Volf, Miroslav. *Exclusion and Embrace: A Theological Exploration of Identity, Otherness, and Reconciliation.* Nashville: Abingdon, 1996.

———. *Free of Charge: Giving and Forgiving in a Culture Stripped of Grace.* Grand Rapids: Zondervan, 2005.

Wedekind, Carl. *Politics, Religion, and Death: Memoir of a Lobbyist.* Louisville: Kentucky Coalition to Abolish the Death Penalty, 2006.

West, W. Gordon, and Ruth Morris, editors. *The Case for Penal Abolition.* Toronto: Canadian Scholars' Press, 2000.

Whitman, James Q. *Harsh Justice: Criminal Punishment and the Widening Divide between America and Europe.* New York: Oxford University Press, 2003.

Williams, Rowan. *Christ on Trial: How the Gospel Unsettles Our Judgment.* Grand Rapids: Eerdmans, 2000.

Wood, Chris. *The End of Punishment: Christian Perspectives on the Crisis in Criminal Justice.* Edinburgh: Saint Andrews, 1991.

Wray, Harmon. "An Eye for an Eye." *Comin' Out* (Fall–Winter 1987).

———. "Models of Criminal Justice Ministry and Resistance: A Southern Christian Perspective." *VOMA Connections* (Fall 2003) 1, 10–11.

Wray, Harmon, and Peggy Hutchison. *Restorative Justice: Moving Beyond Punishment.* New York: General Board of Global Ministries, The United Methodist Church, 2002.

Wright, Kevin N. *Great American Crime Myth.* Westport: Greenwood, 1985.

Zehr, Howard. *Changing Lenses: A New Focus for Crime and Justice.* 3rd ed. Scottdale: Herald, 2005.

Zimbardo, Philip. "The Psychological Power and Pathology of Imprisonment." *Society* 9 (April 1972) 4–8.

Žižek, Slavoj. *Violence: Six Sideways Reflections.* New York: Picador, 2008.

Essays of the original *Katallagete* (Winter-Spring 1972) issue

"The Good News From God in Jesus Is Freedom to the Prisoners," Will D. Campbell and James Y. Holloway.

"Southern Prison Camps," Marc Hacker.

"Security and Rehabilitation and God In a Godless World," A. Puchalski.

"Doin' Time," Jane Kennedy.

"The Impossible Conspiracy At Soledad Prison," Madison Flowers, Jr.

"Memories of Danbury," J. R. (Bob) Jones.

"Children of Parchman," Sherry Jones and Mary Johnson.

"Dear Joyce," Albert Johnson.

"The Draft Resister in Prison," David Miller.

"My Name is George Wilson," George Wilson.

"Church and State in Prison," Patricia Glennan.

"Prison," James Douglass.

"One Meaning of Prison in America," Norm Barnett.

Scripture Index

Genesis

4:13-15	80n25
39	82n27

Exodus

21:24	80

Leviticus

19:33-34	57
24:20	81
25	223
25:1-10	83

Deuteronomy

10:17-19	57
15	83
19:21	81
22:1-13	81

Ezra

7:25-26	82n27

Job

1:6-12	84

Psalms

69:1-2	84
69:15	84
69:33	84
99:4	58
107:10	84
130:3	68
146:5-9	83

Isaiah

9:2	253
10:1-2	83
42:7	83
61	16
61:1-2	83

Jeremiah

34:15-17	83
37:15	82n27
38:6	84

Lamentations

3:34-36	83

Amos

5:12	83

Micah

7:3	83

Zechariah

3:1	84
9:9–12	83

Matthew

5	205
5–7	223
5:38–39	81
5:43–48	57
10:16	193
10:22	193
10:32–33	193
25	203
25:5	5
25:31–46	83
25:35–40	4
25:36	98
25:44	253

Luke

1:68	83
4	35, 188
4:14–30	56
4:16–19	58
4:16–30	16
4:18–19	84, 187
6:27–28	80
10:25–37	57
22:31–33	84
23:32–34	68
23:43	21

John

1:5	63
8:1–11	148
8:44	198

13	206
18:14	85n32

Acts

12:1–11	84
16:25–34	84
21:33–34	82n27

Romans

12:14–21	68

1 Corinthians

6:1	83
13:1	69

2 Corinthians

5	6
5:15–20	57
5:16	21
5:16–20	58

Galatians

3:27–28	200

1 Peter

3:8–22	68

1 John

3:14b-15	198
4:18	197

Revelation

2:10	84

Subject Index

Academy, 5, 47, 177, 235, 240, 242
Afghanistan, 198
Agamben, Giorgio, 59
Albany Movement, 209
Alley, Sedley, 151, 157
Amberson, William, 10
American Legislative Exchange Council (ALEC), 52–53
And Also With You, 8
Anti-Drug Abuse Act, 37
Apartheid, 70, 219
Aramark, 44
Arizona, 52, 60,
Assault, 39, 48, 62, 114, 220
Association of Private Correctional & Treatment Organizations, 52
Autobiography of Malcolm X, 244

Babel, 66
Ballie, Gil, 194–95
Banjo Lesson, The, 238
Baptism, 174, 177, 183, 199–200, 202
Barnett, Norm, 89
Barth, Karl, 84, 85n32
Bastards, 7, 12, 14, 15, 132
Battle of Nashville, 194
Beatitudes, 203–6
Becker, Ernest, 12, 12n17
Beisswenger, Don, 258
Beloved Community, 6, 177, 179, 182–83, 212; *see also* "Community"
Bentham, Jeremy, 71–72, 235
Berrigan, Dan, 17, 19
Berrigan, Phil, 17, 19
Beuys, Joseph, 241

Beyond Prisons, 39
Bible, 19, 23, 72, 81, 83, 99, 100, 102, 130, 140, 141, 176, 181, 194, 195, 203, 204, 206, 253, 260, 262
Black Nationalists, The, 210
Bradby, Dennis, 49
Bredesen, Phil, 173
Brother to a Dragonfly, 67n34
Brothers Karamazov, The, 68
Brown, Cyntoia, 14, 210, 230–34, 241
Brueggemann, Walter, 65, 189–91, 223
Bundy, Ted, 219
Bureau of Justice Statistics (BJS), 34, 40
Burkett, Dennis, 197
Bush, George H. W., 38
Bush, George, W., 38, 79

Cabral, Joao, 270
Caesar, 27, 130, 176, 220–21
Calley, William, 17
California, 35, 43, 47, 80n25, 194
Calvary, 19, 21, 99
Campbell, Charles, 13n21
Campbell, Will D., 3n2, 4, 5–15, 29, 33, 41, 56, 58, 67, 87, 129, 130, 131, 181–82, 203, 209–12
Canteen Services, 44
Capital punishment, 25, 42, 129–30, 132, 155, 221; *see also* "Death penalty"
Capone, Al, 40
Carceri d'Invenzione, Le, 235
Cash, Johnny, 29–30
Cassatt, Mary, 239, 239n6

Caudill, Harry, 23

Cauthern, Ron, 175

Chaney, James, 27

Chiaroscuro, 228

Christ, 6, 11, 13, 15, 24–27, 58, 132, 133, 174, 193, 198, 200, 253; *see also* "Jesus"

Christian Century, 209–10

Christianity and Crisis, 210

Christmas, 21, 75, 108, 151–53, 155

Christmas Eve, 252–53

Church, 4, 5, 12, 19, 99–101, 110, 138, 139, 158, 169, 174, 176, 193, 197, 198, 252–53, 255, 261, 262, 266, 267, 269, 270, 274

City Paper, The (Nashville), 54, 60, 61

Civil disobedience, 3, 71

Civil Government, 193

Civil rights, 14n22, 22–25, 210

Civil War, 73n8, 194, 238

Classism, 76

Clinton, Bill, 38, 51

Cold War, 217

Coleman, Thomas, 14, 14n22, 24–27

Colt, Samuel, 73n9

Committee of Southern Churchmen (COSC), 3, 33, 87, 129

Community, 4, 6, 6n5, 7–15, 18, 19, 21, 30, 34n5, 35, 36, 49, 57, 58, 63, 64, 71n4, 73, 73n10, 76, 77, 84, 88–91, 96–97, 99, 101, 105, 108, 111, 118, 126, 129, 158, 177–79, 182–83, 185, 187, 189–92, 194–95, 210–12, 215–17, 221, 223–24, 225, 236, 240–42, 244, 248, 250, 251, 254–56, 259, 260, 262–63, 266–67, 269–70; *see also* "Beloved Community"

Confession, 17, 82, 133, 183, 187–90, 193, 198, 212

Correctional Medical Services, 44

Correctional Privatization Commission, 49

Corrections Corporation of America (CCA), 35, 44–45, 47, 49–52, 55, 56, 60, 120, 121, 123, 124

Couture, Pamela, 253

Cox, Renee, 238

Cradle, The, 239

Crashing the Idols, 3n1, 6n5, 13n20, 210n4

Crime and Delinquency, 50

Criminal(s), 15, 17–21, 29, 33, 34, 40–43, 45, 46

Criminal justice system, 34, 41, 42, 45, 50, 51, 56, 58–65, 69, 89, 113, 185, 190–91, 195, 213, 215–17, 219, 222, 223, 230–31, 234, 247, 254, 258, 262, 267, 270–71; *see also* "Justice"

Criminal Justice Task Force, 52

Cross, 98, 101, 173, 175, 176, 179, 183, 221

Crucifixion, 18, 98

Cuba, 218

Daniels, Jonathan, 13–14, 14n22, 25–27

Dark, David, 29, 30, 66

Davis, Angela, 17, 39, 73n8, 80n25

Death penalty, 33–34, 42, 119, 129–31, 136, 138, 139, 143, 178, 185, 213, 220, 222; *see also* "Capital punishment"

Death row, 136, 140, 147, 153, 155, 156, 178

Death sentence, 29, 42, 66, 136, 139, 158, 173

Department of Correction, 49, 108, 126, 188; Florida, 49; New Jersey, 47; New York City, 51; Tennessee, 108, 126, 188, 199

Department of Criminal Justice, 203; Texas, 203

Department of Defense, 51

Department of Justice, 25

Dismas, 15

Dostoevsky, Fyodor, 68

Douglass, James, 87–88

Drug Enforcement Administration (DEA), 37, 39

Dylan, Bob, 186–87

Easter, 21

Ecuador, 26

Eddy, Sherwood, 9

Electric chair, 30

Elizondo, Virgilio, 262

Elkins, James, 240

Ellul, Jacques, 73n10, 88

Embrace, 100, 182; *see also* "Reconciliation"

Empire(s), 65, 78, 176, 218, 261

Enemy, 19, 20, 24, 26, 29, 37, 57, 65, 67, 69, 80, 88, 131, 194–98, 209, 210, 217–18

England, 72, 75, 76n14, 78

Enola Gay, 132

Eschatological, 84, 183

Ethelbert, 74n12

Evers, Medgar, 27

Fair Labor Standards Act, 36

Faith, 26, 70, 76n14, 84–85, 87, 89, 158, 175–76, 186, 198, 200, 217, 221, 228, 230, 270

Falwell, Jerry, 131

Farley, Wendy, 67

Federal Bureau of Prisons, 34, 46, 52, 193, 195–96

Federal Correctional Institute, Englewood, 195

Federal Probation Journal, 48

Florida Commission on Ethics, 51

Forbes, 35, 55, 60, 61

Forgive, 11, 26, 59, 68, 83, 102, 175, 222, 227, 228, 232, 234, 245, 269

Forgiveness, 11, 67–68, 89, 167, 172, 186, 191, 229, 258

Foucault, Michel, 60, 71n4, 72n5, 127

Franklin, Sam, 10

Freedom, 16–21, 22, 29, 58, 61n19, 65, 66, 73, 83, 84, 93, 95, 106, 111, 122, 123, 126, 154, 182–83, 187, 190–92, 197, 200, 202, 249, 262

Freedom Riders, 3

Freire, Paulo, 262

Fry, Elizabeth, 72

Frye, Northrop, 85

Furman v. Georgia, 33, 42

Gandhi, Mohandas, 70

Garb, Tamar, 239

Garner, Thad, 29

GEO Group, 44–45, 49, 53

Georgia, 42

Gilmore, Gary, 131

Girard, Rene, 194–95

Glad River, The, 183

God, 6, 7, 9, 11, 12, 12n18, 12n19, 16–21, 25–27, 56–59, 61, 63, 65, 68–69, 73n10, 80n25, 83, 83n29, 89, 100, 102, 116, 130–32, 141, 142, 147, 158, 162, 167, 168, 171, 173–79, 182–83, 189, 191, 194, 196, 197, 199–200, 202, 203, 212, 220, 221, 224, 227–28, 230, 233, 234, 253, 264, 265

Golgotha, 85

Good Friday, 15, 132

Good News, 6, 13, 17–21, 27, 56, 58, 65, 84, 182, 187; *see also* "Gospel"

Goode, Richard C., 254

Goodman, Andrew, 27

Gospel, 16, 19–20, 23, 26–27, 58, 68, 82, 85, 85n32, 187, 191, 196–97, 198, 204, 262; *see also* "Good News"

Gospel Advocate, 193–94

Gospel Missionary Union, 26

Gospel Nonviolence, 196–97; *see also* "Nonviolence"

Grace, 7, 11, 22

Grady, Ben, 199

Graham, Billy, 131

Gray, Duncan, 8–9

Gregg v. Georgia, 42

Griffith, Lee, 12n19, 13, 211

Hamerton-Kelly, Robert, 194

Harris Act of 1914, 76

Heidegger, Martin, 64

Henley, Steve, 135–43, 171

Hernando County Jail, 47

Heroic humility, 12n18

Hitler, Adolf, 7

Holloway, James Y., 4

Holy fools, 13n21, 56

Hope, 6, 11, 12, 25, 30, 63, 77, 83, 90, 97, 99, 108, 111, 115, 127, 138, 142, 145, 153, 167, 169, 170, 173, 181, 183, 185, 189, 192, 199, 210,

219, 229, 230, 250, 252, 256, 257, 260, 270, 276
House, Paul, 140
Howard, John, 72
Human unity, 6, 7, 13
Hutschnecker, Arnold, 80n25

Iconoclasm, 5, 6
Idolatry, 176, 220–21
Idolatry of heroism, 6, 12–13
Imaginary Prisons, The, 235
Immigration, 54, 55, 60, 67
Immigration and Customs Enforcement (ICE), 46, 52
Institution(s), 5, 6, 6n5, 7–11, 13, 15, 35, 41, 48–49, 55–56, 58, 63–65, 71n3, 72, 73, 77, 82n27, 84, 88, 90n7, 91, 106, 114, 132, 135, 144, 173, 177, 182, 195–97, 199, 210–12, 217, 230, 234, 236, 240, 242, 243–44, 247, 249, 255–57, 260; *see also* "Principalities and Powers"
Institutional church, 19, 177; *see also* "Steeples"
Iraq, 8, 78, 81, 195, 198

Jackson, Jimmy Lee, 27
Jackson Sun, 197
Jesus, 5, 16–21, 24, 27, 35, 42, 58, 65–66, 80, 81, 84–85, 85n32, 98, 100, 130, 132, 141–42, 173–77, 183, 187, 188, 192, 194, 196–98, 200, 202, 204–6, 220, 223, 257, 262; *see also* "Christ"
Johnson, Cecil, 173–75, 177, 178
Johnson, Don, 175
Jordan, Clarence, 9
Jubilee, 83, 223
Justice, 9, 13, 14, 19, 24, 30, 40, 42, 43, 45, 46, 53, 56–67, 69, 73, 73n10, 80, 80n25, 81, 87, 89, 118, 125, 129, 143, 145, 151–52, 154, 162, 167, 178, 179, 185–92, 209–10, 215, 217, 218, 220, 223–24, 227, 230–34, 239, 245, 254, 255, 259, 269, 270; *see also* "Criminal

justice system," "Restorative justice," "Retributive justice/punishment"

Katallagete, 3–4, 13, 16, 22, 33, 34, 87, 89, 129, 130, 211, 273, 287
Kilpatrick, Lawrence Elbon, 193
Kilpatrick, Lawrence Marlin, 194
King, Martin Luther, Jr., 70
Kingdom of God, 59, 142, 176–77, 179, 182–83, 196, 197, 200, 206
Koinonia Farm, 9
Kristofferson, Kris, 3n2
Ku Klux Klan, 210
Kudzu, 5

Lawrence, Jacob, 238
Lee, Herbert, 27
Legalism, 23–24
lex talionis, 81
Liberation, 5, 17–18, 56, 69, 70, 83–84, 202, 242, 262
Lipscomb, David, 193–94
Lipscomb Initiative for Education (LIFE), 185–92, 225, 228, 236, 237, 241, 242
Liturgy, 9, 264–65
Logan, James Samuel, 35
Lohfink, Gerhard, 10
London, 78
Lord, 4, 17–21, 42, 68, 89, 142, 143, 175–76, 183, 187, 211, 253, 257
Lord's Supper, 142

Magnani, Laura, 39, 258
Malcolm X, 78n20, 244–45, 248, 250
Mammon, 220
Mandela, Nelson, 70
Marion, Jean-Luc, 64
Mars, 220
Martyr, 12, 26, 202
Martyrdom, 20, 178
Massachusetts Institute of Technology, 78n20
Maximum Times, 157
Mays, James, 57, 61–62
McCaffrey, Barry, 79
McCormick, Michael, 140

McCoy, Donna, 59, 90, 125
McVeigh, Timothy, 195–97, 216, 219, 222–23
Medical care, 34, 44–46, 104, 113, 121, 124, 178, 214
Medicine, 104, 258
Menninger, Karl, 19, 79
Merton, Thomas, 3n2, 11n15, 12n18, 179
Metanarrative, 240; *see also* "Narrative"
Mier, Golda, 7
Miller, David, 88
Mississippi, 3, 9, 24, 49, 211, 273
Mohammad, Elijah, 245
Morisot, Berthe, 238, 239n6
Murder, 14, 19, 21, 24–26, 42, 62, 68, 77–79, 81, 102, 103–4, 111–13, 118, 124, 126, 136, 137, 139, 140, 143, 145, 173, 174, 178, 179, 196, 198, 220, 222, 230, 231, 232
Murphy, Wendy, 209

Narrative, 85, 183, 188, 192, 240; *see also* "Metanarrative"
Nation of Islam, 245, 250
National Council of Churches, 13n20, 211, 273
National Public Radio, 60
Neibuhr, Reinhold, 9
Neighbor, 4, 9, 12, 15, 17, 20, 30, 75, 78, 107, 124, 133, 144, 210, 250, 275
Neville, Charlotte, 250
Nichols, Terry, 195
Night Comes to the Cumberland, 23
Nixon, Richard, 33, 36–39, 76, 80n25
Nonviolence, 3, 73, 196–97, 259
Norfolk Correctional Facility, 78n20
North Korea, 218

Office of National Drug Control Policy, 79
Oklahoma City bombing, 78, 195, 223
Organization of Petroleum Exporting Countries, 33
Orr, William F., 83
Orwell, George, 30

Palmer, Parker, 210
Panopticon, 71, 71n4, 235
Paris Peace Accords, 33
Paul, Saint, 18, 19, 22, 23, 58, 68, 82n27, 83n29, 84, 174, 200, 202
Peace, 30, 73, 73n9, 89, 105, 116, 126, 141, 142, 161, 172, 175, 176, 194, 195, 199, 214, 223
Peacemaker, 73n9, 205
Peacemaking, 73, 73n9
Persian Gulf War, 195, 267
Peter, Saint, 18, 84
Pharmakon, 195
Pharmakos, 195
Philemon, 23
Pilate, 85
Piranesi, Giovanni Battista, 235–36, 242
Politic(s), 17, 18, 67, 74, 89, 138, 182, 215, 238–39, 239n6
Political, 6, 12n17, 13, 17–18, 39, 43, 46, 50, 51, 53, 56, 59, 60, 62, 67, 70, 77n17, 81, 84, 88, 154, 156, 176, 215–18, 220, 237, 240, 243, 244, 246, 250
Political party, 8, 10, 231
Political prisoners, 19
Political Science, 6
Political Theology, 74n12
Politicians, 78, 120, 154
Polycarp, 26
Power of Art, 237
Powers, *see* "Principalities and Powers."
Pride, Walter, 199–200, 202
Principalities and Powers, 5, 6, 7, 9, 36, 41, 55, 56, 64, 66, 69, 70, 82, 82n27, 84, 88, 91, 132, 177, 183, 212, 230, 232, 262; *see also* "Institutions"
Prison, *passim*
Prison Health Services, 44
Prison-industrial complex, 5, 14, 15, 36, 42, 44, 45, 51–53, 55–56, 60–65, 69, 87, 89, 90n7, 217
Prison population, 34–39, 41–46, 96, 105, 111, 113, 116, 125, 256
Prison Realty Trust, 51

Prison system, 5, 35–36, 43–45, 47

Prisoner(s), 4, 16–21, 31, 34–36, 42–46, 48–50, 53, 54, 56, 58–63, 65, 67, 69, 70, 71, 71n3, 71n4, 72, 72n6, 73, 75, 75n13, 76–78, 80–85, 88, 113, 156, 177, 182–83, 187, 195, 200, 203–4, 206, 213, 214, 248, 249, 255n3, 256–58, 260, 261, 270

Private Correctional Facilities Act, 52

Private prison(s), 8, 35–36, 43–53, 60–61, 216, 220; *see also* "Privatization"

Privatization, 41, 43, 46, 50–52

Prophet(s), 18, 30, 56–58, 66, 83, 85, 130, 187, 196, 223

Prophetic, 6, 29, 30, 39, 130, 183, 189–90, 255, 259, 262

Prophetic Imagination, The, 189

Providence Community, 9–10

Prisoner Transportation Services of America (PTS), 44, 54

Public Safety and Elections Task Force, 52

Punishment, 14, 19, 25, 39, 42, 44, 59n14, 63, 70, 72, 73n8, 76n14, 78, 79, 93, 101, 111, 129, 130, 132, 149, 154, 155, 177, 183, 188, 196, 197, 209, 214, 219–21, 224, 231, 250, 260, 261

Punitive, 71, 72n5, 77n17, 82, 129, 219–21, 241

Quaker(s), 20, 72, 75, 75n13, 76n14

Racism, 76, 186, 187, 222

Radical, 7, 9, 22, 70, 81, 191, 203, 205, 206, 236

Rainey, Lawrence, 27

Rape, 68, 74n12, 126, 178, 205, 219, 220, 259

Ray, James Earl, 17

Reagan, Nancy, 37

Reagan, Ronald, 37, 38

Reason Foundation, 51

Recidivism, 35, 46, 49–50, 53, 77–78, 269

Reconcile, 13, 18, 190, 224

Reconciled, 6, 7, 9, 15, 58, 68, 69, 129, 130, 174, 175, 178, 200, 212, 234

Reconciliation, 6, 7, 9, 13, 14, 16, 18, 30, 63, 67, 69, 73, 73n9, 82, 83, 83n29, 89, 130, 177, 179, 183, 188, 191, 200, 210, 231, 232, 233, 244, 257, 269, 270

Reconciling, 16, 91, 202, 228, 233, 252

Rector, Stacy, 141

Redekop, Vern, 195

Reeb, James, 27

Rees, John, 52

Reform, 17, 19–21, 45–46, 53, 71–73, 73n8, 118, 218, 227

Rehabilitation, 17, 18, 49, 76–78, 84, 88, 94, 96, 97, 100–102, 104–6, 111, 118, 126, 213–15, 223, 235, 236, 269

Reiman, Jeffrey, 39–40

Resurrection, 18–21, 27, 63, 84, 130, 173, 189, 229

Restorative justice, 178, 209, 213, 215, 220, 223–24, 236, 254, 269; *see also* "Justice"

Retribution, 30, 31, 34, 42, 66, 68, 76, 80, 80n25, 81, 84, 87, 129–30, 178, 186, 188, 213–15, 221, 223, 231

Retributive justice/punishment, 67, 70, 73n10, 80n25, 214, 217, 222; *see also* "Justice"

Revenge, 12, 25, 81, 129, 130, 151–52, 167, 172, 185–86, 219, 221–23

Riverbend Maximum Security Institution (RMSI), 135, 173, 175, 182, 199, 354, 255, 259, 263, 269

Robertson, Pat, 131

Rome, 17

Saar, Bettye, 238

Sabbath, 76n14, 83

Saint, Nathaniel, 26

San Francisco Chronicle, 90n7

Sawabona, 252, 267, 271

Schama, Simon, 237n2

School of the Americas, 259

Schwerner, Michael, 27

Scottsboro trials, 210

Security, 8, 17, 20, 25, 44, 46, 48, 71, 89, 93–94, 97, 122, 135, 165, 173, 175, 182, 188, 197, 199, 214, 221, 237, 254, 255, 256, 263, 265

Sentinel Offender Services, 44

Sermon on the Mount, 99, 194, 204, 223

Shalom, 9, 223, 234

Shanblum, Laurie, 52

Shipp, Preston, 185–86, 188, 210, 225–30

Show trials, 216

Sikona, 252, 267, 271

Slater, Philip, 71n4

Slavery, 73, 73n8, 83

Society, 5, 11, 12n17, 13, 17–21, 29, 53, 56, 57, 59, 65, 71, 71n4, 72n5, 73–78, 82, 85n32, 90, 93–99, 101–2, 103, 105, 106, 109, 118, 119, 124–27, 131, 164, 174, 177, 178, 186, 187, 194–96, 209, 216–21, 227, 231, 233, 236, 239, 242, 250–51

Soelle, Dorothee, 270

Solzhenitsyn, Aleksandr, 68

Soul Among Lions, 132n2

South Africa, 70, 219, 252

Stafford, Fred and Edna, 138–39, 142

Steeples, 5, 211; *see also* "Institutional church"

Stephen, Saint, 178, 202

Stevens, William R., 144

Stories of Art, 240

Stringfellow, William, 64, 69, 90

Supreme Court, *see* "United States Supreme Court"

Sussman, Peter, 90

Tanner, Henry Ossawa, 238

Tennessean, The, 173

Tennessee Coalition to Abolish State Killing, The, 148

Tennessee Prison for Women (TPW), 112, 116, 126, 185–89, 231, 235, 236

Terrorists, 218

Texas Senate Committee on Criminal Justice, 48

Theology, 6, 13, 74, 74n11, 138, 153, 195, 215, 254, 255, 261

Therapeutic Community Program, 105

Thomas, Charles, 51

Thompson, Ron, 47

Through the Looking-Glass, 79

TransCor, 44

Transformation and Reconciliation from the Inside Out (TRIO), 269

Tucker, Carla Faye, 131

Tyburn Hill, 78, 78n20

Ubuntu, 266

United States Supreme Court, 33, 42, 51, 129, 131, 168

Unity, *see* "Human unity"

University of Mississippi, 211

Vanier, Jean, 11

Vietnam War, 33, 88

Violence, 30, 38, 40, 41, 45, 46, 48–50, 53, 56, 58, 62, 63, 69, 78, 82, 84, 120, 138, 139, 143, 155, 183, 193, 194–97, 206, 210, 216, 217, 219–21, 248, 259, 267

Vocation, 3, 56, 96, 210, 211

Wackenhut Corrections, 44

Walker, Kara, 238

Wallace, Foy, 194

Walther, James Arthur, 83

War on Drugs, 36–42, 44, 76

Warfare, 16, 62

Washington Sentencing Project, The, 108

Welborn, Jerry, 175

Welch, Bud, 223

Wesley, John, 253

West, Cornell, 67

Wiggins, Brad, 52

Williams, Rowan, 85n32

Wilson, Pete, 80n25

Wimberly, Edward, 266

Wolf, Janet, 212, 224

Workman, Phillip, 151, 156–58

Wray, Harmon, 39, 89, 130, 210, 213n1, 224, 254, 258, 259

Writings on Reconciliation and Resistance, 5n4, 6n5, 7n9, 56n6, 58n13, 181n1, 203n1

Ybanez, Felicia, 14, 212

Zabelka, George, 196
Zehr, Howard, 220